ADVANCE PRAISE

"A TRULY GREAT BOOK! Cleared Hot is intense, compelling, instructive, humorous, and brutally forthright. It is also truly inspirational. It takes the reader on an extraordinary journey—through the formative years of a fiercely independent and competitive individual and then into the cockpit of an Apache attack helicopter engaging in ferocious combat with a tenacious enemy in the most challenging environment and context imaginable. It explores the challenges of dealing with family issues on the home front during a time of war, as well. Brian Slade also guides the reader on a very instructive examination of the use of traumatic experiences to foster the development of mental resilience. Cleared Hot provides for a heck of a ride!"

—GEN. DAVID PETRAEUS, US Army (Ret.), former Commander of US Central Command and the NATO and US Forces in Afghanistan and former Director of the CIA

"Truly a one-of-a-kind war story, Cleared Hot vividly captures the shock and awe of battle from the perspective of the ultimate close-quarters combat war machine—the Apache. Do you think they are insulated from casualties? Think again! From laughter to outrage to heartbreak and back again, this book is a must-read for anyone wanting to know the truth of what these warfighters bring to the battlefield!"

—SCOTT MCEWEN, co-author of The New York Times #1 bestseller American Sniper

"Brian Slade is a tough-minded and candid individual who, out of a concern for the wellbeing of others, is eager to share his personal experiences. His extensive military leadership and combat experience give him credibility that can be earned in no other way. Cleared Hot is a superb amalgamation of his experience and insights. Readers will be drawn into his compelling narrative and emerge with insights on facing the demands and adversities of life with vigor and a ready mind."

—**DAVID S. WOOD**, PhD, MSW, assistant professor at Brigham Young University's School of Social Work and operational psychologist in the Utah Army National Guard, holding the rank of major

"Cleared Hot is the Chicken Hawk of the Global War on Terrorism's generation and a book long overdue. Too much of the Afghanistan War has been clouded by hyperbole, politics, and rumor. Brian Slade's experiences as a US Army AH-64 Apache Attack Helicopter Company Commander show how the issues of 21st-century warfare are complex—not only the general topic of soldiers at war but also combat at home involving different people, times, and locations. Cleared Hot puts a human face on the Clausewitzian idea that while the character of war changes, the nature of war—and its impact on individuals—remains the same."

—**COL. JAYSON A. ALTIERI (RET)**, US Army, Task Force Corsair Commander, 2007-2008

"Brian Slade masterfully weaves lessons about leadership and life with adrenaline-pumping stories of life-or-death situations as an Apache pilot in Afghanistan. Brian pulls back the curtain to reveal the whole story—the wins and the losses—and, by so doing, delivers lessons that we are often too afraid to share ourselves. Cleared Hot is real, tough, and fantastic!"

—**CARSON HOWELL,** PhD, Vice President of Snow College

"Brian is a leader, a warrior, and a combat-proven aviator. Having served with Brian in Afghanistan, I can personally attest to his character and calm under fire. As a company commander and leader, there were none better. His book captures the stress, split-second decision-making, and confusion that comes with modern combat operations. Brian also perfectly describes the challenges of leading through adversity and personal pain. This is a book about modern warfighters. It's a book about facing and overcoming adversity. Simply stated, it's a book about success-fully leading through hardship."

—**COL. CRAIG J. ALIA (RET),** 1st Battalion Deputy Commander,
Virginia Tech Corps of Cadets

"An engaging and inspiring story from one who has successfully navigated extreme and prolonged stress. Lt. Col. Brian Slade shares his amazing account with unique insights into how to prepare and protect one's mind during intense personal suffer-ing and war."

—**STEVEN HOFFMAN, PHD,** assistant professor at Brigham Young
University's School of Social Work

"Cleared Hot *captures the chaotic intensity of combat in Afghanistan. The narrative is gripping, putting the reader in the cockpit with Brian as bullets and RPGs whiz by. But the book is more than just another war story. It's about overcoming obstacles, growing as a leader, and, more importantly, as a person. Throughout* Cleared Hot, *Brian finds the connection between growing up in Utah and his response to combat and command in Afghanistan. Facing life's challenges with a positive attitude, as Brian does throughout the book, helps us become a better version of ourselves.*"

—LTC SCOTT TAYLOR (RET), US Army, Director of Transfer and Veteran Admissions at Syracuse University

CLEARED
HOT

CLEARED
HOT

LESSONS LEARNED ABOUT LIFE, LOVE,
AND LEADERSHIP WHILE FLYING THE APACHE GUNSHIP
IN AFGHANISTAN and WHY I BELIEVE A PREPARED
MIND CAN HELP MINIMIZE PTSD

LT. COL. BRIAN L. SLADE
AND MICHAEL HIRSH

HOUNDSTOOTH
PRESS

CLEARED HOT
Lessons Learned about Life, Love, and Leadership While Flying the Apache Gunship in Afghanistan and Why I Believe a Prepared Mind Can Help Minimize PTSD

ISBN   978-1-5445-3377-3   *Hardcover*

       978-1-5445-3376-6   *Paperback*

       978-1-5445-3378-0   *Ebook*

CONTENTS

For my son Axel

Every day his spirit embodies
the bright future that lies ahead

AUTHOR'S NOTE

I wrote *Cleared Hot* with the belief that sharing the things I learned in combat might do more than just entertain my readers, that it would offer them—you—an opportunity to learn and eventually practice some of the techniques that protected me from much of the negative impact that stress and trauma can have on all of us. That's why throughout the book you'll find occasional reminders that I've posted videos at www.clearedhot.info/lessonslearned that elaborate on those methods in an audio-video format. I see how these techniques saved me and pray they can help you and others. I want to hear from you if they do; please share your experience with me at brian@clearedhot.info. I will respond personally to every email.

There's a glossary of terms at the back of the book that will explain some of the jargon. You'll also find three maps that will provide some geographic perspective on my missions.

This is a work of nonfiction. Our best efforts have been made to ensure the stories are accurate through interviews, video, journals, and more. That said, some of the names have been changed for reasons that will be apparent, and elements of several combat missions have, in some instances, been combined in the narrative. The opinions and views expressed by the author in this book do not constitute endorsement by the United States Air Force, the United States Army, or the Department of Defense. Thanks for coming along for the ride.

—Lt. Col. Brian L. Slade

INVICTUS

Out of the night that covers me,
Black as the Pit from pole to pole,
I thank whatever gods may be
For my unconquerable soul.

In the fell clutch of circumstance
I have not winced nor cried aloud.
Under the bludgeonings of chance
My head is bloody, but unbowed.

Beyond this place of wrath and tears
Looms but the Horror of the shade,
And yet the menace of the years
Finds, and shall find, me unafraid.

It matters not how strait the gate,
How charged with punishments the scroll,
I am the master of my fate:
I am the captain of my soul.

—WILLIAM ERNEST HENLEY

BLACK ON AMMO

As we come over the ridgeline, we can see muzzle flash firing downhill on our patrol. *As soon as we're past the bad guys, they're going to redirect that fire at our backside.* Now we're down almost into the treetops, taking that toboggan ride downhill no more than fifty feet above ground level to keep that cushion of air under us. I am carrying a little more smash than I had expected, and have every bit of power applied at this point. Now it's a finesse game. I see fire coming up through the trees all around us. *I was wrong. The Taliban aren't waiting for us to pass them to shoot. This might not have been a great, or even a good, idea. We're going to come in hard. No other "survivable" way to do it.*

I'm not sure if I'm holding my breath, but if I am, the landing knocks it out of me. I know Brett, my copilot/gunner in the forward cockpit, can hear my OOOOFF! over the voice-activated intercom. It isn't a crash, but it's definitely not a landing my instructors at Rucker would be happy with. I can almost hear them saying, "Lieutenant, are you *trying* to break my helicopter?" And that's what's going through my head: *Did I break it? Are we gonna be able to fly out of here? I know this wasn't a good idea, but it's the only idea we had. A Hobson's choice. If we don't do it, these guys are gonna wait another hour or more for ammo. How many of them will die in the interim?*

Brett is sarcastically complimentary. "Well, it worked. Uuuugly, but it worked."

"Able 6-2, we've got ammo for you. Come and get it."

As several of these dudes break out of the wood line, stumbling toward the left side of our bird—where most of the enemy fire is coming from—others continue firing uphill, and I can see one still trying to make it uphill to this saddle from down below. He's dragging a wounded buddy, while firing his M4. All of them are exhausted; it's clear they've got nothing left. The camo on their faces is streaked with dirt; their uniforms are soaking wet. *These guys are completely whooped. They look like death. They've been in a firefight and getting their butts kicked. All freakin' day. They look like zombies, emotionally spent. How long have they been fighting their way up this mountain? These guys don't even have enough energy to look scared. Pinned down, black on ammo, and resupply doesn't show up all day?* I don't have time to be angry right now, but it'll come.

"Oh, crap!" I say it aloud, suddenly realizing that they can't figure out how to open up the freakin' compartments. They're repeatedly banging on the lower fuselage to no effect. I can see Brett in the front seat, frantically pointing at the compartment they should be trying to open. I even hear him shout, "No, that's the wrong compartment." But of course, they can't hear him.

"Brett," I shout, as I pop open my canopy, "they can't figure it out. I'm getting out!"

"Oh, hell no. I've got this." And before I can respond, he rips off his helmet and contorts his way out of the forward cockpit, Cuban cigar firmly clenched between his teeth. The second he hits the ground, he darts around the nose of the Apache to the left side and pops open the correct storage locker. All the while, incoming rounds are literally puffing up dirt all around us. He reaches in and pulls out a black garbage bag filled with loaded magazines, and it splits open, spilling half the load back into the compartment. One of the infantrymen takes the bag, as others come up to grab as many loose magazines as they can carry.

Brett is working like a madman to empty that compartment. Another garbage bag breaks and the routine continues, but by now there's a ragtag bucket brigade, passing magazines up to the guys waiting in the tree line, who immediately lock and load and begin returning fire. I can see that there's this huge, crazy-eyed grin on Brett's face. It's like I can almost hear him doing an Oprah give-away: "You get ammo, and you get ammo, and you get ammo." But then a sobering thought strikes me: *If he gets hit...if that happens we're screwed. How long have we been sitting here? Way too long.* Rounds continue to come in. *They want to destroy this helo.* I imagine Brett going down, knowing that I'd have only two choices, both bad. *I couldn't leave him. I'd have to get out of the cockpit, muscle him back into the front seat, and position him so he can't foul up the controls—hands or feet.*

I see him point to the open locker, urging the guys to keep unloading it, and then watch him run around the nose of the bird and crack open the locker on the other side. I can't talk to him because he's taken off his helmet, but I actually shout, "Look out!" after a bullet strikes the ground right in front of him, probably missing his crotch by mere inches. It makes me flinch. He reacts to the flying dirt by stopping in his tracks and then turns and gives me two thumbs-up. I shake my head. I can see his cigar has taken a real beating. *Holy crap! He's fifty freakin' years old and acting like a kid in a messed-up candy shop.*

Sitting on the ground, we are able to hear our wingman pouring all the firepower they can expend on the ridge above us, to the right of us, and to the left of us. Although I can't feel them, I'm sure we're taking hits from the Taliban's 7.62 Kalashnikovs as we sit here. *We need to crap and get off this pot. Please, God, no RPGs today,* I think, with one eye on the engine page of the display, just waiting for something to go red.

Several of the ground pounders who followed Brett around the nose of the bird join him in emptying the starboard compartment. When it's empty, he closes it, slams that compartment shut, climbs up, and shimmies back in. But I have no intention of waiting for him to plug in before we lift off. There's now a song playing in my head, and it's from another era. I chomp a new wad of gum while singing along with The Animals, "We gotta get out of this place, if it's the last thing we ever do."

The first words I hear from Brett as soon as he plugs back in are something about being good to go: "No master caution lights."

I pick up, sensing through the controls that we've got a little more power margin now that we've dropped all that weight and burned a little fuel. Though I don't feel it, I'm certain Brett is shadowing me on the sticks. Immediate problem is there's low bushes and then trees in front of me, but it's downhill. I pull as much power as I possibly can, we split the trees—well, actually our wheels and the belly of the bird probably scrape through them—then dive down the descending terrain and we're flying.

"You do know that they were shooting at you?" I ask, ready to poke some fun.

"You're wrong, college boy. They were shooting at you. I was just closer to them." *Uh-huh.*

"Now," I say to Brett, "you ready to blow some stuff up? I know I am!" It feels personal.

CHAPTER 1

WORDSWORTH WAS RIGHT

The Power of Positive Perspective

My heart leaps up when I behold

A rainbow in the sky:

So was it when my life began;

So is it now I am a man;

So be it when I shall grow old,

Or let me die!

The Child is father of the Man;

And I could wish my days to be

Bound each to each by natural piety.

—WILLIAM WORDSWORTH

Never thought I'd be a member of the Dead Poets Society—or writ-ing a memoir for that matter—but Wordsworth got it right! The kid I was foretold the man I've become.

AAAAAH!! Pain-riddled screams blast through the earcups in my helmet, interrupting radio communications; they are from my copilot through the intercom system in the helicopter.

"AHHH! I'M SHOT! AHHH! THEY HIT MY LEG!!"

My heart rate just jumped from sixty to, I don't know, two thousand beats per minute. I am in the middle of an aggressive bank turning inbound, trying to line up a shot against very tenacious Taliban unleashing on us with everything in their arsenal. Their weapons have just ripped through our aircraft, giving us instant feedback on their resolve, requiring me to alter my plan or succumb to theirs.

As crazy as this may sound, I have more pressing matters to deal with right now than my screaming copilot, who is obviously in excruciating pain.

"Rotor RPM low. Rotor RPM low."

It's the audio alert telling me my rotor blades are slowing down, that we have lost an engine. I am weightless in my seat and we are falling out of the sky, causing my stomach to take up residence in my throat. I need to adjust my flight controls. Crap! They don't budge! They are frickin' jammed. What else can go wrong? Still falling. Hypotheticals I had previously run pop into my head. Stay calm, use the adrenaline surge to act quickly, be decisive. We just fell one hundred feet with only two hundred to go, and that number is shrinking rapidly. I need to do something now—but what?

We will get to that story, trust me.

It is my belief that everything that happens can be turned to benefit us in some way. Life provides us with tests, trials, and obstacles, and they can either beat us down or we can use them as building blocks to shape and refine the absolute best versions of ourselves. I feel my life has been one blessing after another, though many of those blessings were disguised as difficulties. I have enjoyed the journey so far and plan on enjoying whatever is next—be it good or bad. Now, looking back, I can't help but think that all the things I have experienced and learned from are being wasted if they only serve to benefit me. Hence, this book.

I am guessing most of you have not ever had hundreds of hate-hardened fighters try to shoot you out of the sky with heavy machine guns, rocket propelled grenades, and even surface-to-air missiles. Maybe you have, but it's not the type of thing most people have on their bucket list, right? Maybe that sounds like an entertaining story to you; maybe it doesn't. Bottom line is, who cares? I don't mean that flippantly, but really, aside from being entertained, why would you care about my story? How does it relate to you and your life? How can my story benefit you? How about this: have you ever suffered something painful or had a life-altering traumatic experience that carried with it residual effects? I bet I got a lot more up-and-down head nods on that one. There are actually more similarities between my war experiences and yours than most realize. Even though they may be different in context, coping with life is coping with life. Impact is impact.

Maybe this will help explain it. This book chronicles my experiences in Afghanistan. My Afghanistan. I am willing to bet you have an Afghanistan or two. It doesn't have to be war. Just experiences that result either in PTSD—post-traumatic stress disorder—or PTSG—what the experts have begun to call post-traumatic stress growth. Statistics show that one in three Americans have experienced a significant trauma in their life. That makes it likely that either you or someone you love and care about will deal with extensive trauma in their lifetime.

Although combat scenarios might not be directly relatable to all, the lessons derived can apply to many situations. Basically, any situation that has the potential of negative impact carries with it certain commonalities. Maybe it's not trauma; maybe it's just getting the most out of a challenge. Dealing with—or even better, preparing for—these types of impactful moments in our lives can ultimately dictate outcome. There are really only two things that can happen. You can grow from the experience or be damaged by it. My intention is to share, through my Afghanistan journey, some ways to increase the possibility of that outcome being growth-oriented, by applying simple techniques anybody can use. I learned some of them by accident in combat.

But before I can tell you about multitasking for a year in Afghanistan as a US Army Apache gunship pilot, as the commander of an attack helicopter company, and as a husband whose marriage was coming unglued, let me give you a little background on where I came from. I really want you to understand the lens through which I viewed these leadership challenges, life-and-death situations with the enemy, and my relationship struggles. I believe many of the tools I used and lessons I learned—sometimes the hard way—can help anybody overcome or even avoid trauma's devastating effects and, in turn, be an all-around healthier human being.

Mom and Dad raised eight kids on his teacher's salary—yup, you heard that right, eight of us in ten years in the small Idaho town of Mountain Home. They were churchgoing Mormons, priding themselves in self-sufficiency, whose parents taught them not to expect somebody else to take care of them. Mom, Connie Slade, says, "We needed to be responsible for our personal, financial, and spiritual needs."

Which means for my folks it was a conscious decision not to get food stamps, though they would have easily qualified for them as well as many other welfare plans. Nor did they ask the church for help, even though LDS doctrine had led to the creation of the "Bishop's Storehouse," which evolved after World War II into a complex churchwide production and distribution system, all based on the belief that members of the church should care for themselves and each other. Members were also discouraged from seeking assistance from government or social service agencies if they could find other means.

Quite honestly, I'm glad my parents didn't get help. It's a point of pride for me now when I talk about how they fed eight kids on a teacher's salary—with no help from anybody. Was it tough for them? I'm sure it was. But they made those life choices and proudly owned them. It taught me a lesson that would be pivotal in the roles I would later fill: ownership.

Mom treasured motherhood and struggled with the fact that she couldn't afford the ingredients to make cookies for us kids. Recently, she told me, "There were times when we lived on whatever I could make from the whole wheat and beans we had as our food storage, because there was no money to go to the store. It was always a challenge." Don't get me wrong, I know many have it way worse. I don't have negative feelings about my upbringing. We did not starve, but we were indeed poor.

Here comes the Wordsworth affirmation: If I drill it down, poverty taught me that although it may not be pretty, you can always make it work. Gratitude is key. It gave me an understanding of the difference between a *need* and a *want*. We didn't get a lot of wants; we lived mostly off needs. How awesome and rare it was to learn that at an early age in America, where wants abound. That distinction got refined even more a decade later, when I lived in a third world country on my two-year mission. What I learned is that we aren't owed anything, and if we are grateful for what we have, our outlook is positive no matter the situation.

As a company commander twenty years later in Afghanistan, I had little patience for entitlement or laziness. Didn't want to hear, "I don't have this," or "That's not fair," or "I don't have that." I'd tell them, "There comes a point where you either need to suck it up or get me somebody who won't be hampering our mission."

A lot of that attitude I also attribute to lessons I learned while playing high school sports. One of my favorite coaches, John Srholec, told us, "Show me commitment, engage the unknown with courage, and together we will increase our capability as a team to win." I would add that after you see that process in action, you gain confidence, and with that perspective you are armed to attack the next challenge. The tripwire to that process—the one that would get me—was becoming overconfident. From there, the tendency is to make reckless decisions, only to be curb-checked back to reality. This tripwire is there so we can continue to learn, but in war, that trip can mean death. It's important to recognize earlier rather than later where healthy confidence morphs to dangerous pride, and check yourself before reality does it for you. One thing for sure, throughout the whole process, complaining about how bad things are only hamstrings growth potential.

Perhaps it was seeing my parents struggle with poverty—or my childlike understanding of it—but I knew I needed to earn money. Right then. So I sought out ways to do so from a very early age. At the age of ten, I hired on to move irrigation pipes on a nearby farm growing sugar beets, potatoes, and alfalfa. This was hardly the first time I performed this kind of work; it was merely the first time I got paid for it, which was a welcome change. At first, I could barely lift the thirty-foot water-filled pipes, but with time, it became easier. Call it early-age CrossFit training. The desire to have more options to eat than beans and rice, as well as to wear something other than third- and fourth-hand clothing, drove my work ethic. When I experienced the fruits of my labor, it motivated more of the same. I am grateful for learning that lesson early on.

At twelve years of age, I was driving a dump truck for a local farmer and making what I considered to be serious money. Having that cash allowed me to play at an elevated level as well.

In class, I might have been considered a class clown, never passing up a chance to crack a joke or play a prank. I didn't respond well to authority and found myself in the principal's office on a fairly regular basis, but because my folks insisted I get As and Bs or I couldn't play sports, I always made good grades. I left junior high my way, by starting the biggest food fight they had ever seen on the last day of my freshman year. It was epic—never seen so many french bread pizzas being used as ammunition. I wasn't a bad kid, just had a lot of energy. In fact, on the flip side of that coin, I was an Eagle Scout and church youth leader, and because Mom was into it, I tried out for a play put on by Missoula Children's Theater. I landed the part of a comical villain in my first production. I actually enjoyed it and I must've been good at it, because a few years later, in high school, I auditioned and landed the role of lead villain again. #typecasting. Shock of shocks. As a result of that performance, I was offered a drama scholarship at Missoula College. No way I was taking that scholarship. Although I did enjoy the stage, I did not relate to drama folk.

It wasn't until my sophomore year in high school that I started playing football. At first, I wasn't very good. I was not naturally a super athlete, but I am super competitive and really enjoyed the game. I played hard, frankly, because I didn't like sucking and I didn't like losing. I weighed 160 pounds that year but was strong for my weight, what with all the lifting of heavy things I'd been doing to earn money. Coach had me playing offensive guard, but I didn't know what I was doing. I was lost in the sauce, didn't understand the rules, who to block, how to block. He would yell at me, really yell, "Slade, stop holding!"

"Sure thing, Coach," thinking, *Holding? What's holding?* I hadn't grown up like a lot of the other guys watching football on TV with my father. Dad wasn't into sports.

Finally, they switched me to defense, told me I was now a nose guard. That was easy for me to do. My job was to get through the line and attack the quarterback, or if he handed the ball to somebody else, go after him. It was kind of like a *Waterboy* moment, if you're familiar with the 1998 Adam Sandler film where he plays a college kid with Asperger's syndrome. "S'ss'so I go after the quarterback, a-a-a-and if he doesn't have it, I go after the other guy..." I could understand that. I'd found my spot. They began starting me at nose guard, and then toward the end of that year after JV season ended, they moved me up to varsity, and I played a few games before that season ended.

But it was really in my junior year where it just kind of clicked. The game started to slow down and suddenly I could read the field. I played with reckless abandon and began racking up tackles and sacks. They had me playing offense and multiple positions on defense, as well as special teams. I rarely came off the field, and I loved that! I did not want to be on the sideline. I had shown the commitment and the courage Coach talked about, to go full throttle, and it indeed was resulting in added capability and confidence.

Without realizing it, I was also learning things that aided in my success. I began practicing mindset and perspective control—skills that would cushion my brain from trauma's effects later on. *I go into more detail on how to do this in a video you can watch at www.cleared-hot.info/lessonslearned.*

Around the same time, I was having conflict with my dad, and it got to the point where he said, "You're doing your own thing, you're completely disregarding our rules, so you've got three choices: you have a week to decide whether you're going to stay here and keep the rules, go to juvenile detention, or go out on your own." I opted for independence over being controlled either at home or in a cell. It's not that I was a bad kid; I was just an over-amped, very independent teenage boy, doing crazy adrenaline-fueled antics. We'd jump off cliffs into lakes and rivers; race cars; hang out the window of a speeding truck, firearm in hand, hunting coyotes. We'd jump any kind of conveyance, and I do mean *any.* The best, of course, had motors. Once I caught about eight feet of air in an empty ten-wheel dump truck. Man, if we had video-capable cell phones back then, I would hate to see what else we would have come up with.

We also bungee jumped and played train dodge. Pretty stupid actually.

I guess I should explain that last one. It's where you stand on the train tracks as long as you can, feel the ground shaking like an earthquake as the train gets closer, and at the last second, you jump off. It was kind of thoughtless on our part; I never considered what the engineer must be thinking while he's hitting his brakes and blaring his horn, but that just added to the thrill. Those are the things that people, including my parents, were worried about. "He's gonna kill himself before he gets…" But luckily, I made it. Had a good time, too. Learned to work hard for what I got and play to the extreme when not working.

Now, in my forties, I go dirt biking with my brothers and I'm the one saying, "Hey, man, that looks a little sketchy…" They laugh at the irony, telling me, "That's a thought process you never had in the past." It wasn't like I had a death wish at all; I just didn't think anything would hurt or kill me. That's the danger of overconfidence. Fortunately, I did grow out of that one. Afghanistan can do that to you. Even though confidence came in handy at times, I would learn just how vulnerable the human being is, physically as well as psychologically.

But back to my youth…

Now on my own, I lived in the basement of my best friend, Heath Schilz, for a bit, then in an apartment with roommates who were legally adults and could sign a lease. I worked the sporting goods counter at Kmart in the evenings to pay rent.

To be clear, I didn't completely cut off my relationship with the folks. I didn't harbor any ill will, just accepted it as differences in opinion. Although we didn't interact very much, they actually came to watch me play football. Then there was the time that I had to ask them for a note giving me permission to keep playing.

It's the end of the second quarter, the running back just cut toward me. I lower my shoulder, pumping my legs, accelerating into the collision. My arms instinctively wrap around him as I make contact. Simultaneously, one of my teammates hit him from the other side before my arms could completely wrap him up. In the process, he hit and jammed the middle finger of my left hand, pushing it all the way back into my hand. Yeah, you heard that right: finger pushed into hand. It folded on itself and slid in there, so it looked as though I didn't have a middle finger. Of course, I felt it, and as you can imagine, it hurt, but I didn't look at my hand. I just kind of shook it hoping the pain would subside. It didn't. I went to line up for the next play, and as I was getting set in a four-point stance, I put my hand down on the ground and instantly noticed I did not have the return pressure I anticipated from my middle finger. I anxiously looked down and that's when I saw there was no middle finger; there was just blood where the finger had been. My reaction? "Oh, crap! My finger got ripped off." But the play was already in motion, so instinctually, I launched at the snap of the ball and actually got the tackle. Standing up, I staggered toward the sideline, tapping my helmet to signal to the coach that I was coming out.

As I got closer to the sideline, Head Coach John Srholec says, "What the hell you coming out for?" It was an appropriate reaction, because I never came out. I never wanted to come out. I truly loved being on the field from start to finish.

Holding up my left hand, now showing only three fingers and a thumb, I say quite seriously, "I'm not sure, Coach, but this doesn't look right." His eyes got big and his face went white.

He uttered a few expletives as some assistant coaches hollered, "We gotta stop this game and look for a finger."

Meantime as trainers head my way, I'm standing there, holding my hand and staring glassily at the field, hoping they find my finger. A moment later, one of the assistant coaches, Tony Kerfoot, takes a closer look at it, sees my fingernail sticking out of the loose skin, and says, "I think your finger is in your hand." Not something you really ever expect or want to hear.

He says, "I think you just need to pull on that," pointing to the disguised fingertip.

So I squeezed the bloody tip with fully functioning fingers on my right hand and I pulled on it until it came out. The slimy form just slipped out of the bloody hole, reminding me of an animal giving birth. Right then, that finger is a worm that'll bend any way you want it to go. That's when I got queasy. Coach grabs me and asks, "You okay?"

"Yeah, little dizzy. Didn't know I had a finger in there." It hurt badly. I had busted the bones in my hand, which is what made room for the finger to shoot back. A trainer shot some cold water in my mouth, and man, cold water never tasted so good. It woke me up; the black haze that was clouding my vision subsided.

When we went into the locker room at halftime, the coach asked me if I could still play. I told him yes. Commitment and courage, right? I can see the finger is loose and the hand had swollen to where it looked like a baseball mitt. So we just taped three fingers together, padded my hand, and I played the rest of the game. It hurt like crazy, but that was one of those test-your-mettle moments for me, a true opportunity to put what Coach had been preaching to the test. Double up your commitment and your courage, put your head down, and get through it. If you're going to sit here and tell me how bad it is, you won't. I decided to heed the advice. Even if playing with a busted hand may not have been what he was referring to, I thought it was applicable. Honestly, whether that was the type of situation Coach was referring to or not, it didn't matter. His charge stuck with me, and this incident would prove to build my confidence by leaps and bounds.

After the team doctor examined me, Coach Srholec said I would be allowed to play, but he added, "I think we need permission from your parents for you to play with a broken bone."

I said, "I'm emancipated—not legally—but I'm living on my own." That didn't fly, so I went to my dad, and he wrote a note that said, *Brian has my permission to be an idiot if he wants to be, to include playing with a broken hand.* And he signed it *Larry Slade.* My coach framed that note and hung it in his office. I played the rest of the year. And the next.

I was a good football player but didn't realize just how good. I just enjoyed the game and went as hard and fast as I could, increasing capability and confidence as I gave it my all. As my coach promised, commitment and courage had, indeed, resulted in increased capability. I began getting letters from colleges here and there trying to recruit me, and at the end of my senior year, I got the all-state recognition for my position, got most tackles in the state—stuff I wasn't tracking because I didn't have parents who followed sports like that, so I didn't know to do it myself.

Football season ended. My roommates got evicted, so by association, so did I. The last six months of my senior year I lived in my truck. Winters in Idaho were cold, snotcicle cold, below-zero cold. So truck living meant lots of blankets, a gearshift in your back as you slept, and showers at school and truck stops. I could have gone home at any time. I knew that but was determined to prove I could do this independence thing. I didn't want to just say I could make it on my own. I wanted to prove I could do it right, by still playing sports, working a job, maintaining grades, and ultimately graduating. Staying in my truck allowed me to save money for college. I saw it as not only a challenge but also an adventure. Perspective was key.

I realize now that my football coaches burned into my soul two fundamental lessons that served me well in the life-or-death situations I confronted in combat: first, lead by example, and second, lead with intensity. Do that and people will follow you. They will absolutely follow you when they know you are more than willing to do what you are asking them to do. I was a fierce Mountain Home Tiger. Coach had taught me that my toughness and aggressiveness were assets when used correctly. He taught me not only how to use them but how to grow them and bring them out in others as well. I could change the tempo of a game by motivating guys with emotion and action-based communication saying, "We're not done. This isn't over. Let's go! I'll meet you at the ball!" Then I'd go do it, and they'd follow me. We'd run the play; we'd meet at the ball, and I would look at them in the pile of bodies and say, "Yeah! Let's do it again!" That was the first inkling I had that I might be a *leader* and that I could really move those around me to do what we needed to do without being a complete jerk. This would play out over and over in my military career, building camaraderie, cutting out problems, challenging each other, and meeting at the proverbial ball.

It was at my graduation party that Dad pulled me aside to ask if I was planning on serving a mission. A two-year stint for the church, often abroad, was typical for LDS kids just out of high school. I told him that I wasn't.

"Why?" he asked.

My answer wasn't glib. "I don't doubt that a mission is a good thing, that it helps people and teaches them a belief that if applied sincerely will help them through life. But I don't believe it strong enough that I'm going to take two years and talk to people about this."

It wasn't that I didn't believe in a higher power. I believe there is that influence in our lives. I knew that most religions teach "This is the path. You take our path, and you get to heaven, swargaloka, nirvana, jannah, or whatever paradise that path is supposed to lead to." I just wasn't convinced ours was the only path. I felt it was a good path. It wasn't wrong, just not the only path.

Dad looked at me. I waited for what I was sure would come.

"Okay, that's a fair answer. It makes sense."

That took me by surprise. Both my parents were devout, and Dad was definitely a my-way-or-the-highway type of guy, which is what caused me to leave home in the first place. There had to be more, and there was.

"Will you do me a favor?" he asked.

"What's that?"

"At some point in your life, you're going to question what your purpose is in life. Why are you here? Why do you even exist? Where did you come from? What's the plan? You're going to have those types of questions. And when you have those, I just want you to promise me you'll kneel down on your knees and you will pray to your Heavenly Father, and you will ask Him if whether this gospel, as we teach it as a path, is the right path."

I immediately agreed, because in my mind, I wasn't worried about having those questions. I was happy with life and didn't feel the need to delve into its purpose. Just be a good person, build your team, compete, and win—that's where I was at.

A day later, my buddy Lee Long and I hit the road for Arizona, driving my $900 bargain 1977 Chevy Custom Deluxe pickup, which was neither custom nor deluxe. The truck and I were almost the same age, but it was much worse for wear. It was two-tone gray, or three-tone if you consider rust a color, and what was left of the suspension seemed to allow for as much up and down travel as forward. Top speed might have been eighty-five mph, and I could see the pavement through what remained of the floor. I was reminded of that defect every time I reached for the four-on-the-floor gearshift. It was completely paid off, though.

In Arizona, I strengthened my résumé: Lee and I worked as security guards at Hoover Dam and got hired to do road paving work. In Arizona. In the summer. I would advise against that unless you have an affinity for surface-of-the-sun-type work and don't mind drinking water by the barrelful. But they paid us $15 to $19 an hour, so we were happy—happy enough that the summer slid into fall, and I missed the start of the school year at Boise State.

I needed a plan. A girl I'd dated in the past happened to be in Naval ROTC, and she's the one who clued me into the ROTC scholarship setup, which I applied for. I decided to move to Logan, Utah to attend Utah State. There, I actually got an army ROTC scholarship.

My plan was tweaked a bit after I spoke with an army recruiter, who said I could enlist in the army reserves, get paid for my training and monthly drill time, and ultimately do the ROTC thing. But by doing it this way, there were more benefits, and my time in college would count toward retirement. I headed off to basic training at Fort Leonard Wood, Missouri, knowing that the army was going to turn me into a 62B—a heavy equipment diesel mechanic. Why diesel mechanic? Well, I knew it was a temporary position and it had the biggest signing bonus, not to mention a skill I wouldn't mind learning.

Mom was surprised to hear I was joining the army. It just didn't seem to fit the son she knew. She saw me as a free spirit—I'm guessing that's a charitable description—who hated regimentation. She's also a worrier. I recall her asking, "Can't you find something that won't put your life in danger?" Why would now be different than the rest of my life to this point?

Mom's patriotic, big into following elections and voting. I responded, "Mom, you can't be patriotic on the one hand and then on the other hand say, 'Not my family.' That's hypocritical." Now with a son of my own, I get it, especially after seeing and experiencing what I have seen and experienced. I will support him should he choose this life, but by no means will I push him this way. Back then, naive and patriotic, I had a different perspective. I am still patriotic, just not as naive.

As for the forced regimentation part? True, I didn't like being told what to do. But it's different when you choose it yourself. I just channeled my motivation for army boot camp the same way I did for football training. Whenever the drill sergeants at Fort Lost-in-the-Woods told us to do push-ups, I did my best to do them better and faster than anyone else until I simply could do it better; when they made us run, I ran faster until I puked, then ran some more. It's that same recipe Coach taught: put forth commitment and courage. In no time, I found myself getting strong and very fast (increased capability). I wasn't the biggest guy in my platoon, but I could do push-ups all day. Some guys said basic was the toughest thing they'd ever done in their lives. My response? "It's all perspective."

I guess I stood out enough that they made me platoon guide, which was interesting. There were around forty men in my platoon. Only three of us were White. I was the country-boy hick; the other two were from down South somewhere and were definitely rednecks. There's a difference, trust me. You see where I am going with this? I'd grown up around Black kids; because of the air force base near Mountain Home, we had diversity on our teams. Race wasn't ever an issue for me or my family. In fact, years later, the son I adopted would be African American. I was more concerned about the perception from the guys in my platoon. To be clear, I was outperforming everyone at this point, so I had earned the position, but still, perception of those you lead can be an obstacle.

Although most of the guys respected my drive and ability to perform, what initially got me into the good graces of "the brothers" was my sense of humor. In no time, I was rapping with them—actually better than some. The freestyling spilled over into cadence calling, which I had a lot of opportunity to do as the platoon guide.

One day, I decided to do my best impression of our very soulful, large-bootied female drill instructor. Let's just say she had a very distinct way of calling cadence. I copycatted her with a soulful rendition of a cadence I made up on the spot, shaking my booty as we marched to the beat. Laughter could not be contained but was interrupted as she came charging out of the company orderly room, shouting, "SLADY BABY, DRRROP!" I took it as a compliment that she knew exactly whom I was imitating, and so did everyone else. The push-ups were worth it. Even the other drill sergeants doubled over laughing.

Shortly after that is when one of my platoon members said to me, "Slade dawg, you might be a milk drop in a bottle of ink, but we will follow you anywhere." That meant something to me. Truth is, charisma can open the door, but if that's all it is, you'd just have friends, not a team. At the end of the day, it was the same thing as with football: lead by example, with intensity, and be willing to do anything you ask your men to do. If you do that, they'll follow you, even if you are a white hick from Idaho.

AIT, advanced individual training, was next.

It was during one of the punishment formations they gave us when too many guys screwed up that my mind began wandering. There I am, soaking wet in a drizzling rain in the middle of Missouri, and I start thinking, *I've been here for almost three months now; it's been fun; the screaming is now more boring than motivating. What's the point? What's next? Why am I even here?* And this cartoon bubble pops up above my head, and in it is my dad saying, "If this happens, I'd like you to..."

"PRIVATE SLADE, ARE YOU CHEWING GUM IN MY FORMATION?"

Busted! My pondering had made me forget to keep that wad of Wrigley's spearmint in my cheek, and I had started masticating subconsciously. "No, Drill Sergeant. I am just holding it with my teeth."

Laughs were being suppressed all around, but he let me have it. "Drop!"

That night, I knelt down in the barracks and prayed. It's what I promised my dad I would do. I asked Heavenly Father if the church is true and if there's a path that I should follow. I didn't get a strong feeling one way or the other on that, but I got a pretty strong feeling that I should serve a mission. And I remember saying—I don't know if I said it out loud or if I just thought it really deeply—*THAT is not what I'm asking. That's not on the table right now. What I'm asking is, is this true?*

I did that three nights in a row, and every single time it was, "You need to serve a mission." The thought even came to me during the day. I had this nagging feeling, and I knew that it wasn't coming from me, because I didn't want to serve. I'm thinking, *If I'm getting this feeling against what I want to do, I gotta believe it's coming from somebody that knows more than I do, right? About what I'm here for and what I'm supposed to do. And so, I guess that's what I'm gonna do when I get back.*

Within days, I had gotten in touch with church officials and enrolled in a missionary training program that would begin three months after I returned to Utah. I also applied for and was granted a two-year sabbatical from my Army Reserve unit. Everything fell nicely into place.

After two months at the missionary training center, where I learned rudimentary Portuguese, I boarded the plane for São Paulo, Brazil, on my way to the city of Salvador, capital of Bahia State, on a peninsula poking into the Atlantic in the northeast of the country. I was almost twenty years old.

The mission was two years of hard work under primitive conditions, eating beans and rice every day that were cooked in very suspect conditions, hygienically speaking. I remember thinking, *Hey, I've done this before, no biggie, but not for two years straight. Oh well, that's what stomach acid is for.* What stomach acid didn't kill, we got rid of with a pill every six months. I called it exorcizing my internal family, which was a whole different kind of religious experience carried out in the commode.

We would get up at six every morning, study till nine, then work for twelve hours. Our tasks ranged from building houses and rudimentary sewer systems to assisting in orphanages. And, of course, we shared the gospel. It was a huge foundation builder for my life, and honestly, the experiences and lessons learned could be a book in and of itself. That mission service made me feel blessed to be born in the USA and strengthened my patriotic feelings even more. More importantly, it taught me to believe and work for something greater than myself and appreciate the joy that comes from that.

In 1999, I returned to the United States. Because of Defense Department cutbacks, the ROTC program had been disbanded at Utah State, so I decided that I would go to Snow Community College in Ephraim to minimize expenses. While there, I managed to nearly amputate my left arm in a catastrophic snowboarding accident. Reconstructive surgery with no insurance buried me in medical bills, and football was now out of the question. The arm was never supposed to work again, but it does, more or less, thanks to two summers of rehabbing it by whitewater river guiding for Western River Expeditions in the Grand Canyon. It was an awesome job, and it's where I first experienced risking my life to save others. The experience with my arm solidified my belief that the world may tell you matter-of-factly that things are a certain way, but you still have the power to prove the world wrong.

I earned my associate degree in one year, then returned to Utah State with a plan to get my bachelor's degree in just two more years. After my first year back at Utah State, ROTC made a comeback, and I eventually received that ROTC scholarship but did have to extend my college experience from the two semesters I had left to three in order to qualify. I agreed, but like an idiot, instead of opting for Basket Weaving 101 or Underwater Fire Prevention, I asked how many majors I could complete in that time. End result: I carried as many as twenty-five credits a semester, ultimately receiving my BS degree with majors in finance and economics and also a minor in international business. Sounds fancy, but I really did not end up using any of it near term.

My second year there, my arm was working again, so I walked onto the football team and tried out for strong safety. I locked down a second-string position and received the promise of a scholarship for the following year if I kept on my trajectory, but the game just wasn't the same for me as it had been in high school. The vibe was all wrong; the fun wasn't there; there was no team camaraderie. Most players didn't even know each other's names. After one season, disappointed in the game at this level, I decided I was done.

I could have chosen to enjoy it and try to be the catalyst for change, but that thought didn't cross my mind at the time. I loved football, but this wasn't the football I loved. This highlighted to me the importance of camaraderie on a team; it's a truth that absolutely holds true in combat. When bullets are flying at you and you are flinging them back, the patriotism and sense of mission take you only so far. Ultimately, it's for your brothers in arms that you willingly look death in the face, over and over.

Meantime, I did need something to fill the team-competition void I was experiencing, so I organized a squad to compete in the intercollegiate ROTC Ranger Challenge. It tests leadership skills, physical fitness, marksmanship, and military academics. By the end of that year, Utah State finished second at the competition in Monterey, California.

Major Rand Curtis, our professor of military science and my mentor, made it clear that this was a leadership-building exercise for me—and later told me that nobody expected us to even place as a first-year team. Problem was, I expected us to take first (he was happier with second place than I was). The critical decisions were mine—who made the team, and whom I had to face and say the equivalent of "Sorry, despite your best efforts and dedication, you didn't make the cut." We created a unique synergy, and that experience taught me the importance of attitude, of having guys by your side who want to be there, who are willing to work hard so they don't let the rest of the team down. It also helped me be comfortable with uncomfortable face-to-face conversations. These understandings and skills would prove very valuable down the road.

The Utah State University student paper covered my efforts to build a Ranger Challenge Team back in 2002.

In December 2002, I was commissioned a second lieutenant in the US Army Reserve. My mom and siblings attended the ceremony; my dad developed kidney stones on the way to Logan, Utah, with them and got stuck in the hospital. Mom pinned the bars on my collar. At the time, my view was that those gold bars were the reward for the work I had done. What I didn't grasp at that moment is that they signified my tacit acceptance of future levels of responsibility, which would include life-and-death decisions for the troops I would come to command.

CHAPTER 2

SO THAT'S WHAT THAT FEELS LIKE

Preparing the Mind for the Unknown with Chair Flying

My adrenaline spikes as we plummet toward the ground. I'm looking at the very rock we're going to smash into. Seconds earlier, we were looking for very-well-hidden Taliban among trees and rocks when a concussion wave most likely caused by an RPG airburst reverberated through the aircraft and our bodies, vibrating our innards like a Jell-O wave. The blast wave lifted us off our flight path and flung us forward. Our rotor blades are no longer biting the air to produce lift, meaning gravity rules. We are diving down like you do on a roller coaster, but there's no track we can ride to avoid last-minute impact.

That happened during my very first engagement with the enemy. Spoiler alert: I am writing this book—gravity didn't win. You'll read the complete details of that engagement in a later chapter, but it's important now that I relate what I said sarcastically, just seconds after we realized our time wasn't up—at least not then: "So that's what that feels like." It wasn't the first time I had uttered that statement after a significant emotional event. I actually was blessed—or cursed—depending on your perspective, with many opportunities in flight school to hone the skill of staying calm in order to effect the best possible outcome. Those events were also the catalyst for my adopting the practice of chair flying, which I'll explain shortly. I credit the practice with saving my life on more than one occasion and now realize it's something we all can do in order to not only increase the chance of better outcomes in all sorts of endeavors but also to decrease the chance of lasting trauma. Chair flying—this simple technique is applicable to anyone; it is my hope readers will learn to adapt a version of this in their lives.

A profile of the Apache showing the pilot and copilot/gunner in separate cockpits. The only communication between the pilots is by intercom.

Before they let us climb into a helicopter, we had four weeks of OBC, the basic officer leadership course. That was followed by two weeks of preflight instruction...*yawn*. Only then did we start the ten weeks of in-flight training to acquire basic flight skills: picking it up, hovering, landing, and flying a rectangular traffic pattern in an orange-and-white TH-67 Creek (most military helicopters carry the names of Native American tribes; Creek is the only native blood I can claim any part of, barely, and coincidentally, that's the trainer that I got), which is the military variant of the civilian Bell 206B JetRanger, your basic TV news chopper. Each two students had a civilian instructor for that phase, and my "stick buddy" (a female captain) and I were unlucky enough to draw one who was a screaming, condescending prick. His legend was that he'd flown in Vietnam, supposedly racking up an unbelievable 20,000 helicopter hours. Legend or not, what a douche!

Hovering a helicopter requires minimal, very exact movements with both hands and both feet simultaneously. But it isn't really your muscles that make it hover; it's your brain. They call it finding the "hover button." You can't do it, you can't do it, you can't do it—and then you can, from one day to the next, you've found your hover button. Our screaming instructor really helped us relax and focus on learning those very fine motor movements (thick sarcasm intended), while we unintentionally oscillated the aircraft like one of those carnival rides that swing you back and forth. When I finally did find the button, he said, using his typical condescending tone, "Well, look who finally learned how to hover."

I responded, "That's bad news for you, old man, 'cuz when you have your heart attack, I'm just going to keep hovering till you stop kicking." My stick buddy was aghast. My default is to respect my elders, but I'd had enough of his crap. During our table talk after we landed, he ignored the insult and told us our next goal was to solo. Then he proceeded to tell both of us how we were way behind and how he didn't even know whether we were ever going to be ready to solo.

So what happens the very next day? On his recommendation, we're the first pair on the schedule to solo. If confusion is what he was aiming for with this instructional technique, he nailed it. My solo turned out to be quite the adventure. Each student is supposed to successfully take off and land eight times, flying a pattern in between. I'm in the pilot's seat, my stick buddy in the copilot seat next to me. After we'd done four or five laps and I was feeling pretty good about myself, I suddenly felt excessive feedback in the controls, indicative of a hydraulic failure. I had only ten hours in this bird, not nearly enough to be equipped to handle erratic control inputs, yet it's not like you have a choice. Unlike football, I couldn't tap my helmet signaling a sub to come in from the sidelines.

I knew enough to call the tower and request immediate clearance to go straight to the apron adjacent to the control tower and land. Like a drunken sailor, I shot a very edgy approach, got the helicopter into a quasi-hover about three feet above the tarmac and relatively stable—emphasis on *relatively*—and planted the thing hard enough that the back door popped open. Remember, I could barely hover. Doing it with added resistance and feedback in the controls was a big deal for me. The touchdown wasn't pretty, but we were safe with no damage to the aircraft.

Our instructor—whom we'd taken to calling Boss Hogg—comes stomping out of the tower. He tells my stick buddy to exit and climbs in, screaming at me. "You chicken! Making up reasons to land! I'm taking it up." He doesn't get it any higher than a five-foot hover and immediately brings it down. "Yep, it's hydraulic failure; those never happen." Score one for the new kids, not just on correctly identifying the emergency but actually landing without incident. Another instructor pulled me aside and said, "Your instructor won't tell you this, but you handled yourself outstanding; many students would have panicked and crashed. Any experience like this, you can both walk away from and learn from, is a good experience." That phrase would stick with me.

I still had four more patterns to complete, so we went up again the next day. A similar routine, only this time I feel a high-frequency vibration in the pedals. "You feel this?" I ask my stick buddy, who puts her boots on the pedals to check. With uncertainty, she says, "Maybe." So once again, we tell them we need to land forthwith. That vibration could mean imminent tail rotor failure, which would almost certainly be unsurvivable even if you are experienced, let alone greenhorn status. As much as I did not want to execute yet another precautionary landing, the risk of me being right in my malfunction analysis was enough to call yet again for an emergency landing.

Same thing happens with Boss Hogg declaring that we're full of crap, then picking it up to a hover and bringing it right back down. "Yep, high-frequency vibe." This time, he discovers that the air-conditioning belt had broken and was lying on the tail rotor drive shaft, causing the feedback in the pedals. So it turned out to not be a dangerous situation, but I read the indications correctly, and the only way to know it wasn't dangerous was to land and check.

Over the course of flight school, I had fourteen legitimate PLs—precautionary landings—earning the honorific PL King from my classmates. I don't recall putting it together at the time, but later I figured out that the PLs were great training for the combat emergencies they foreshadowed. Actually, those first two solo crises fostered a habit in me to imagine every scenario I could think of involving emergencies. Then I would systematically picture what I would do with every part of my body, what my frame of mind would be, and how I would communicate. This is the practice known as *chair flying* and is something I do to the nth degree, even today. It's something that I am absolutely positive saved my life several times downrange, in emergencies that, if handled incorrectly, indecisively, or without the requisite expedience, would have resulted in my demise.

After finishing the third phase of flight school, basic instrument flying, and learning how to cope when visual flight cues are absent, I moved on to the fourth and final phase of training: basic combat skills. We traded in our orange-and-white Creek trainers for the military green OH-58 A/C Kiowa. This is where we received low-level flight experience and learned tactical night operations using night vision devices. For some unknown reason, I felt more comfortable in these scenarios than with the simple flying we'd done in previous phases.

It's also where I experienced my first—and to this date only—*real* autorotation. What is an autorotation, you ask? Short version: it's bad and has the potential to be the last thing you do in this life. It happened at night. We're flying over some of Alabama's heaviest forests. We're about fifty feet above the trees, which is roughly one hundred feet above the ground level (AGL). My job is to navigate and cross-check instruments. My stick buddy is asleep in the back. Suddenly, the engine sound changes slightly, drawing my eyes in to the instrument panel, and I see that the N_1 gauge measuring engine rpm is going in the wrong direction. I know that at a certain point, it is going to indicate an engine shutdown.

"Hey! Look at the N_1?" I urgently suggest, with a question in my voice. Was I really seeing and understanding what I thought I was understanding? The N_1 drop triggered the "engine out" audio warning. The engine had died, and the instructor pilot quickly puts us into autorotation. Glancing out the window, I see that the dense trees are giving way to about a half-mile opening over a farmer's pasture. How fortuitous.

Helicopters are not like planes; you can't just glide and steer to a comfortable landing. At the instant of engine failure, the main rotor blades are producing lift and thrust by a combination of their angle of attack and velocity. When engine power fails, the drag component will rapidly reduce or decay the rotor speed, turning the aircraft into a rock. The flight manual will stipulate a minimum rotor rpm, below which it may be impossible to recover. To avoid this, the pilot must immediately *reduce* collective pitch, which has the effect of decreasing both lift-induced and blade profile drag. As a result, the helicopter begins an immediate *descent*, which produces an upward flow of air through the rotor system. You're falling with intent, but you still feel like a rock. This upward flow of air through the rotors keeps the spinny thing spinny. This provides sufficient thrust to maintain rotor rpm throughout the descent, while also producing some lift. If you've done it right, the moment comes when you're able to increase the pitch in the blades and slow yourself down enough to land without compressing your spine. So as I said, it's bad. *More detailed video explanation found at www.clearedhot.info.*

We are dropping fast, and as we come down to about treetop level, I can see that he has us lined up to hit the solitary, gigantic tree in that field. I say, "You do see that tree, correct?" He immediately slides us to the right. Guess he hadn't. But his slide to the right lines us up to land on the only fence in the pasture, which is now visible through our night vision goggles (NVGs). We're at twenty feet AGL, now flaring to slow our impact. "You do see that fence, right?" Another quick shift, and we are on the ground with a thud, the fence just outside my door.

The landing was eerily quiet, no engine, just the drone of the rotors spinning down. I knew I should feel some intense emotion, but really, it was more like we finished a maneuver with a little different ending. Even at that moment, part of me saw it as experience I could take with me for the future. "So that's what that feels like," I said.

I'll never forget the instructor kicking open his door, bending over at the waist with his head out the door, and spewing chunks. I knew that this was not his first real-world autorotation. He had one previously where he went down in the trees, causing serious injury to himself and his copilot and damage to the aircraft. Not too many guys have two real autos under their belt and still have a pulse, so I get why his dinner made a reappearance. It turned out that they'd given us bad gas, which grounded the entire flight school fleet.

About a month later, when flight school ended, I ranked third in my class, which disappointed me. At graduation ceremonies outside the US Army Aviation Museum, I was presented my wings by one of the instructors. I had studied and worked harder for those wings than I had for my four-year degree. They indeed meant something to me. *I am now officially an aviator.*

From Fort Rucker at the end of February, I immediately headed to Apache school at Silverbell Army Heliport, home of the Western Army National Guard Aviation Training Site (WAATS) in Marana, Arizona, just north of Tucson.

Throughout all my initial rotary wing training at Fort Rucker, I felt a level of stress triggered by the basic *Will I get through this and reach my goal?* thought. At Apache school, I felt that I'd arrived. The machine was awesome! The updated description on the army's website reads this way:

> The Apache AH-64D/E is the Army's attack helicopter. It is capable of destroying armor, personnel and materiel targets in obscured battlefield conditions. The Apache is a twin-engine, four-blade tandem-seat attack helicopter equipped with an M230 30 mm cannon, Hydra-70 2.75-inch rockets, and HELLFIRE missiles (both laser-guided and radio frequency). The current

Army Aviation fleet contains both AH-64D Longbow Apaches and AH-64E models. The Apache is fielded to both Active Army and Army National Guard armed reconnaissance battalions and cavalry units. The aircraft is designed to support Brigade Combat Teams across the full spectrum of warfare.

This is why they call the Apache the deadliest helicopter in the world. It can carry multiple armament configurations. Displayed in this US Army image are the choices that can be made before a mission. From left to right on the ground: extended range fuel cells, rocket pods holding nineteen rockets each (which can be exchanged with the Hellfire racks already mounted on the Apache), 2.75-inch unguided rockets (center, closest to the bird), which are available in a variety of types, including point detonating and proximity air burst and 30 mm rounds for the M230 chain gun (front, center). The Apache can carry up to 1200 light armor-piercing rounds, but we flew with only 300 or so to allow us to carry an extra internal fuel tank. There were times that we carried and fired more than a million dollars worth of ammunition on a single sortie. The versatility of both the machine and its payload makes for a lethal choose-your-own-adventure scenario.

My instructor, CW4 Mike Hilwig, was amazing. The Apache felt so big compared to the little trainers, and the power of those two jet engines was astonishing. I called my parents, excited about the reality that I was actually going to be flying this incredible helicopter. I told them it was like driving a semi that handled like a Ferrari but one that I could make move in three dimensions. And—wait for it—it could blow up a small town if called on to do so. I loved it.

Learning how to fly using the helmet-mounted display unit (HDU) was painful. I'd eventually use this device in nearly every firefight in Afghanistan. Hang with me here as I try to explain. The HDU is a monocle positioned in front of my right eye. It displays all the information I need to fly—altitude, torque, airspeed, forward-looking infrared radar (FLIR) image for night vision, plus several more. The bird's weapon system symbology is also displayed on the HDU, and I can actually aim the 30 mm chain gun using just the HDU. My left eye independently needs to see both inside and outside the cockpit. It's like holding a book up to one eye and reading, while the other eye is watching TV in the distance. I actually had to teach my brain to separate what each eye is doing. They teach us to embrace the HDU by blacking out the cockpit—they call it *being in the bag*. The only thing you can see is in that little monocle in front of your eye. While in the bag, you have to lift off the ground, hover, fly some patterns, and land. Flying that way is more uncomfortable than kissing cousins. Of course, there's an instructor pilot in the back seat without curtains—actually a separate compartment in the Apache—ready to prevent a disaster. But they don't stop the bagged student pilots from making their aircraft wallow around like drunken boats on the sea. Eventually, just as with hovering, the brain figures it out and then that monocle becomes your best friend, feeding you valuable information without you having to look down at display screens inside the cockpit.

While I was training at WAATS, I picked up intel that the co-located 1/285th Attack Reconnaissance Battalion, an Arizona Guard unit that flies Apaches, was anticipating a combat deployment to the Middle East. I had been jonesing to deploy ever since 9/11, so I quickly requested a transfer from my Utah Guard unit and, after graduation in May, began drilling with the Arizonans while making a living as a financial planner one hundred miles away in Sierra Vista, Arizona, near Fort Huachuca.

My total flight training time: one very fast year. So that's what that feels like.

The art of chair flying is something most people can master. I believe that this kind of visualization actually results in stress inoculation as well as mental preparation, which aids in staving off the negative effects of trauma. *To see a demonstration of my chair flying technique, go to www.clearedhot.info/lessonslearned.*

CHAPTER 3

WHY IS THIS SO HARD?

Staying Afloat by Compartmentalizing

Man, it's dark! I can see where we're going through the monocle on my right eye using the FLIR, but my left eye isn't registering a thing outside the cockpit. It's pitch black. No moonlight, no starlight. We have been working for several minutes with a ground controller to confirm which compound in this village is hostile, when we finally hear that we are cleared hot. "Arrow 0-6, you are cleared to engage on that compound. Keep all fires west of the river."

"Widow 1-9, Arrow 0-6 copies all. In hot from the west."

I tell my copilot, "Okay, Josh, get it locked up in the tactical acquisition display, and hit it with some 30 mm." We are both looking at the same screen on the multifunction display, and I can see him moving the sensor around. "That's it."

"Yeah, I got it."

"Shoot!" The aircraft shakes with the rhythmic recoil of the
30 mm. *Gugutgutgut! Gugutgutgut!* Seconds later, the image
in my MFD turns from a compound to a dust cloud. I can see
the flashes of the explosions with my naked left eye while
looking at the destruction through the FLIR image in my
monocle on my right, when all of a sudden, I lose the image.
Now both eyes are seeing only black, and what's more, the
lights in the aircraft have all turned off and the side tone
of the radios in my ears has gone silent. We just entered a
sensory-deprived black hole. No lights, no instruments, no
navigation, and no radios; just the eerie sound of the engines
and the rotors whirring.

We were flying fairly level before the world went dark, so I
maintain the controls and reach for the battery-operated
night vision goggles I have on the dash. I connect them
quickly to my helmet and flip the toggle, and blackness
gives way to dark green. The goggles aren't great since
there is nearly no ambient light for them to magnify, but
I can make out the ground enough to keep air between us
and it. I adjust the flight controls, head back toward Camp
Bastion. I know my wingman will follow me even though
I can't communicate with them. It's part of our standard
operating procedures. Then we get a surge of power and
all interior lights and the audio come alive. I immediately
key the mic to let them know what happened, only to have
it drop out again before I can get two words out. I yell
forward, hoping my copilot can hear me through the glass
that divides us, even though that's an unrealistic expectation. "WE ARE OKAY! STILL FLYING. HEADED HOME."

Imagine you are driving on a twisting mountain road, on a pitch-black night, cruising at sixty-five mph, listening to the radio and talking to someone on the phone. Suddenly, all the lights in the car inside and out shut off, the radio stops, and the person you were talking to goes silent. You know you saw a turn ahead before that happened, but now all you see is black. Add to that getting shot at and being in the sky, and you pretty much have what happened.

I slow up, hoping my wingman will fly up alongside us, and they do. I wave my flashlight back and forth so they know something is obviously wrong. It works. They take the lead and I stay on their wing. They're the guide dog and I'm the guy with the white cane.

Turned out we took a round to one of the generators. Boeing says the other generator is supposed to be able to pick up the load, but it didn't. Oddly enough, during this event it felt as if I had been there before because I had. Not in actuality, but I had made up a similar hypothetical scenario in my head during a chair flying exercise. I rehearsed staying calm, maintaining aircraft control first, gaining situational awareness by gaining vision from a system not dependent on aircraft power, and then communicating the best I could. Because I had flown this mission hypothetically a few times, I knew what to do and did it with relative calm. When it actually happened, I am sure my heart rate was elevated, but we enjoyed a safe flight home. This was something I had prepared my mind for, and therefore something that could have been catastrophic ended with nothing more than a pretty cool story.

What I was not prepared for prior to my deployment was navigating the intricacies of a new marriage to a wife who, I later learned, struggled with a mental disorder that led to such serious depression that she hinted at suicide. Never even thought about chair flying that scenario.

I was at a promotion party at a club in Tucson when I met Katie Trelhose, a blond-haired, blue-eyed beauty, about five-six, 115 pounds, with everything packaged the way I like it. She was three years younger than I, a respiratory therapist, and motivated to become a nurse practitioner. There was an immediate physical attraction, which led to dancing, which led to dating. More importantly, I actually enjoyed her company. I really enjoyed our laughter and our conversations when we were together, and I found her motivation attractive. I had long since realized that pretty girls were a dime a dozen, but a pretty girl you could enjoy your time with? That's a gem worth investigating. It was only after I started dating her that I learned she was an enlisted medic in my battalion. The fact that she was not LDS didn't dissuade me from wanting to get to know her better, and she had expressed a great deal of interest in my beliefs, attending church with me every Sunday. Months later, I learned her Baptist family was decidedly not thrilled at the notion of having me as their son-in-law. Not that they had anything against me personally' they just harbored a good number of misconceptions about my faith. Her mom actually believed we ritually sacrificed goats. I told her that was only on Wednesdays and totally optional.

We had been dating for about six months—by then, I was twenty-seven, which is long in the tooth for a Mormon boy; friends and family had been asking "When?" since I was twenty-three. I was already seriously thinking about proposing to her down the road—but had kept that to myself, not wanting to jinx it or add any undue pressure—when I got a call from her sister telling me that Katie had been in a serious car accident. She'd been out with friends and the driver had been drinking. Somehow, he got her Ford Explorer airborne. Katie was the only one wearing a seat belt—and she's the only one who got hurt. Everyone else bounced when the car came down, but because she was strapped in, her spine absorbed the entire shock and it shattered.

I immediately jumped in the car and drove like I was being chased to get to the hospital in Tucson. There, I learned that she'd been in surgery and the docs now weren't sure whether she'd be able to walk again. That caused some serious introspection. *If I was thinking about proposing before this happened, and now I'm not going to propose because it happened, what does that say about my character? Is that who I am?*

I prayed about it but to be honest, didn't really get a feeling one way or the other. I just felt the right thing to do would be to act as if the accident didn't happen and make decisions I would have made; whether or not she could walk shouldn't play a role. So even though it was a lot sooner than I'd planned, I actually proposed to her while she was still hospitalized. I wanted her to know I loved her for who she was, and walking is not a determining factor. She was shocked, anticipating I might do the opposite, but she quickly said yes.

The surgeons had spanned the gap in her spine with two metal rods, fusing the vertebrae together, and in answer to our prayers, Katie began walking! She had to wear a hard, white plastic clamshell brace on her upper body that I called her stormtrooper vest. Technically, it's a thoraco-lumbo-sacral support corset—like I said, a stormtrooper vest. With it, as well as a lot of painkillers and other meds, she could walk. Unbeknownst to us, she got hooked on the painkillers.

While we'd been courting, there hadn't been any drama at all. We had gotten along like great friends. We were able to talk amicably through issues as mature adults. Now things were different. She began to go through emotional extremes. This began shortly after she went on the pill, and we both attributed it to her hormones being out of balance. I didn't tell her, but I wondered if there were other factors, such as the physical and emotional trauma she'd been through, that may have changed her body's chemistry.

Much later, we would learn that she had borderline personality disorder, a mental illness that typically shows up in adolescence to early adulthood. The trauma could have triggered it or may have had nothing to do with it. The National Institute of Mental Health has a comprehensive definition for it, but the short version is that it's a mental health disorder that impacts the way you think and feel about yourself and others, causing problems functioning in everyday life. It includes self-image issues, difficulty managing emotions and behavior, and a pattern of unstable relationships. With borderline personality disorder, you have an intense fear of abandonment or instability, and you may have difficulty tolerating being alone. Yet inappropriate anger, impulsiveness, and frequent mood swings may push others away, even though you want to have loving and lasting relationships.

To put it plainly, she was becoming unreasonable in a disproportionate way. On top of that, because she was between jobs at the time of the accident, she had no health insurance or income, and her parents lived paycheck to paycheck, which meant I was paying all those bills. Although I was doing well as a financial planner, we're talking hundreds of thousands of dollars in medical bills. It didn't matter how much money I was pulling down, the bills were going to sink us. My only solution was to marry her sooner rather than later and then go on active duty, which would get her covered as my wife by an insurer that wouldn't disqualify her due to preexisting conditions. We actually moved the wedding date up so I could quickly get her listed as a dependent. Originally, I'd been thinking I'd maintain courtship during the upcoming deployment, propose afterward, and then plan a wedding. But events forced different priorities.

We scheduled the wedding at a Mormon church in Tucson for December. Katie had been baptized and became a member of the Church of Jesus Christ of Latter-day Saints while we were dating. The wedding was a low-key event with just immediate family present. We didn't go on a honeymoon because I had to prepare for deployment, but a couple of days after the wedding, we moved into a new home I'd purchased in Coolidge, almost at the midpoint between Tucson and Phoenix.

I was laying a flagstone patio for our new home, and she'd told me she'd help. I was grateful for that because maneuvering the big stones and leveling the sand underneath was difficult for me to do alone. Katie kept coming out and acting as though she was going to start helping but then finding a reason to go back inside. After several such delays, I was tired of waiting. So out of frustration, I said, "If you're gonna help, help. If not, I would prefer you just stay inside; I'll do it myself." That's how the army had taught me to confront personnel issues. I didn't know enough about being a husband to understand that probably wasn't the best approach. Moments later, while my head was down as I smoothed sand underneath a huge stone I was propping up with the other hand, I got hit with her wedding ring. She'd thrown it at me. I looked up completely shocked and confused. To this point, we'd never had any serious altercations. Sure, she'd flown off the handle a few times prior to the wedding and had increasing mood swings. We'd chalked those up to side effects of birth control hormones. But they were nothing like this, nothing really aimed directly at me.

"What're you doing?" I asked.

"I hate you. Keep it," she said, referring to the ring, and stormed back inside.

I was dumbstruck, even bewildered. Talk about being in the dark. I hadn't chair flown this, nor had I been trained for it. Although I had mentors who guided me in the nuances of flying a combat helicopter, my married friends and relatives had never prepared me for anything like this. My mind simply was not prepared. The *hate* word had never come out before, and *hate* was a term I was raised never to use. I had violated that family dictum just once, with my father, right around the time I left home for good at fifteen. It's been a trigger word for me ever since. I just knelt there for a few minutes in the sand, that $8,000 emerald-cut diamond ring in my hand. Totally confused, I stood up and followed her back inside and was apologetic.

It was clear that she felt extremely hurt by my words. I knew they weren't loving words, but I never thought they would trigger something so dramatic. It was a turning point in our marriage. From then on, everything was a huge deal. "You don't love me...you don't want to be with me..." and on and on and on. The woman I was deeply in love with was now my biggest enigma. I had to figure this out for our sakes.

"Honey, if I didn't love you, why would I propose to you before you could even walk? I chose to get married on an expedited timeline for you because I love you and wanted to make sure you would be taken care of. Can't you see that?" My assurances fell on deaf ears. She was in a new reality now, one where I played a vital role, but unbeknownst to me, what I did really didn't matter. My role now seemed primarily to be the focal point of my wife's insecurities. In the script, I could have a speaking part or not. I could lose my temper or be patient and loving. I could even be hateful in my efforts to bridge our disconnect. But it was all to zero avail.

I had heard guys say, "Once you get married, they completely change." Was this what they were referring to? Literally, one day after marriage our interactions changed completely, and they only continued to deteriorate. Was this how all marriages were, and did people just live this way?

Katie kept going to the ER for things. Her ailments sounded legit, but man, it seemed as though every week it was something different. It wasn't until one of our cars broke down that I realized what was happening. She was still on painkillers and in a big way. Not having the car kept her from being able to get more. She went into nasty withdrawals, vomiting and diarrhea, sweating like crazy. She was in such terrible shape that when I offered to take her to the ER, she didn't want to move from the tub of warm water she had made her home. She had been thin to begin with, but when I walked into the bathroom and saw her pale, skin-and-bones frame, stringy hair, and lifeless eyes, it was very clear to me that whether she wanted to move or not, I had to get her to a hospital.

Once there, the attending physician asked if she was on any prescriptions, to which I responded no. He pulled me aside and said, "It looks like opiate withdrawal. We're going to give her some painkiller, and if she perks up, we'll know."

That is indeed what happened. I felt so betrayed. I was raised in a family where you simply did not lie, no matter how small. Even if the truth was difficult to divulge, I had to tell the truth. The fact that she had lied about coming off painkillers, yet was doing things to keep using the pills behind my back, hurt. But like an idiot, I masked that hurt with anger. I was in the dark again, with no training, no chair flying, just winging it. That method leads to crash after crash. I chastised her for lying. She was apologetic, then justified her deceit. Next came anger at herself, followed by rage directed at me. And then we went full circle, and she was once again apologetic.

I made her agree to come off the opiates cold turkey. When she told me that was dangerous, I didn't believe her. *She's just being weak.* The suck-it-up-and-drive-on part of me was in full force even though it was counterproductive. I had self-doubts. *Am I being the jerk husband here?* I attacked Katie's medical issues just like I'd attacked every obstacle in my own life: aggressively, head-on. In fact, I saw her obstacles as my obstacles, and rather than empathizing, I put myself in her shoes to attack the problem. It's a typical guy-thing to do. By trying to make her do it the same way I would do it, I caused her an immense amount of physical and psychological pain.

The next week was hell. Katie was very sick. She screamed and manipulated, trying to get more narcotics. This time, I'd been prepared with IV bags and electrolytes to keep her hydrated until she finally seemed to be coming through to the other side. I later found out she just found a way to get her drugs and never fully came off of them anyway.

Then came a big surprise. Katie had gone off the pill because she couldn't keep them down during detox and forgot to go back on once she finished treatment. Nature took its course, and she got pregnant. Although it had always been my thought that we wouldn't have kids until after my deployment—and I certainly didn't want her going through a pregnancy while I was in Afghanistan—neither one of us viewed this negatively. In fact, I hoped it just might be the thing that brought some immediate joy into her life, providing something positive to focus on. Unfortunately, about six weeks after we confirmed the pregnancy, she lost the baby. As you can imagine, it was devastating for both of us but especially so for Katie.

She was also cursed with incredibly bad luck. No matter how carefully I worked with her to plan things, it seemed as though Murphy's Law was always enforced. If it could go wrong, it would, at the worst possible time. She would either take full responsibility for what happened in a very excessive way, emphasizing how terrible she was and how she didn't deserve me, or find a way not to take responsibility for it at all, justifying and blaming others—usually me, in some way. I've got broad shoulders, but these constant circumstantial crises that I had to bail her out of were taking a toll. It felt like bailing her out had become my full-time job—often quite literally. More than once, she hadn't taken care of traffic tickets, and when she'd get pulled over, her one phone call came my way. As it should have, but still.

I was also getting blindsided by thousands of dollars in debt I'd been unaware of, by collection calls, by her car being repo'd, and on and on. I really wanted to be a loving, supportive husband, but this was taxing, and despite my best efforts to let it go every time, resentment was building.

Nevertheless, I so badly wanted to reach her, comfort her, and work as a team on our new life, but nothing I did seemed to help. I just had to suck it up because the gears of the mighty military machine were grinding, and my unit was going to deploy to Fort Hood, Texas, where, before deploying to Afghanistan, we'd get certified to fly the latest version of the Apache, the AH-64 D-model Longbow.

Five months after saying, "I do," five months of way more heartache and strain than I had anticipated, the 1st/285th deployed from Silverbell to Fort Hood, near Killeen in central Texas, on what would turn out to be eight months of camping in the woods and playing war so we could be ready to go to war.

I never understood the army's need to practice *suck* repeatedly. Maybe once, to see if you can hack it. But can't we agree that we remember that it sucks? I mean, breathing in CS gas so we appreciate our gas masks is actually a periodic requirement. They call it a "refresher." Yeah, I remember well that it feels like you're breathing fire, and more liquid comes out of your nose, eyes, and mouth than you thought possible. There's no need for the refresher.

Our stay at Fort Hood was topped off with a capstone field training event. We were told we'd be fighting a mock war: executing movement to contact. Intel painted a pretty robust enemy force with which we would need to contend. I was pumped; this should be cool. I expected to use the skills of an air mission commander (AMC) that I'd just been taught. To my acute disappointment, none of that happened. It turned out to be nothing more than an exercise in communicating within a conflict zone, merely flying from one phase line to the next.

During the well-attended after-action debrief, I publicly expressed my dissatisfaction with the second-rate conclusion to our eight months of practicing the suck. What I actually said to the colonel in charge of the training and my battalion CO—call sign Desert Hawk 0-6 ("0-6" is a call sign given to the commanding officer of an army unit)—turned out to be a bit too direct for the occasion. At least that's what he told me afterward. "To be honest, sir, I feel like I have tactical blue balls." Too direct? Maybe, but it accurately conveyed my feelings. The reaction was decidedly mixed: the suck-ups' jaws dropped, while the rest were either roaring with laughter or desperately trying to hold it back. It was a feedback session, after all. I gave mine, respectfully.

Katie came to see me twice, when I was allowed out of the field and could spend time in a barracks on base, where I had my own room. On both trips to Fort Hood, she managed to get into car accidents. This would become a recurring theme. Murphy hung out with my wife nonstop. My family began referring to it as "Katie's black cloud." The only luck she had was bad. Some she brought on herself by lack of preparation or just plain bad decision making, but some was no-kidding-just-plain-bad luck. How bad? Brace yourself: Katie got pregnant, this time while on the pill. Unfortunately, lightning struck twice, because again, she miscarried, leaving added heartache and feelings of inadequacy in its wake.

I was well aware that I was about to be sent eight thousand miles away from her, and knowing her history, that was concerning. I was still struggling with this gigantic question in my head, "Why is this so hard?" I naively believed that any two people can make a marriage happy if they just work at it. But this wasn't coming together. I'd always taken things in stride and didn't obsess over anything. But after a relatively short time married to Katie, I was different. She was constantly on my mind but not in the best ways. It was clear to me that in order to succeed during our deployment to Operation Enduring Freedom, I'd have to be vigilant about compartmentalizing job from marriage. Doing that when your spouse keeps mentioning how bad things are—even alluding to suicide—can leave you with quite the conundrum. Intuition told me that most of what she said was unlikely to be enacted. But what if I was wrong and she did opt to do something drastic? So even though compartmentalization was absolutely necessary, it was also very important that I continue to work with my wife in order to avoid something none of us wanted.

At that point in my life, I didn't believe in therapists. It was up to me, alone, to figure it out. I stubbornly believed I could but really had no clear path as to how.

The day finally came when we deployed to Afghanistan. I honestly don't remember saying goodbye to her. I think that's because things were so shaky between us that I've managed to suppress those memories and can't seem to be able to recover them—even for this book. I did leave, and she did cry. I know that happened. But I just can't remember the details of how that happened. I think, in a way, that leaving was a relief. Boarding that C-17, I put on my headphones and the words of U2's "With or without You" resonated:

My hands are tied

My body bruised, she got me with

Nothing to win and nothing left to lose

And you give yourself away, and you give, and you give,

And you give yourself away

With or without you, I can't live.

With or without you.

Although the song epitomizes the futility of effort I was feeling, my state of mind was *I know there are lessons to learn from this; I just don't see them clearly. I know we can succeed; I just don't know how. I know I'll have to deal with this. I know we have to figure out our marriage, but I have to compartmentalize those unknowns and focus on my job right now. I have to focus on leaving the country.* Little did I know it was about to get a lot harder.

For more on the art of compartmentalization, go to www.clearedhot. info/lessonslearned.

FORWARD OPERATING BASES IN AFGHANISTAN

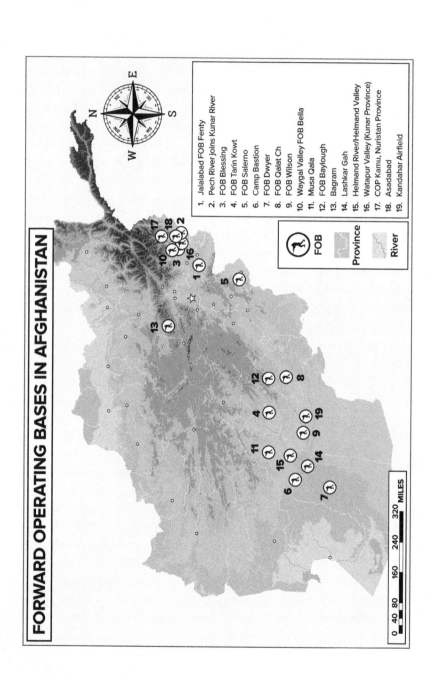

FOB

Province

River

1. Jalalabad FOB Fenty
2. Pech River Joins Kunar River
3. FOB Blessing
4. FOB Tarin Kowt
5. FOB Salerno
6. Camp Bastion
7. FOB Dwyer
8. FOB Qalat Ch
9. FOB Wilson
10. Waygal Valley FOB Bella
11. Musa Qala
12. FOB Baylough
13. Bagram
14. Lashkar Gah
15. Helmand River/Helmand Valley
16. Watapur Valley (Kunar Province)
17. COP Kamu, Nuristan Province
18. Asadabad
19. Kandahar Airfield

0 40 80   160   240   320
MILES

CHAPTER 4

BAGRAM—BULLY IN THE RANKS

Building Trust by Fighting for Your People

Aboard C-17 Transport—February 2007—"MRFDA BALABKA DEBRRM. Soon." I can barely make out what the formal announcement sounds like over the intercom, what with the earplugs I'm wearing to dampen the ambient noise. But as I wipe the crud out of my eyes and look around, I see that the entire cargo compartment of this giant C-17 Globemaster has a *Friday the 13th* feel with an eerie red glow, an almost theatrical lighting change that goes nicely with the hot, acrid odor of hydraulic fluid in the air we'd been breathing for the seven hours since departing in late afternoon from Rhein-Main Air Base near Frankfurt. This was the second leg of the flight from Killeen-Fort Hood Regional Airport in Texas. Then I figure it out. We must be over enemy territory and it's time to unass the hammock I'd strung beneath one of the three Apache helicopters we were escorting to our new home at Bagram Air Base, Afghanistan.

Minutes later, I strap myself into a fold-down seat on one side of the huge jet next to the other member of my advance team, Staff Sergeant Joel Mann, and take a moment to contemplate the residue in my mouth of the half dozen Kudos nutty fudge granola bars that served as my dinner and midnight snack. I could have had an MRE cooked by a chemical reaction that re-created the smell of a hot porta-potty, but no point in spoiling myself with the good stuff this early in the tour. Then I look at my buddy. He looks like a bear contemplating hibernation. Over his fatigues, he's wearing every bit of black fleece the army issued and possibly a few more he'd acquired along the way. No one had told us to bring sleeping bags, Eskimo coats, or fire-building materials for the flight, and it had been brutally cold.

"Warm enough?" I ask him.

"Almost," he says through chattering teeth. "I've been thinking about those Seabees we met in the Frankfurt terminal."

There had been a group of them in line for a plane heading back to the United States as we were moving to board our flight. "What about 'em?"

"Remember when they said, 'Be safe'? It wasn't casual. I think they meant it; they actually seemed worried about our safety." This was totally in keeping with Mann's character. He's soft-spoken and very pensive. Not quite what I'd expected in a guy whose civilian job is Arizona state trooper, especially one who actually pulled me over for what he claimed was excessive speed, but that was before I became his boss. During our pre-deployment adventure at Fort Hood, his thoughtfulness occasionally led him to see things that I'm not sure were there, but the flip side of that is that he doesn't miss much. I value that. He also let me off with a warning when he pulled me over, so two thumbs-up in my book. Still, he does have a point regarding the Seabees. They did have a very sincere tone, and I noticed a dullness in their eyes that surprised me considering they were on the good leg of this all-expenses-paid round-trip vacation. It caused me to wonder, *What are we getting into?*

The intercom interrupts our conversation. And now I can hear the announcement more clearly. "Seat belts on. We're getting ready to do our tactical descent into Bagram." I have no idea what that means.

All of a sudden, we're in a forty-five-degree dive, buffeting side to side, and I'm only being held in place, uncomfortably, by the seat belt, the law of gravity having been temporarily repealed inside that aircraft. For a while, it's Splash Mountain but with no water. Break right. Break left. Corkscrew (okay, maybe it wasn't a corkscrew, but you get the idea). Accelerate to the ground. I've done maneuvers like this in my Apache, but hell, this is half a million pounds of airplane, and as far as I knew, Boeing didn't build it to do aerobatics.

"Is this necessary?" I'm not sure if I actually said it to my sergeant or just thought it. And then we pull up. I can feel the Gs. This is a lot of weight. We've got three helicopters inside this thing, each of them longer than a New York City bus. Sure, they're chained down and cranked down, and they're still on the deck. But I see them lift, the struts kind of stretch out, then compress as we pull out of our dive. *Seriously?*

And then they level us out and do a basically normal landing. I'm thinking, *I don't know if that was necessary. Those air force pilots must be like, "Yeah, we're allowed to do this because we are in a combat zone, so we're going to do it."*

A few minutes of taxiing and along with the second C-17 carrying three more of our unit's Apaches, we're parked on a ramp. (The third C-17 with two more helos and some of our company somehow got sent to Kandahar in southern Afghanistan and would take a week to make the two-hour flight to Bagram with the rest of our troops.)

It's early morning, before sunup, twilight actually, and as I get up from the seat, I can sense that the crew has started to open the rear loading ramp. It's a clamshell, with the top retracting into the roof and the bottom beginning to angle down. It's winter and the air is cool, dry, and brisk. The first shock is that it smells pretty nice, clean. Didn't expect that. When I look toward the ramp, I get my second shock: the place looks like Utah or Montana; ignore civilization in the foreground and you see beautiful snow-capped mountains in the distance.

I'm taking this in when suddenly I hear Joel screaming, "Stop! Stop!"

It takes a fraction of a second to see the problem, and I join him. "Stop! Stop! Stop! Stop! Stop!"

On this flight, since three Apaches were packed in like sardines, the tail wheel of the last one to be loaded is chained tightly to the up-angled ramp in the back of the plane. Those chains were tight to begin with— they had to be in order to keep the thing in place during the flight. Especially during that frickin' tactical descent. As the loadmaster lets the ramp down, it's tightening those chains guitar-string tight, and we can hear a nasty sound. Something is about to give in a bad way.

"It's the airframe," Joel yells. And now we both keep screaming at the loadmaster to stop lowering the ramp before the tail boom buckles.

I look at Joel. "Dude, seriously? This guy has never done this? Is this the first time?" This would become a running joke. "First time?"

Disaster averted, it takes a few minutes to unhook the chains, drop the ramp, and then hop down to the ground looking for the team that is supposed to meet us and help offload. Down the way we can see a tent city, admin buildings, and lots of vehicles. But it's beginning to look like they didn't know we were coming, even though there were

BAGRAM—BULLY IN THE RANKS

more than a hundred members of the Tennessee National Guard whom we're there to replace. They knew we were coming; I'd sent them the itinerary and updates all along the way. You'd think they'd be waiting on the ramp, very happy to see us.

Ten minutes later, we're still waiting for someone to tell us where we're supposed to park our helicopters when one of the guys from the other C-17 walks over to us. I can tell by his body language he's not happy. The loadmaster on his plane failed to unlock the chains before letting the ramp down as well. Nobody was there to holler "Stop!" Apparently, that's what's required to keep them from trying to origami your aircraft. She bent the frame on the Apache tied down to the ramp.

Staff Sergeant Mann, one of my best maintainers, has that look on his face. "Lieutenant, this isn't covered in the battle damage manual, and I don't think there is any way possible we can fix it here in Afghanistan."

I respond calmly but sarcastically, my frustration showing as I shake my head. "First time?"

I'm thinking, *This is disheartening. A $52-million aircraft totaled before it even touches the ground.* It's a Class A accident and the C-17 crew is told they can't leave. Everything stays in place. All three helos are stuck on the plane. That Globemaster isn't going anywhere for a few days, at least not until the investigation is complete. I look toward the disaster thinking, *Some incompetent loadmaster just did more to debilitate our fighting force than the Taliban has. Combat loss due to stupidity. I'm the officer in charge until my commander makes it to country, so I have to notify the command we will be tasked to support that they are down one Apache. How do I explain this to the Task Force Pegasus commander? These are going to be his assets and he is down one from the get.*

Finally, someone shows up to give us some direction to our TOC, the tactical operations center, which turns out to be just a hut made out of plywood. You know, the kind you build as a kid to be a fort in some random field or backyard. We swing the squeaky door open and announce ourselves: "Hey, we're the new guys. Where are our digs?" In my head I'm thinking, *Thanks for the reception and the help when we landed.*

A twenty-minute walk from the TOC—to the other side of the base— and we're standing outside the transition tents, barely adequate shelter that would be our home until the old guys leave and we can move in. Honestly, that's a dick move. They should have vacated the permanent digs so we could get situated and get to work, rather than have to do what amounts to two move-ins while we're simultaneously trying to get to know the area and establish a battle rhythm. I am already taking notes on how we'll do this better when we receive our replacements. Heck, I'll put mints on their pillows to facilitate the transition when the time comes, but that honestly is so far down the road at this point that I just jot it down as a reference to come back to.

The tents are terrible. They're dank and reek of a powerful combination of mildew and body odor. We're going to have I don't know how many dudes in each of those tents, stacked up like cordwood on literally stinking, bunk-bed-style olive drab canvas cots. And the tents are definitely not waterproof. It's raining off and on, so you have these little rivers flowing along the floor. It looks like a 5,000-foot view of the Amazon right where our gear is going to be sitting. Pretty nasty, but what can you do? I lived in a truck for six winter months and in third world accommodations for two years; we could suck it up for a couple of weeks in a swampy tent. It's a challenge. Perspective, right? I joke about the circumstances so we can laugh and get the job done, despite the less-than-ideal situation. This is what we have to work with; let's get to it. Our job as advance party is to get things figured out so when the rest of our guys roll in, we can give them an outline or itinerary. We also have to start unfolding aircraft.

Two days later, our guys arrive and we all begin in-processing. "Do this, do that, don't do that. This is where Taco Bell is. Don't run here. Don't step there—the Russians left a lot of mines when they pulled out." I'm thinking, *But they left in 1989 and the place is still mined?*

It blows my mind that there's a Pizza Hut and a Taco Bell in Bagram. It doesn't taste the same, but they're here. They call Bagram the ant hill, and for good reason. Once the sun comes up, it's just people moving everywhere, all over the place. And the thing that's crazy? For some dumb reason, you have to salute. It is so crowded and your rank is showing, as a young officer you have to salute every dude that goes by because you either outrank them or they outrank you, so you're saluting double-time, every single person! It's ridiculous. I learn quickly: wear a beanie and a fleece with no rank on it. So now I'm an enlisted man or contractor as far as anybody else knows, so I don't have to keep popping salutes. That cuts it down to maybe five salutes a day to high-ranking officers instead of five hundred to every enlisted guy I pass. It's just ridiculous. Why are we doing this?

In the midst of all this mission takeover and admin chaos, I would try to call Katie. It was always at night when I could get away, so the time difference between Afghanistan and Arizona worked. Because I couldn't anticipate how things would go if I managed to get through, I couldn't chance calling from our office where everyone could hear the conversation. So I'd catch a ride or walk to the Morale, Welfare, and Recreation (MWR) building on the other side of the base, where they had phone booths offering some semblance of privacy. At MWR, I'd wait in line until my turn came up, then place a call, which would invariably go unanswered. Or to voicemail. I'm downplaying things when I tell you that it was annoying. I knew she hadn't gotten a job and should be at home in the morning or early afternoon. But she rarely picked up the phone. The most frustrating part is that I am pretty sure it wasn't on purpose. She simply wasn't putting forth the effort to ensure her phone was charged, turned on, and close enough for her to hear the ring. I knew she was likely lying in bed, struggling mentally to be motivated enough to get up. I considered having a phone readily available a minimum effort and something you should want to do to be able to communicate with your loved one who is in a combat zone. So I would take a deep breath, hang up, go to the back of the long line, and do it all over again. And sometimes, again and again. Then go back to my tent and try to fall asleep. As you can see, I was very focused on how what she was doing was affecting me rather than trying to fully understand what she was dealing with. That was primarily because I was truly ignorant as to why she couldn't just suck it up and drive on.

Two weeks later, we got to move into our permanent quarters. Mine was an eight-by-eight plywood room that the previous tenant had made some custom upgrades to. I had a shelf for my clock radio, a little trapdoor where I could stick stuff, and some drawers that reluctantly slid in and out of a built-in cabinet. All in all, a pretty cool room. Who would've thought that you roll into quarters like this and think, *Ah, I finally made it?* But that's the way it is. It provides an odd sense of stability. So grateful to be out of those nasty tents. A dry eight-by-eight you can call your own might as well be the Taj Mahal.

Almost as soon as our maintainers got the Apaches ready to fly, we began getting missions from the unit we'd been assigned to, the army's 82nd Airborne Division. We weren't getting TIC (troops in contact) missions, just the routine escort assignments, making sure that Black Hawks and Chinooks carrying troops and gear to forward operating bases (FOB) got there safely.

The escort flights were actually great for acclimating us to flying through the Afghan mountain ranges. We'd practiced mountain flying back home in Arizona and Colorado, but this was different. Even though the mountains we were flying through on these missions weren't heavily contested, on my first combat patrol as a copilot/ gunner in the front seat, my head was swiveling so much while scanning for muzzle flashes from Johnny Taliban that the circumference of my fullback-type short neck was rubbed raw by my load-bearing armor-plated vest. Eventually, I learned how to comfortably wear the gear and also understand that constant scanning was necessary only over contested terrain, and although very little terrain was completely uncontested, there were areas to be concerned with, and then there were areas to be *concerned* with.

Some of that understanding came from the chair flying I did after I'd climbed into bed at night. (I'd become mentally adept enough that I didn't actually need to be sitting in a chair to visualize and enact scenarios.) I'd take myself through multiple situations, doing mental gymnastics for an hour. It had become a type of meditation for me and would help me fall asleep.

At Bagram, I'd often fly with the unit's senior pilot, Chief Warrant Officer Gino Prepotente (not his real name), who was assigned to instruct me in preparation for my eventual upgrade to AC, aircraft commander. Quick explanation for nonmilitary types here: There is our company commander, who holds the top position of leadership within the unit. The company is split into two platoons, which each have platoon leaders who work directly for the company commander. Then there are levels of responsibility in the aircraft itself that have nothing to do with the company hierarchy: copilot gunner (CPG) and aircraft commander (AC). Additionally, in the air, there is the position of air mission commander (AMC), who may or may not be an AC. How does that happen? It's likely he is a trusted enough leader and tactician to run a combat mission but may or may not yet have enough hours or flying skills to be an AC. So my leadership position within the unit is platoon leader, and in the aircraft I am a copilot gunner but also an air mission commander. I know, confusing. According to our senior pilot and other pilots' evaluations of me, I was ready to take on the added responsibility and upgrade from CPG to AC. Sorry for the alphabet soup. Honestly, I think it was more a factor that we needed more ACs, and even if I wasn't ready, they deemed me competent and hoped I'd rise to the occasion. I shared their hopes.

In addition to flying, I'm spending a lot of time in command meetings. Our boss is Capt. Jeremy Pfeifer, the company commander. I'm the attack platoon leader and 1st Lt. Ryan Pixler is recon platoon leader. We had a lot of stuff to work out. Who's going to which meeting? What's our flight schedule going to be? What crews were we going to stick together as a form of risk management? Who'd be dealing with which problem child? All this is referred to as a battle rhythm, and right now our tune is not discernable as music. But we're refining and expect to be playing Mozart soon...or at least "Chopsticks."

After hours in the office, I had time to check my email, and *if* Katie had responded to either a voice message or an email from me, it would invariably be something negative: the sky is falling, our relationship is terrible, or you shouldn't have left me. On rare occasions, I could detect elation in connecting with me, but that was really rare.

My commander, who is only a year older than I, knew the situation to some degree because he'd been exposed to it at Fort Hood, and he'd talked with me about it briefly. His approach was half-joking, more or less "Dude, I see you're dealing with some tough stuff. If it gets to be too much, you'll let me know, right?" He never actually said those words, but that's what he meant. It was as much to be there for me as a friend as it was to say, "I'm going to be leaning on you a lot, and I need to know you'll be able to handle it." Actually, he was helpful, getting me to understand that although women are generally more emotional than men, my wife was extreme. That realization somehow helped me double up my efforts, knowing my wife had some extreme imbalances, so I wasn't sure what she could control and what she couldn't. At times, the three of us—Pix, Pfeifer, and I—would swap wife stories. Unfortunately, I could always one-up them, and that was only sharing the lowlights. I wouldn't share the highlights because I would feel as if I would be betraying my wife's confidence by making her look bad. Most of the time, I would play it off as comical and self-deprecate my inability to figure it out.

There were no concerns that my home situation was negatively affecting my flying because it clearly wasn't. I don't remember ever being distracted while I was flying. Once I got into the aircraft, that's gone. That's in the back, and it's not ever gonna come to the front. It could be on my mind right before we climbed in, then gone. We'd land, and it could pop right back in. But during? I can't think of any time I've had an issue with that. I think that ability to compartmentalize might go back to high school football. Once I got on the field, I wasn't conscious of anything else: not the crowd in the stands, not how I was going to pay the rent that month, not the test I bombed that morning or the one coming up the next day. I was like a horse with blinders— in my case, mental blinders. Never thought of it this way, but that was good training for my current mission.

I will admit that although it didn't affect my flying, those times when Katie just went off the grid for weeks at a time were troublesome. She'd just disappear. No email. She wouldn't pick up the phone when I called her late at night my time, which was midday hers. I walked around wondering whether she was even alive. I knew she was suffer- ing from deep depression, and these disappearing acts kept the back of my mind wound tight.

There are all sorts of growing pains involved in the adjustment from stateside to a combat base. Turns out our biggest issue, right from the start, is that we have a bully in the ranks. And he is a significant problem because he has rank. In fact, he's the guy doing my aircraft commander instructional rides. CW4 Gino Prepotente, in the civilian world, is a US Customs officer. In our activated National Guard unit, he holds the position of senior pilot and is supposed to be our most professional guy, policing and standardizing all the other warrants, who constitute most of our pilots and copilots. We didn't have a whole lot of experience working with him. Right before we deployed, we got him on a trade with Alpha Company that was going to be flying out of Kandahar because he had what they told us was a personality conflict with the A Company commander. Go figure. We all knew the A Company commander was a class A douche, so we figured the commander was likely the problem. Turns out they were two peas in a pod, which made for a great deal of friction resulting in their problem now being our problem.

Initially, he seemed a little boisterous, lacked a little military bearing, but not too bad. But as time went on, we could see he had his nefarious hidden agendas, and he began manipulating people. Basically, he was like a dirty cop, planting evidence to hang anyone who got in his way. For example, he took a fellow warrant officer's ID and put it somewhere that would cause the guy to get a security violation. He was from the Bronx and looked like a slightly overweight Vin Diesel, talked like Vin Diesel, and was bigger than Vin Diesel. So he's an intimidating person to begin with, and he would buddy up with the commander. He's a very assertive person, and he'd keep working the commander to get what he wanted. He would also be browbeating the guys below him to the point that they were afraid to do anything.

Right off the bat, I start talking to the company commander, like, "Sir, Prepotente is a problem that we have to deal with now; it's not going away." Captain Pfeifer is no idiot; he knows what's going on. The problem is that he's a really good guy, very charismatic, friends with everybody. But that is also his weakness. Good thing is, he knows that too.

Pfeifer is an average-size guy, a former Marine, but outside of his high-and-tight haircut and ability to complete a twelve-mile ruck march in under three hours while carrying a seventy-pound load, he just wasn't your typical jarhead. He's a jovial, quick-witted, intelligent, married father of a two-year-old daughter who owns him. An eminently likable guy. Not saying jarheads aren't likable, just that in my experience they are much sterner and mission-only focused.

Back in Arizona he acknowledged, "This is my weakness. I really want to please everybody. And I know that you can't always do that as a commander." Then he looked at me and said, "Slade, you're my hammer. You don't have a problem sticking somebody in their place when you need to. So when that needs to happen, I need you to be the bad guy." Truth is, I didn't like doing that. But it was worse letting an issue fester, so I would do it if I felt something needed to happen.

So I became the hammer when needed. Pixler, on the other hand, fit the computer nerd stereotype, glasses and everything. The man had my respect, though: he can handle tech stuff; he's good at geek-speak; good at figuring out crypto. Spreadsheets and PowerPoint slides came out so much better when he had created them. Even before we deployed, the captain had pointed to me and said, "Hammer." Pointed to himself as "Boss." Looked at Pix and said, "Tron. These are your roles." And that worked, in addition to our responsibilities as platoon leaders where we both had stewardship over warrant officers and enlisted maintainers. It was a good lesson in leadership. Pfeifer knew his weaknesses and utilized his people's strengths to compensate for them. I would employ this lesson over and over down the road because, even though I have my strengths, my list of weaknesses isn't too short—and those are just the ones I know about.

Problem was, Prepotente didn't fall into either of our platoons. As senior pilot, he's part of the command staff, along with the first sergeant and us as platoon leaders, and that puts him primarily answering to the boss, not Pix, not me. I try telling the captain he needs to do something before morale in the ranks is destroyed by this jerk, and although he sees it, he keeps putting it off, holding out hope that he can turn Gino from the "dark side."

Finally, we have an official meeting to talk specifically about the problem, and I say, "I'll do it. It probably should be you, but I have no problem cutting out this tumor. It needs to happen." I was really pissed that Prepotente had been disrespectful to Ryan and others on multiple occasions, making fun of them in a condescending way in front of other people. Don't get me wrong, there is teasing and camaraderie-based ball busting that I think is fine, even constructive, but that is not what Prepotente was doing. This is a big issue. This is a command climate issue, undermining authority, right? He never talked like that to me, but he did talk like that to a couple of other lieutenants and even the first sergeant. I was getting fed up with it, but the captain had given me marching orders not to jump in yet. He wanted a little more time to see if he could bring Prepotente around by doing things his way. Got to admire his optimism. I just didn't think we had the time for rehabilitation; this tumor was metastasizing quickly.

What finally does it is when 2nd Lt. Christina Thomas, the highest ranking female in our company, says something and Prepotente goes off on how dumb and incompetent she is. His level of disrespect—as well as ignoring that there were others in the room when he did it— is setting a rotten precedent. I am in a meeting on the other side of the room with the first sergeant and a couple of admin sergeants, not even involved in the conversation between the two of them, but I overhear the boisterous blathering of a pompous bully and I am incensed.

"That's it. Everybody out but you and you," I say, pointing to Thomas and Prepotente. It seems as though everyone has an uncomfortable mental pause while trying to understand what's happening, even while they stand up and move to the door. I kept Thomas as a witness.

Prepotente walks over, not even realizing that I'm angry at him. I don't think he'd been confronted too many times in his life given his physical stature and assertive personality. Well, I guess those uncomfortable one-on-ones Major Curtis had me do are about to pay off. At least I hope so.

Recognition sets in as he sees my posture and my glare. He realizes this is aimed at him. I'm watching his head turn slowly like a vicious dog who knows he's cornered and is about to lash out. He says in his thick New York accent with a menacing tone, "What's wrong, LT?"

I stare at him intensely as my mind reels. I realize I may have just overstepped with respect to the guidance I had been given by Pfeifer. *Should I go through with this? Yes, I need to. I am committed at this point. Backing down isn't an option.* "This is a one-way conversation. You need to shut your mouth and sit down right now." I need to set a tone, so he knows he is not going to hijack this conversation. His brain is churning now, looking for the angle. But he still doesn't get it. He's trying to transition from intimidator to manipulator.

"What, LT?"

"I said, this is a one-way conversation. That means you shut your mouth and listen."

He's a big freaking dude and knows he's big too. I'm a big guy, right? But he dwarfs me. I'm behind the desk, so he changes tactics again, switching from manipulative passivity to intimidation. He leans toward me with his big bald head, staring at me with a half-crooked smile. But I lean toward him and say, "This is your only shot. If you're going to swing, swing now. I don't think you're that dumb, but go for it. Otherwise, sit your ass in that chair." His head is red hot and not from the temperature in the room. I can actually see sweat beading on his forehead, which is only about three inches away. It's literally a face-to-face testosterone-charged stare-down. He's angry, but he's smart. He knows that if you punch an officer who's telling you to do something because of something you did that wasn't appropriate, you're not going to win that fight in the long run. I don't know that he would win in the short run. I've got forty to sixty seconds of fury; I've boxed, wrestled, MMA, rugby, and football, so physicality is not something that scares me. I might be able to hang or even win—at least that's what I believe until someone proves me wrong. But he sits down slowly, staring at me the whole time. I just stare back into those angry, dark Italian eyes for a few seconds that feel like minutes. Then, forcing myself not to yell, I begin to lay into him.

"Gino, you're a malignant tumor within this company. The way that you interact with individuals does nothing but negatively affect the company in the following ways." And I give him a list. And then pause. He starts to say something, but I stop him. "No. You are mistaken. I'm not pausing for you to speak. I'm pausing for air and I'm pausing to calm down so I don't yell at you." Eventually, I say, "I'll be honest. I'm going to do my best to make sure that you're no longer in this company." His brows furrow, showing the indignation of a belligerent toddler. "I'm going to call you back and put all this in writing. We'll make sure that this is an official formal counsel later. Are there any questions?"

Ever the manipulator, he says, "LT, are you still thinking about doing Border Patrol when you get back?" Remember, this is a National Guard unit and nearly everyone has a civilian job, and his is working for US Customs. He knows people at the Border Patrol.

I say, "Don't you backdoor threaten me right now. I don't give a damn who you know or what you know. Right now, I'm dealing with you as you are: a bully who has pushed everyone around to get what he wants."

"I don't know. The way I carry myself has always worked out."

I'm still pissed. "For you! That's because most people fear you, Gino."

"Yeah, they do."

"Hey, Gino." He glares at me and I return the glare. "I do not fear you, so that ends now! Get out of my sight."

He leaves, and Lt. Thomas says, "Oh, my gosh! This is gonna be..." because she knows that the guy is going to employ all his manipulative skills on this one.

I interrupt and say, "Okay. So that happened."

Thomas is generally soft spoken, used to staying in the background. She came into the army as a private, worked her way up to being the admin NCO for the schoolhouse where I learned to fly the Apache, then got her college degree and went through the Basic Officer Leadership Course to get commissioned a second lieutenant.

She almost whispers when she asks, "Now what?"

"Well, he's gonna run right to Captain Pfeifer, and I need you to get to the captain first and get Captain Pfeifer over here as soon as you can. That's your job."

She gives me a "Yes, sir!" and takes off like the Roadrunner on steroids. I start typing while it's fresh in my mind and fueled by the adrenaline of the moment. In a couple of minutes, Pfeifer shows up and I let him know what happened. "I need your back on this, Boss. If this doesn't carry teeth, nobody in this company is going to believe that we have their back. Nobody in this company is going to believe that we're gonna take care of this bully. I really need your back on this."

There's no hesitation. "You got it. I'll back you on this." I can tell Pfeifer is not in his comfort zone with how this happened or even the role he now has to play, but he knows it's the right thing to do, and to his credit, he pushes through the discomfort. Sure enough, the weasel does go to Pfeifer with a twisted version of what happened. But the boss already knew what was going on, so it wasn't like I had to prove anything to him. But as soon as that happened, we opened an investigation, because that's what you do in the military. The word spread like wildfire through the company that I had stood Prepotente down and said enough is enough. Almost immediately, the one-on-ones began to flood in without any invitation. This was proof our actions as leaders build trust. That is huge.

They say things like, "He did this to me... He's been threatening me with this... His wife's a mail carrier and I haven't had my mail for four weeks..." On and on and on. The guy was actually pulling strings in federally illegal ways. But the troops now clearly believed in their command, that we had their backs, which we'd made obvious through action taken. So we commenced what is called a Commander Climate Survey.

Basically, I wrote all the questions. "Does your commander comport himself in a professional manner? Yes or no? If no, please explain. If yes..." Every loaded question—and they were 100 percent loaded. I put the commander on there. The first sergeant was on there. Put the two platoon leaders on there. And, of course, the senior pilot, CW4 Gino Prepotente. All the same questions for every single person in a leadership role. Every single one of those surveys came back just tearing that dude apart. Except for one. There's one guy who was still scared of him. He didn't say good; he didn't say bad. He just said nothing. But other than that, everybody else just tore him apart. We brought the results forward to the leadership, and they said, "Yeah, there's stuff in here that warrants a criminal investigation. You know, it could be prison time for some of the stuff he was doing."

There's no mercy in my response. "I don't care where he goes. He needs to be gone outta here 'cuz we gotta focus on the mission."

They sent Prepotente down to FOB Salerno. And then, of course, like a bunch of spineless bureaucrats that they are, they don't follow through, so nothing really happens beyond that relocation. Our problem just became someone else's problem and the circle of ineffective leadership continued.

That was one of the first real leadership challenges that I had on the deployment, right when I got there. A path of extreme resistance that needed to be taken for the good of the whole. Prepotente's presence was weakening the company, compromising the integrity of the chain of command; by dealing with it, we united the company and had those guys absolutely believing "Our bosses have our back. They're gonna take care of us. Doesn't matter who it is. If threat is from the inside or threat is from the outside, they got us."

A postscript to the bully saga: a few days after I dressed him down, Prepotente sneaked into our clerk's office one night and changed the written flight evaluations he'd given me on my upgrade syllabus from positive to negative, hoping to scuttle my advancement to aircraft commander. But I'd predicted he would try that, so keeping the commander in the loop, I had already pulled my records, copied them, and then put them back so he could hang himself further. Just one more nail in what should have been the guy's coffin.

I did confront him on it. I said, "You changed my grades on the rides I had." He smiled devilishly and said, "I don't know what you are talking about."

That's when I pulled out the copies and said, "The brigade senior pilot already has these." His smile deflated immediately. I am not going to lie. That gave me a little bit of joy.

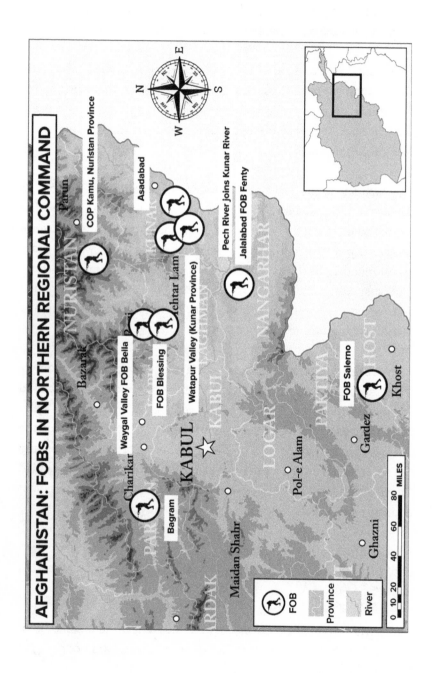

AFGHANISTAN: FOBs IN NORTHERN REGIONAL COMMAND

Parun

COP Kamu, Nuristan Province

Asadabad

Pech River Joins Kunar River

Jalalabad FOB Fenty

NURISTAN

Bazarak

Waygal Valley FOB Bella

Mehtar Lam

FOB Blessing

Watapur Valley (Kunar Province)

NANGARHAR

Charikar

KABUL

KABUL

KHOST

FOB Salerno

Khost

Bagram

PAKTIYA

Maidan Shahr

LOGAR

Gardez

Pol-e Alam

WARDAK

Ghazni

FOB

Province

River

0 10 20   40   60   80 MILES

CHAPTER 5

REDCON-1 QRF

Teambuilding: Synergizing All Team Members' Strengths

FOB Fenty, Jalalabad, February 2007—I climb out of the Apache after a quick 110-mile flight south-southeast from Bagram and take a moment to enjoy the fact that it's about twenty degrees warmer here. Jalalabad is on a plateau at the junction of the Kabul and Kunar Rivers, less than one hundred miles south of the Hindu Kush Mountains, which rise to more than 19,600 feet. I can see some of the ominous peaks poking through high clouds and think, *Not so good for helicopters.* Jalalabad is the fifth-largest city in Afghanistan and sits on the highway that links the capital of Kabul to the west with the storied Khyber Pass to the east, leading to the city of Peshawar, Pakistan. The area outside the Hesco barriers that surround the forward operating base (FOB) at Jalalabad Airport is definitely not friendly; the bodies of beheaded local translators left at the FOB's perimeter had made that point all too clear. I'd already been warned that incoming fire, both direct and indirect, happened irregularly. This is already a lot different than Bagram, and I've yet to see action.

The Tactical Operations Center (TOC) at JBAD. Running at top speed from the TOC to the helicopter on those rocks was a challenge.

My assignment from Capt. Pfeifer is to assess, and if needed, fix things. "You're no longer a platoon leader; you're the detachment commander. Just take charge and make good decisions. I trust your judgment and resolve." Very short version: Pfeifer had been receiving emails from many in the detachment here at Jbad, dealing with all kinds of concerns—from mission frequency to leadership issues to personal drama. Some of them were contradictory in nature, making it clear to him that he couldn't accurately identify, let alone fix, the problems with emails and phone calls from company headquarters at Bagram. My orders are clear, and he gave me the latitude to carry them out as I see fit. "If need be," he said, "use your hammer." *Oh, geez, why can't this just go smoothly? We have great guys, talented in what they do. We all just need to unify and focus on the right priorities, and we will be fine.*

I'd only been given the new job earlier that day and was traveling light with just a duffel bag stuffed with some uniforms and sundries, my M4 rifle and M9 sidearm, and the load-bearing vest and helmet

I'd worn on the flight. My other gear was back in Bagram. Frankly, bringing along a separate flak vest and Kevlar helmet to wear on the ground was more trouble than it was worth. It's a prioritization game: how much to carry? Risk versus reward. I figure getting hit by the occasional incoming would be lottery odds gone wrong. If there's incoming, I'll duck and cover.

I drop my gear on the porch of the TOC, which happens to be adjacent to the chopper pads, and go inside. The guys seem glad to see me as I enter, excited to be able to share their Jbad adventures with me as well as ask about life at Bagram. Someone tosses an Icom walkie-talkie my way. "You'll need this, sir. Keep it close." I clip it to my belt. That radio would be within arm's reach for the next four months—sort of like wearing a court-ordered ankle monitor, but this one can yell at me. Taking a look at the flight crew assignment board, I ask which copilot wants or needs a break. CW4 Richard Schiffli says his copilot had been jobbing it and could use a spell, so I crew up with him for that day.

As I'm sitting on the porch getting the lowdown on battle rhythm, CW4 Mike Hersteller shows up. I hadn't seen him in two months and have to hide my shock because I almost don't recognize him. The guy must have dropped forty pounds. Hersteller had once been the battalion's senior pilot, but he had a run-in with the boss and was reassigned to a line company. Although I don't know the details of that altercation, what I know of Mike and of Desert Hawk 0-6 from our time in Arizona and at Fort Hood leads me to believe Mike must have challenged the boss on a valid point involving taking care of his people and got sacked for his efforts.

As a result, Mike had come downrange with us, and we were grateful to have him. I could never understand why staff positions are sought after to begin with; the operational company is where the rubber meets the road. When we sent him to Jbad from Bagram, he might have been carrying a few extra pounds, but now he's just skin and bones. His two-piece flight suit is hanging loose, and I'm sure if the belt didn't have a chokehold on his waist, the pants would be around his ankles. And now he's smoking—chain-smoking from the look of his nicotine-stained fingers.

I probe gently, "Mike, you're kinda dropping some serious pounds."

"No, sir, I don't think I've lost any weight."

"Oh yeah? Have you seen a mirror lately?" I laugh, but he doesn't. "When did you take up smoking?"

"Used to smoke long time ago. Decided to take it back up." His answers are curt and he looks down while he talks, at no time making eye contact. Unlike a lot of the other pilots, Mike had never been an extrovert, but this is much different.

"So how you doing?"

"I'm good. Taking out effing ragheads whenever I get the chance, sir." But now he's looking me in the eye, and I see anger. "Libby and I got into 'em really good." That statement had much more venom in his voice than I'd ever heard come from him before.

"Mike, which way to the 82nd's TOC? I need to check in." He points me in the direction of a two-story building, about two hundred meters away, and I head off, telling him it's great to see him, that I'll catch him later. I need to figure out what is going on with him, but now isn't the time.

With all sorts of radios humming in the background, the brief I receive from the 82nd's operations officer, Major Smith, is efficient.

He is direct, to the point, and I can tell he only cares about mission and people, not any crazy ancillary military requirements. That's a breath of fresh air after some of the rank-chasing task force leadership in Bagram. After I absorb the intel dump and meet the battle captain, he says, "You need to get out there. You need to see what these guys are doing." I don't know whether he's telling me there's stuff I need to straighten out or that he won't trust me until I see it myself. Maybe a little of both. I mull it over on the run back to our own almost embarrassingly barebones TOC.

Going through ops reports, briefing books the major had given me, and intel situation reports of recent enemy interaction, I quickly discover that unlike Bagram, where we were doing mostly escort flights on ring routes and only occasionally expending ammunition or launching the quick reaction force (QRF), our crews up here are being tasked to support a number of combat ground units including 82nd Airborne assets based at Jbad and other FOBs, 10th Mountain Division units, and foreign coalition fighters, as well as respond to OGA (other government agencies) who need high-impact assistance. This long list of customers has led to the unit ceaselessly responding to troops in contact (TIC) calls.

Initially, it seems like an opportunity to showcase what we can do with the efficiently lethal Apache Longbow. But I quickly surmise, after several conversations, that the opportunity might not be such a good thing; with this ops tempo, there is definitely no way for our guys to get the required eight unbroken hours of crew rest, and some of them are just too exhausted to fly safely. I'd begun to pick up on that at Bagram by reading some of the emails Pfeifer had been receiving, but here, it is in black and white. A lot of times, the guys weren't even legal to fly. That's a sure way to get someone killed. I get why they keep launching—I would do the same thing when troops are desperate for help—but we have to figure out a better method.

Just as I'm beginning to get my mind wrapped around the limiting factors I have to deal with, the radio on my hip lets loose with an obnoxious screech: *"Gunmetal! Gunmetal! Gunmetal! Go Redcon-1!"* All crew members respond via their radios.

"Schiffli moving!"

"Steele en route!"

"Hazon on my way!"

I key the radio and state, "Slade en route!" as I fall in right behind Schiffli, but he's running so awkwardly that he's got me laughing. As I jump off the TOC's porch, he warns me to watch my step. Some genius had decided to surround the chopper pads with an assortment of ankle-breaking rock riprap. Racing through it is a challenge. Quick feet, quick feet. Parkour!

"Gunmetal! Gunmetal! Gunmetal! Go Redcon-1!"

Okay, we're coming. Take it down a notch. So much for my first-day-on-the-job plan to take time to understand the flight crew mixes and challenges, figure out how best to pair them up, and create a schedule that would accomplish the mission yet still keep everyone legal. When I arrived six hours ago, Schiffli and I were number five on the callout list. Time flies when you're trying to eat the new elephant you've been served. When we get to our aircraft, it's already gassed up and fully armed with a basic load of rockets, 30 mm, and a single Hellfire. We had previously set up our cockpit; M4 rifles are already secured in their brackets. I get into my vest, which I'd left hanging on a rocket pylon, then reach in and pull my helmet off the front seat where it has been baking in the sun. For $125,000, you'd think they could figure out how to keep the thing air conditioned. I'm copilot/gunner on this sortie. I was supposed to have completed my check ride at Bagram in order to qualify as aircraft commander and fly backseat. Plans changed. Pfeifer told me to get it done at Jalalabad. Clearly, it won't be happening today; from the looks of things, maybe not tomorrow either. So we start it up and are off the ground in minutes. This is in response to troops in contact, so there are two of us spinning up. The other bird is a little ahead of us; I hadn't had practice running up so quickly, but next time, I wasn't going to be the one who slowed us down. I decided right then to practice when we got back.

The flight to the TIC should take only fifteen minutes based on the eight-digit grid we've been given by the unit requesting help. On the way, Rich briefs me on what he has been experiencing. "These bad guys are really hard to find, fix, and kill. They can hide in plain sight. And muzzle flashes are nearly impossible to pick up in bright sunlight, but you know that." I knew that in theory but to my knowledge hadn't yet seen any muzzle flash.

I confess to being more than a little amped because we're heading to a known fight. We're not just flying escort or waiting around for something to happen. Good guys and bad guys are exchanging lead, and if the good guys weren't in a hurt, they wouldn't be calling for us.

Rich is going to handle the flight controls; I'm on radios and guns. "Beastmaster 0-6, this is Iron 1-6. We are one minute out. If able, can you mark your location for us?" There's a thirty-second pause.

"Iron 1-6, we've just popped purple smoke."

"Confirm purple smoke, Beastmaster. Can you give us azimuth and distance to target?" Ground troops can mark their location in the daytime with colored smoke or with a fluorescent reflective panel. The smoke is better for us; it shows us wind direction. But it also tells the enemy where the good guys are. In this case, the enemy was already very aware of where they were, so smoke didn't do anything but obscure their fields of fire.

"Estimated azimuth is 120. Distance 300 to 400 meters."

"Beastmaster, Iron 1-6. Near that big pine tree just east of the rock outcropping?"

"No, drop fifty."

I look below the tree and see a group of bushes on rocks with striations going east to west and describe it to the ground commander.

"That's it. In that area somewhere is where it was coming from. But as soon as you showed up, enemy fire stopped. We don't have positive ID of enemy at this point." *In that area somewhere? Estimated azimuth and distance? Crap! That's not enough to pull the trigger.*

We're running weapons tight, which means we need clearance from the ground unit or have to positively identify the enemy ourselves in order to engage. At one hundred feet and one hundred knots, we fly over our own troops, desperately looking for bad guys.

"Beastmaster 0-6, are you certain there's no more incoming fire on your position? We'll take it around a few more times and see if they're dumb enough to fire on us."

He confirms that it's quiet on the ground. Meantime, we see abad-abas, but they're just looking up at us as if to ask, "What're you Americans looking at? There's nothing here but us and our goats." Their guns must've gone somewhere. Under a bush, beneath their man-dress (more politically correct, a kameez shalwar).

I try again. "Beastmaster 0-6, you're not seeing hostiles 300 meters southeast your position, in the area of rock outcropping? Can you confirm that we're clear to engage that area?"

"Negative, Iron 1-6, unable to PID [positively identify]. Looks like they'll behave as long as you're here, and we aren't sure of their exact location."

We agree to remain in the area for a while, circling, watching for muzzle flash, flying directly over the described area, basically baiting them to play with us. This does allow the friendly forces to break contact and continue on their way, but the bad dudes live to fight another day. "Beastmaster, we are bingo on fuel. We have to return to base."

"Thanks, Iron 1-6. Maybe next time." We can hear the resignation in his voice. He could probably hear it in mine too. We all know that as soon as we head off, the abadabas are going to start taking potshots at them again. (A note about the word *abadabas*: I was really uncomfortable with all of the racist characterizations of the enemy that our troops were using. Yeah, I know, it was ever thus in wars. So I started using a nonsense word I'd once heard in a *Saturday Night Live* sketch featuring an impersonation of Rev. Jesse Jackson about the Middle East conflict. And in my unit, *abadabas* became a non-racist, non-rancid shorthand for the enemy.)

Neither Schiffli nor I are thrilled about the way this sortie developed. I start chattering at him on the intercom, lamenting about the rules of engagement. "It's like we're here to play the big game. We've trained for it; we're ready; we show up. Everybody's cheering in the stands; the band's playing. And just as we're set to come busting out of the locker room onto the field, the coach says, 'Nah, just kidding.' But I know the other team is there; they wanna play."

Schiffli commiserates. He's flown down this road before.

I respond, "You know what? I've got a case of tactical blue balls." He keys his mic, but all I get is a snort of laughter. "Oh, so now you're makin' fun of me? You know you feel my pain." In a way, I guess the training at Fort Hood did prepare me for war, since that was the last time I felt this way.

When we land back at Jbad, we're still the on-call crew. The deal is you can fly no more than eight hours in a twelve-hour period without a request for extension—we're nowhere close—and you can't be on call for more than twelve hours, starting with your first flight, after which you're supposed to get eight hours of uninter- rupted rest. By my calculations, I'm on the clock for another seven hours, up to eleven with extension approval, which means I've got time to grab something to eat and then try to get more admin work done.

I'd just finished a sandwich that one of the guys brought me from the high-class mess tent just set up by military contractor KBR when WO2 Jim Steele comes into the TOC looking like he has some- thing to tell me.

I like Steele. He could be blunt, to a fault, but I'd rather have that than beating around the bush when you're trying to get to the bottom of something. At one meeting, Pfeifer was reading some new orders from battalion, and Steele said, "There's no way in hell we're doing that shit."

The captain looked around at the nodding heads and said, "What Jim means to say is, maybe we should look at a different way of approaching this."

"Yes, sir, that's exactly what I meant to say, sir." I smile, reliving that moment. Mostly because I can sympathize with him; that's how I am too, but I've learned to taper it. At least, in my opinion.

"So what's going on, Jim?"

"I need to tell you about Mike. He and Libby were on a TIC in the Korengal. The way Libby tells it, they were on a slow troll right next to a cliff that's got a lot of trees. These two young kids, teenagers probably, busted out of the tree line pointing AKs at them, getting ready to shoot. They're less than a hundred feet from their bird, on the left. Mike has a really good view. He wazzes the gun and it points right where he's looking. Blows them up. It was a righteous shoot."

"Sounds like it."

"Yeah, but he sees them explode. No identifiable pieces left. You know what a 30 mm does. And they were kids, about the same age as his own kids back home."

And just that quickly, it explains everything going on with Mike. I know that I have to give him a change of scenery, a mental reprieve, but I also know with the shortage of qualified pilots, it will take a while.

Schiffli and I have one more TIC on our shift that evening. I significantly decrease my startup time, but it's more of the same. We never get cleared hot. I get back to Jbad exhausted, take a shower, and hit the rack. I forgive myself for skipping chair flying that night.

Then I see my laptop out of the corner of my eye. Crap. I get out of bed and reluctantly go to open it up, but I stop myself. If I open email and find the usual drama-riddled email message, it'll just roil my guts and I won't get to sleep for hours. But if I do check email and there's nothing, then I'll lie awake wondering if something bad has happened to her again. I intuitively know that black cloud over Katie's head has never gone away. And if I don't open the laptop at all? Like I said, crap! It's just a no-win situation whatever I do.

Next morning, after a decidedly inadequate amount of revitalizing REM sleep, I send an email to Pfeifer, telling him we need to build a cycle-out plan, or a number of these guys were on a quick trip to burnout. I know the company is short on qualified pilots, but some sort of systematic rotation from Bagram, where the duty is less taxing, has to be established quickly before really bad things happen.

Problem is, I have to deal with the crew rest issue right now. We get so many Redcon-1 calls responding to troops in contact that we keep all three crews—just six pilots, seven if you count me as a relief guy—on call, in priority from one to three. If you aren't flying, you try to sleep or eat, because you know your number is going to come up quickly. The hope is that you can grab eight uninterrupted hours of rest at some point in a twenty-four-hour period, since that is what's required in order to be legal to fly. The guys have told me this place is so busy that there've been times all three crews have been unable to get legal rest, thus rendering our ability to respond legally impossible. But when it's TIC time, they go, regardless.

Now I'm in the mix, and I realize that even if I can fall asleep, the walkie-talkie next to my bed is like wearing a leash and collar, maybe more accurately a shock collar. Every time it goes off, it yanks us all awake, and we have to try and figure out if it's our turn to go. Now try getting back to sleep. Not so easy. The problem is simply that we don't have enough pilots at Jbad.

I know that Bagram doesn't have any spare bodies; they were getting legal crew rest, but it takes everyone they have to fly their ring routes and still be available for the rare QRF mission and all the BS required meetings. I smile and shake my head, thinking, *Poor, Pixler.* The only solution I can devise is to cycle our folks back to Bagram on a much more regular basis. Some of my guys have been here since we arrived in country more than two months ago, flying every day, and they are showing the strain.

I also have to deal with some pilots who just aren't cutting it. Since there is no way to pull all of them off TIC missions, I have some heart-to-hearts and tell the senior warrants to do remedial training with these guys while they're en route to and from TICs. It's a field expedient, but it works. Sort of. I do give Hersteller a break from missions, designating him to fly special training flights with a couple of the front-seaters who really need help. And I also ask him if he can finish up my AC upgrade in the next week. I figure getting him in the cockpit doing noncombat-type stuff might help. He doesn't say it, but I can tell he's relieved to unplug his shock collar for a bit.

It's likely my number is going to come up soon for another Redcon-1 TIC, and looking at the board, I see that I'll be flying with CW4 Doug Ehrle, a regular army pilot on loan to us from the 82nd Airborne. He had been in country for a while and we were really glad to have him. Doug and I had been in the same Apache A-model-to-D-model transition course at Fort Rucker. It had been designed to take seasoned Apache pilots and teach them the differences between the A-model and the new Longbow—the D. It was *not* designed for second lieutenants just out of the basic A-model course, yet there I was. When I walked through the classroom door the first day, everyone assumed the dumb butter bar was lost and actually needed the full-up course down the hall. "Nope," I said with a smile, "this is the class on my orders, so looks like I will need you guys to help me through it," as I simultaneously displayed the extra-large box of doughnuts I'd brought with me. The class of senior warrant officers laughed, essentially saying, "Here's an LT who gets it."

This was my Apache Longbow upgrade class at Fort Rucker, Alabama, where I took the A-model to D-model transition course. I had to bribe a bunch of gnarly chief warrant officers with doughnuts to help me through a class that was not designed for 2nd lieutenants with minimal flight hours. Doug Ehrle is left front. I'm third from left.

The rest is history; they helped me out a lot. So who would have thought that about a year later, I'd be strapping into a helicopter with one of the guys from that very same class? I don't say anything to Doug, but I experience a real level of comfort knowing I'll be flying with him. He's much younger than most of our senior warrants, in his mid-thirties, but he has something our older warrants who deployed with my Arizona National Guard unit don't: he had been in multiple contested combat situations. An aggressive pilot, Doug was a mentor and much more.

The first radio call from Titan 1-1, the ground commander of an element of the 3rd Squadron 71st Cavalry, part of the army's 10th Mountain Division, clues me into the fact that my combat action status is about to change. I can hear a variety of weapons rattling off in the background of his radio call. We roll around this corner of a big, steep mountain, almost a sheer cliff, maybe a little slope to the bottom where there's a little creek. On one side of that narrow valley, we can see that Titan's convoy of Humvees and MRAPs (mine-resistant ambush-protected vehicles) has been trying to advance along a rough dirt road built on a ledge about 300 feet above the valley floor, paralleling the creek. It's immediately apparent to us that an IED had gone off in front of them, stopping the entire convoy. They'd been ambushed, and now Titan 1-1 tells us he's taking effective fire from three different directions, but he can't be specific on where exactly it's coming from. The terrain offers great concealment for the enemy: lots of trees, super steep jagged rocks full of shadows and crevices to hide in. He can't see them, and neither can we. The fire seems to be coming from the other side of the valley, where there's also a shelf about 300 feet above the valley floor.

We start at 400 feet above that floor—which actually puts us only about one hundred feet higher than the shelf—both of us scanning for muzzle flashes. Our wingman takes an overwatch position about 500 feet above us. This technique is known as high-low. The low bird snoops and poops, engaging what he sees, and the high bird is supposed to obliterate anything that messes with us that we are not seeing. Seeing nothing to shoot at, Doug opts to descend and fly over the terrain really slow and low. We've become a flashy, noisy bass lure, trolling for fire. *Hmm, maybe we should change our call sign from Iron 1-6 to Rat-L-Trap.*

Now we're only twenty or thirty feet above the ledge at just thirty knots, kind of combing over this area. *We're kind of vulnerable here; Doug has big balls, but this is the guy who's been here, done it.* So I don't question it.

While Doug concentrates on flying, I'm on the tactical acquisition display in the front seat, scanning, zooming in, and changing optimization like crazy in order to identify anything hostile. But no luck. Unlike my previous TICs, our presence has not caused the enemy to stop firing. We just can't pinpoint from where. As we come across the edge of the cliff and out over the valley, our altitude above terrain changes instantly from 15 to 280 feet, when *KABOOM!* It's as if we are literally in thunder as it cracks, shaking everything. We're rocking; the whole aircraft lifts up, shudders. We get peppered with debris. You know how it sounds when you're behind a dump truck on the highway and pebbles hit your windshield? That's what it sounds like on my canopy. But now we're falling like a rock, nose down, right into that creek bed just 200 feet below and getting closer by the second. My stomach is in my throat and my point of view is straight down, and I'm thinking, *We're hit, we've lost power, and that's where we're going to crash. This is it, my first engagement and we are getting shot out of the air.* I can actually see the rock we're going to impact on at the bottom of the valley.

But I'm also thinking, *What am I gonna do when we hit the ground? I'm gonna make sure I got my weapons; I'm gonna get Doug and start egressing, and we're going to try to get on the handheld radio and call Titan 1-1 because these bad guys are right there!* It's my chair flying kicking in. This is all happening in a blink.

But we hadn't lost power. Doug is handling things. He counterintuitively reduces collective power, changes direction, and actually dives away from that vortex created by the explosion until the rotors can grab some air. We dive all the way down to fifty feet before our bird starts to gain altitude and begins flying out of it. But it really looked like we were going in. *First fight; I lose; that'd suck!* Apparently, the juicy target we made ourselves into enticed an abadaba to take a shot at us with an RPG. I'm not sure whether it actually exploded in the air below us or hit the ledge we were flying next to. Either way, it created a vacuum of nasty air, which caused the Apache to freefall—officially, it's termed "settling with power or vortex ring state."

Unofficially, it's termed "Holy shit!" which is precisely what I hear Doug say, followed immediately by a string of eight to fourteen-letter nouns and adjectives preceded by the word "those—!" I'm generally not given to cursing—there are exceptions—so all I can manage is, "So that's what that feels like."

Doug's attitude is, "Vengeance is mine!" And as crazy as it sounds, he takes us right back to where it happened. (Note to self: isn't there something they call people who do the same thing twice, expecting different results?) Let's be clear: I am right there with him, just less vocal. To use a boxing metaphor, the enemy just landed a stun punch; my nose is stinging, my eyes are watering; it's time to shake my head, refocus, and counterpunch.

I've reacquired my bearings and reimagine the situation. Rather than being over-amped, I come down a couple of notches. I'm even speaking in a lower tone of voice than before. Yeah, I have adrenaline coursing through my veins to be sure, but I think it must be how I'm wired. That and the chair flying. "Doug, there's no way that RPG could explode underneath us coming from the side that we're looking at. It had to have come from the other side of the valley."

That's the moment I began to understand that the little flickers I'd been seeing—actually, not really *seeing* as much as *perceiving*, usually out of my peripheral vision—are actually muzzle flashes. They just hadn't registered in my brain as enemy fire. *I am seeing muzzle flashes.* I think it, and then I say it. This is a true aha moment for me. "I'm seeing muzzle flashes." I call Titan 1-1. "Confirm you've got no guys on the north side of the valley?"

"That's affirmative. Iron 1-6, you are cleared hot!"

"Then engage," Doug orders.

GUTGUUTUGUT. The standard thirty kick and vibration shakes the aircraft. What isn't standard is that this is the first time that by squeezing the trigger I have taken lives. It doesn't slow me down, but it feels differently than blasting targets. "Arrow 1-6, this is Titan 1-1. The small arms firing has ceased." He can actually hear the bad guys shooting (in the helicopter, we can't).

We continue our low-and-slow, occasionally firing on muzzle flashes coming from various directions. Doug is getting very aggressive, trying to provoke the enemy, when it happens again! In almost exactly the same spot as the first time.

BOOM! Big pieces of rock are hitting our bird, leading me to believe this RPG either hit us directly or impacted the cliff right underneath us. No little *tink, tink, tink* of pebbles on the airframe. These are rocks. *Or are they pieces of us I'm seeing fly through the air?* It's apparent that some douchebag across the way has this spot dialed in and he's just been waiting for us to come through there again. This one is even worse than the first, if that's possible. It shakes us up; a shock wave comes through the cabin, reverberating, hammering through my muscles and inner organs. It's like my body is a tuning fork and my guts are vibrating way off key. *That was closer!* Again, we're falling, but this time we're going in sideways and angled down because the explosion has really thrown us. (Try this: take the book or device you're reading this on and tilt it hard to the right and down; then lean over sideways with it and fall out of your chair. Now you understand.) But this time, my eyes go right to our instruments. We have power—I know what's going on. Ten-minute-old experience is already being called upon. And as before, Doug flies us out of it. Nice!

"Dude, that was really close. We just got blasted with another RPG," I tell him. Luckily, God saw fit to give us another chance to learn.

Titan 1-1 had been observing the enemy fire and tells us he's marking it with 50 cal tracer fire, but in daytime we can't see it too well. So he gives us an azimuth and distance to the shooters. Doug lights up the point of origin with rockets, and I put down some 30 mm for good measure.

A wrestling match is three two-minute periods of exhausting, often painful exchanges of hand-to-hand combat. The match itself is not enjoyable per se, but at the end, when you walk to the center of the mat and they raise your hand as the victor—the ref raises it because you are so exhausted you can't—it feels amazing. This feels similar. The enemy started this fight and we just ended it, terminally for many.

Without the hail of enemy fire, the ground troops manage to clear the blockage on the road, and they begin to move out. As quickly as it started, it ends. "Iron 1-6, Titan 1-1. No longer receiving enemy fire. Thanks for the help. We were in a bad way there." We stay with them for a bit and then get released.

Doug and I analyze the encounter on the forty-mile flight from the Narang Valley back to Jalalabad airport, but it's pretty much tech talk. Once we land on the pad, everything gets shut down. I unhook my five-point harness and step down out of the cockpit, take off my helmet, hang my load-bearing vest with the armor plates on the rocket pylon, and feel solid ground beneath my boots. That's like the exclamation point at the end of a sentence. It means, "Mission complete. You're still alive."

Then it hits me. *That's real? Those guys were actively trying to kill us, to shoot us out of the air, and they came pretty dang close to doing it. They were tenacious, continuing to fire from multiple points, trying their best to kill the guys on the ground and shoot us out of the air.* There's a bunch of abadabas who are no longer breathing as a result of our actions, as a result of my trigger pulls. This has a perceptible impact on me. I know we're at war, but I don't think I expected this particular feeling. Truth? I had no idea what to expect after I wielded the weapons system the army has provided. I look at the machine that I am entrusted to employ and am awestruck at how this aircraft, with its menacing look, can be manipulated in such a dynamically acrobatic way, with firepower that can be employed in an instant. It is truly a fierce force to be reckoned with.

In school, they told us that "the enemy has a vote." Now I say, "Let them vote" but become nimble enough to answer with a response that causes the jihadis to think twice before voting again; to think twice about their cause; and to think twice about whether they're ready to leave this world the same way their buddies just did—sadly, in pieces. Maybe, just maybe, by us responding to their violence with such a menacing, overwhelming flying tank, they will just go home and make babies instead. On second thought, maybe that's a bit too optimistic. Their fight for Afghanistan did begin in the year 708, and for them, it never stopped. In a weird way, I respect that level of resolve, even if I do not agree with what they are trying to bring to the world. Taking their lives gives me no joy, but knowing their level of commitment means I have to act decisively in these engagements or their commitment will be rewarded at the expense of our brothers on the ground or at our expense, rather than the other way around.

On a personal level, I recognize the need to ramp up my chair flying with more real-world combat scenarios, initially concentrating on how to keep actively flying the aircraft even when it feels as though it's not flying. That was a new one for me today. Thank goodness Doug was on the controls. "Keep the spinny thing spinny" is now my official mantra. All actions must effect that result. I need to tattoo it on my eyelids.

As a leader, I know I need to synergize our team to the max extent possible. Ideally, I want to pair guys who've logged maximum flight hours with those who have heavy combat experience. That would truly bolster our tactics, techniques, and procedures going forward.

But under my current manning limitations, I'm not able to put two ACs in the same bird, with one of them designated co-pilot. That would leave two co-pilots sitting around the TOC playing gin, because neither is officially qualified to command the airframe. So the reality would be that I've effectively reduced the number of available crews, and that won't get the job done.

Logically, what we must do is get more of the copilots who already have combat experience upgraded to AC quickly. They're battle-tested, and that should count toward the upgrade. But that's not how the system is set up. There are lots of boxes to check. Problem is, back in Arizona we had the time to check those boxes, administer the written tests, and fly the test flights. Here, in country? You kidding me? I know why the testing standards were written, and if we weren't downrange, I'd do it by the book. But right now, I need to get Bagram to acknowledge that embracing the spirit of the law, rather than precisely following the letter of the law, is just fine. After all, all those boxes were created to train a guy so he could fly in the situations these guys are actually flying in, so I'd consider that box checked. It's clear to me that sticking to the rules is hamstringing us. Screw that.

Right now, here at Jbad, the most critical *attitudinal* adjustment I have to encourage is to get the guys to be willing to learn from each other's engagements, regardless of rank or age. Combat has created a new dynamic. The senior warrants, the pilots in their late forties and early fifties, are the ones we had always looked to for answers because they had the most flight hours. These older guys were, indeed, my mentors and instructors; they'd literally taught me everything I know about how to fly a helicopter. We had an easy mentor-mentee interaction, partly because of an unspoken acknowledgment that the natural order of things is that age and experience take youth and immaturity under their wing.

But what happens when wisdom is attained out of that natural order?

The way things have played out in Operation Enduring Freedom is that more of our younger guys had been in more scraps with the enemy and had figured some important things out. My job is to get everyone to set egos aside, and tweak tactics as needed. It would prove to be easy for some, not so easy for others. After being "the man" for so long, losing that honorific to a kid can be difficult to deal with. It's not something I can resolve overnight.

After my Titan mission, I decide that the first tactical issue I want to address is the matter of being aggressive versus being overaggressive. There's nuance for you. In our first story-time-with-a-whiteboard, a casual-but-mandatory sit-down I initiate for all pilots, I use trigger questions to try to get the guys to talk through their engagements:

- After taking fire from that area the first time, what was your plan of attack?

- Anyone here been in that situation? Have another way to respond?

- So what did you do with your power setting when that RPG almost blew you away?

- It's freakin' hard to find, fix, and kill these dudes. Has anybody come up with something that beats flying in circles?

- How did you manage to spot daytime muzzle flash?

My immediate problem in that first session is that the younger guys automatically assume their position as students and mostly listen to what the older warrants had to say, even if the younger guys actually had more pertinent real-world experience at this point. And some of the older guys, CW 3s and 4s, still think it's their job to play wise man, stroke their long gray beards, and sow pearls of wisdom. Well, actually it is still their job; now they just have company. This should be seen as a good thing by all, but human nature doesn't work that way.

Just because we're all living the suck together, wearing the same uniform, doesn't necessarily mean we're mentally committed to playing on the same team. I know that building synergies will not only impact mission success but also help create the resiliency we all need to deal with inevitable traumatic events. *You can learn more about this at www.clearedhot.info/lessons learned.*

This truly will be a test of my leadership skills. I need to create an environment where everyone is willing to ask questions and where anyone, regardless of rank or years in service, can offer solutions.

Then, when those solutions are offered, they need to be acknowledged and listened to by everyone, irrespective of who offered them up. Of course, we are going to get some crappy suggestions, but we'll also get some gems that will make us all more proficient and efficient, such as *use white phosphorus rockets to help develop the situation.* More to follow on that one.

Maybe instead of finance, it would've helped if I'd majored in group psychology.

CHAPTER 6

CHECK RIDE COMPLETE: IT'S ALL YOURS

Embrace the Challenges
That Confront You

FOB Fenty, Jalalabad, late February 2007—The game is Texas hold'em. It's a $20 buy-in for $1,000 in chips; blinds start at $4 and go up every fifteen minutes. "I'll open," CW3 Steve Kearney says, tossing a five-dollar chip into the center of the table. It's nearing 21:00 hours and there are only five guys left out of the eight who had shown up three hours earlier. Our regular Saturday night tournament in the TOC was part of my morale-boosting/get-your-mind-off-the-craziness-of-our-new-norm program. That's what I told Major Smith when he walked in on us last week, discovering our buy-in money in a box on my desk. I'm still not sure how he knew to amble right past us directly to the box, which he opened and then looked up directly at me with a judgmental smirk.

Officially, gambling and drinking are verboten for American troops in OEF. Hey, we're not drinking, so I figure one out of two ain't bad. Of course, I don't drink, so the second one isn't hard for me, but for some guys, that's a real sacrifice. To my surprise, the major actually asked about joining us this week, but he hadn't shown up. Maybe the war intervened. It happens.

I catch Kearney looking down at his cards, then turning to glance at me on his right, and back down to his hand. I figure I'll poke him. "Just five bucks for openers? Don't get too gutsy on us, Steve." The other three guys call. I have a solid hand with my pocket kings but don't want to scare everyone out, thinking, Hey, let's build this pot. "I'll raise," I say with no emotion in my voice but only add another $5 to make it $10 to play. I casually toss two red chips into the pot.

All but one call, leaving four of us still in the game. Lt. Brendon Libby deals the flop. A ten and jack of spades, and looky, looky, looky—the king of hearts. Steve checks. "Steve, don't you know if you got 'em, you gotta bet 'em? I know you fly with more guts than that. I've been up there with you. Maybe it'll help if you put on your flight helmet; we will wait for ya." I say this with thick sarcasm and a jovial smile. The bravado should make them think I'm bluffing.

I don't want to bet too big here, since I want somebody to call. But I don't want to play against three guys chasing either. "Twenty-five," I say, pushing in a green. Everybody but Steve folds. Worked like a charm. "And then there were two," I say with a crooked smile, acting as if I had Steve right where I wanted him. No sarcasm this time, completely contradicting the tone of my previous taunt.

"Raise," says Steve, putting in two greens.

"That's more like it." But I hesitate, glance at my hole cards, and purse my lips. "I promise I won't tell your wife you think that spade flush draw can beat me." I stare at him as if I am trying to read him. At this point, I want him to be considering one thing: I'm chasing spades, and my flush draw is not a high one. Of course, I am actually hoping a spade doesn't fall, keeping my three kings good. That way, I can milk him for more. I take a few deep breaths and hesitantly call. Those acting chops I developed in high school are paying off big time now.

"I knew you were bluffing," Steve says, probing. "And thanks for reminding me to phone her when we finish."

"You're welcome."

"No, really, I mean it. She's been on my case for not staying in touch more. I tried telling her we're flying 24/7, but she's not buying it. It's just—all she does is complain."

Brett Brown and Sean Hoover guarding the HardRocket Café.

Brendon burns a card and deals a ten of clubs, faceup onto the table. I don't react to the full boat the poker gods have just delivered. Instead, I very subtly slouch my shoulders, hoping Steve notices and thinks I'm worried because I didn't catch another spade. "Up to you," I say with feigned resignation. Steve fans his hole cards and looks at them. "Steve, they're still the same as when you looked at them thirty seconds ago."

"I'll go twenty-five," he says without a lot of conviction. Although firm with his voice, his bet tells me he doesn't believe in his hand.

I don't want to drive him out. *Let him think I've got doubts.* "Call."

Dealer says, "Pot's right, last card," then places the queen of spades faceup on the table, aligning it next to the previous four cards. *Best card that could have hit!* There's now ten, jack, and queen of spades on the table. I know the spade king is in my hand. *He probably has his flush, but does he have the eight? Is it a straight flush? I don't think so. Odds are, I'm sitting on the nuts. Only one way to find out.*

"To you, Steve," says the dealer.

He doesn't hesitate. "Two hundred," he gloats, a smirk on his face.

I'm thinking, *This is great. He has the flush, no doubt. But the straight flush? I don't think so.* I feign stress and thought, twist in my chair for a bit, relook at the cards a couple more times to indicate a monster decision. Then I just stare at Steve for an uncomfortable minute. I want him to think I have a flush but not ace high. If he believes mine isn't as strong as his, the likelihood of him calling on what I am about to do increases dramatically. "Screw it, I am all in," I say as I shove roughly $2,000 worth of chips into the middle. What I know of Steve says he will not hesitate here; he's already invested too much ego and a decent amount of chips.

"Call," he says with a huge smile, confidently laying down his ace and seven of spades. He has the flush but not the straight flush.

I nonchalantly toss my hole cards on the table, just below the king and pair of tens. "Kings full."

Steve's face melts; he got played and can't figure out how it happened. Two hands later, all the chips on the table are in front of me. Brendon says, "I guess that'll pay for your Monsters the next couple of weeks." Although I'm not exactly addicted to energy drinks, I never take off without several cans in the cockpit. And everyone knows it.

As I begin putting the chips back into the custom-built case I've dragged with me since college, Steve looks at his watch and says, "It's lunchtime back in Tucson. I need to call my old lady before she goes out shopping. Again."

"Wait a sec," I say cheerfully, "you mean your wife actually gets out of bed before noon? And she goes *out* to shop? Doesn't live on Amazon? Really? How'd you get so lucky?"

"Lucky? You should see my Visa bill. I can't keep up with her."

"Hey, you think you're special? I've got eight years of savings being used as kindling for an online shopping bonfire. I have to take your money at these things just to stay ahead. At this rate, we'll both hit the bottom in a month or two. You can't keep up with yours? I can't get ahead of mine."

Although there are smiles all around, domestic bliss—or more often, the lack thereof—was messing with the mental health of several of our fliers, present company included. Participating in recreation such as our poker nights helps dampen the frustration of home stress. It also allows both young and old guys together to talk casually about tactics, which was one of my hopes when I'd instituted the games. Of course, that, and I needed a way to pay for Monster drinks.

Personally, I can still keep domestic stress out of the cockpit when we're weapons clear and stuff is going down, but while piloting those yawn-inducing missions, I'd caught myself mentally replaying the combative sat-com phone calls Katie and I had been having whenever I could get ahold of her—*if* I could get ahold of her. And that isn't good.

What a great thought to rack out with.

Sunday morning at bustling Jalalabad. I don't think there were any *Gunmetal* calls overnight, but I'm not really sure. It was one of those nights where my body told me, "Hey, Slade, I'm running a six-night deficit, and whether you're with the program or not, tonight's the night we're catching up." Thankfully, I wasn't on call. If the radio went off, I never heard it.

But right now, I'm thinking, *KBR has finally gotten its act together and they're cooking real food this morning. Chow hall time.*

I'm just finishing up a loaded omelet with a side of fresh fruit, washing it all down with the last Monster in my stash, when an infantryman with an M4 slung over his shoulder comes in, looks around, and then yells, "Anyone in here know Iron 1-6?"

Oh, crap. Who did I piss off now? I slowly raise my right hand, motioning him my way. "Yo!" As he's winding his way between tables coming toward me, I see he's a captain, so I begin to rise. "Sir?" It's a question.

"You're Iron 1-6? You fly a mission a couple of weeks ago where a convoy got ambushed on a ridge?"

"Yes, sir. I'm Brian Slade. CW4 Doug Ehrle flew with me that day. Something wrong?"

"Sit down, Lieutenant. There's nothing wrong—just the opposite. I'm Titan 0-6. [Apologies, but I've forgotten his name but not his impact.] You were talking to Titan 1-1, my radioman, during the fight. I'm passing through on my way to Bagram and wanted to thank the guys who saved our asses. We were in a bad way, pinned down, till you rolled in and bailed us out."

I'm in a sudden mood reversal. *Here I was revving up inside for a potential conflict, and the guy is saying great things.* A bit of a smile creeps onto my face. *Crap, I hope I don't have food on my face.* "That's very nice of you, sir. Always happy to have satisfied customers."

"I want you to have these," he says, pulling out two-unit coins from his pocket and handing them to me. I look at one of them closely. It's got a bright red border with gold lettering that reads 3rd Squadron 71st Cavalry "Titans" and a blue dragon in the center beneath crossed sabers and a horseshoe. I start to say thanks but can't quite get it out because I feel a bit choked up. He offers his hand and I shake it, suddenly noticing out of the corner of one eye that we've become the center of attention in the tent. "Good luck, Lieutenant Slade. Keep doing what you're doing! It matters. It matters a lot to us." He turns and heads for the exit, while I stare at the coins in my palm and slowly sit back down. *This epitomizes why we do what we do. What those guys do is crazy, and if we can make their day safer, that's all I need to justify lethal force. Not a bad way to start the day. Maybe it's an omen.*

Today's the first chance in the two weeks I've been up here to get my final check ride for certification as an aircraft commander. It's the army's way of telling me that I'm now officially ready to be fully responsible for one of their $52 million Apaches. I guess until now I've just been an intern. I'm in charge of everything in the detachment and have literally hand-receipted half of these birds under my name but never been technically in charge of the one I was flying in.

The truth of the matter is that under stateside conditions, I wouldn't be getting this upgrade so soon. I've got nowhere near the number of hours that ACs are expected to have. But with shooting wars in both Iraq and Afghanistan, we're just plain short on pilots. OEF could use more Apaches too, but that's another story. The reason for all that above-my-pay-grade activity is that our manning compared to our mission load is way out of balance, and even just one more AC—me—will significantly increase the possible combination of crew mixes. Bottom line: needs of the army are fast tracking my upgrade. Back in Arizona, I'd been identified early on as an AC candidate because they felt I had the hands and the judgment to handle it. But I still needed to get hours under my belt as well as get certified.

At Bagram, Pfeifer had asked the brigade's senior pilot, CW5 Dave Swan, to make it happen—or to make me miserable. At least that's how it felt. The guy is a hard ass—okay, maybe that's not fair. Let's just say he is fastidious and demandingly meticulous, with a super-high expectation bar and no apparent concern for the mental agony he's inflicting on his students—in other words, a hard ass. He knows I can fly, but I still have to suffer through hours of questions, all of them asked in a slogging monotone that was driving me crazy. I can't think that slow. Want an example? Out near the aircraft, he says, "You're a drop of gas; take me through the whole system. I want you to explain every component along the way. Tell me what emergency procedures, caution lights, and trickle-down scenarios are possible."

Really? But I do it, thinking we'll move on. Not a freakin' chance.

"Now you're a drop of oil, follow it through."

Seriously? "Mr. Swan, you want me to pass this thing, right?"

"You'll do all right." But it's more like *yooooolll-doooooo-wallllllriiiiiite.*

"If you say so."

Swan sets aside an entire day inside the little wooden building next to the Bagram TOC for the oral evaluation; most instructors get it over with in an hour. I was beginning to hope he'd just waterboard me and get it over with. Finally, I say, "Dave, I'm not sure if you got from me what you need or not, but I need to call this thing."

To my utter surprise, he declares with zero emotion that I'm ready for the first of two required check rides. I wondered if I'd taken that stand hours earlier if I might have avoided the Spanish inquisition. So we go for it. Despite a little trepidation on my part, the flight turns out to be anticlimactic. I fly back seat acting as AC, and we do some escorts. Then he has us peel off and run through some tactical scenarios. And we land.

I hop out and wait for some sort of feedback about the eval: "You're good. You need work. You got bad breath." I get nothing but "Okay, I'm gonna go back to my office now." And he leaves me standing there.

On my way back to my quarters, I run into Pfeifer. "You good?"

"I have no stinkin' idea."

"He didn't tell you you failed?"

"No, but he didn't tell me I passed either."

It took a few days for Pfeifer to finally ask Mr. Swan what was going on. The nonchalant response: "He's good enough. You can have one of your instructors write it up."

So that just leaves the final check ride on emergency procedures before I'm certified, but my move to Jalalabad takes precedence. And here we are.

I catch up on paperwork until late afternoon, when Mike Hersteller comes in. "It's that time; you ready, sir?"

We were one of the two crews going on call, and our plan is to get airborne, check a few required boxes on the qualification forms during daylight, and then finish with a couple of required simulated emergencies once it gets dark. Hopefully, no missions drop while we are in the middle of my testing.

Mike is like a breath of fresh air compared to the hardliner at Bagram. We have it almost all wrapped up—I've displayed the hand skills and judgment he was looking for. Only thing left are rolling landings, including one where Mike tells me I've got an engine on fire that I've got to deal with, and then land safely with our available power cut to 49 percent.

Normally, helicopters shoot an approach to a hover, then set it down. But if you try that without having enough available power, you'll turn your aircraft into a rock and be the first one to the site of the crash. So the solution is to land the Apache like an airplane, which means you're going to come in hot, at least sixty knots, but still go through all the aerodynamic effects associated with landing a rotor-driven aircraft.

What happens is that besides being much faster and imposing a much different sight picture than normal landings, just prior to touchdown the bird wants to drift right. At ten to fifteen feet, it actually slows its descent on a cushion of air associated with the ground, requiring you to refine your inputs mere feet above tire-to-asphalt contact. This is when I remember what they told us in flight school: An overcorrection is self-critiquing; so is an undercorrection. A little subtle for the army, but it makes the point. It requires very delicate manipulation of the controls until you've got all three wheels on the ground.

And that's the other problem. The Apache naturally hangs front wheels low. You can land that way, but the risk at high speed is that you turn the thing into a BMX bike and pop a front wheelie, something Mr. Boeing does not recommend.

Solution? As we get close to touchdown, I give it a little aft cyclic, a little reduction in the collective, and all three wheels settle together, allowing us to roll it out. It's a finesse maneuver a lot of guys screw up, especially early on, but once you get the feel, it's no big deal.

After gassing up at the FARP (forward arming and refueling point), I hover over to our pad and shut it down. Mike says, "Twenty-hundred hours. Check ride complete. Congrats, LT. You're an aircraft commander."

I didn't expect it to hit me this way, but that's actually an overpowering statement. Anything this machine now does, with all its might, is my responsibility. The decisions that have to be made, the liability incurred—it's all on me now. If we get rocked by an RPG, I have to be the Doug and correctly manipulate the controls so we don't end up much shorter than God made us. Although outwardly I'm ordinarily a very self-confident guy, right now on the inside I'm a bit apprehensive because I know there are still some skillsets—mostly night stuff—that I'm not completely comfortable with. Nevertheless, I'm excited at this new step forward. Fixing my self-observed shortcomings should be relatively easy. I've already figured that I'll put myself on nighttime ring routes a few times and get squared away to my own satisfaction.

Only one problem: reality intervenes. *Who was it that said life is what happens when you're making other plans?*

Gunmetal, Gunmetal, Gunmetal, Go Redcon-1. I hear it on the radio that's powered up in the cockpit. We're still on call. This one is a TIC near FOB Naray in Kunar Province, ninety-eight miles northeast of us, roughly a fifty-minute flight up a fairly wide river valley on a pitch-black night.

"Mike, it looks like we're—"

But he interrupts. "Nope, I'm gonna go get you a copilot." And he runs to the TOC.

My reaction? *Oh, crap. This is real. Am I really ready? Nighttime too. I've been an air mission commander many times, but this'll be the first time I am air mission commander and I'm actually in charge of the aircraft itself. I always had a very competent AC taking care of the aerobatics part of engaging the enemy. Tonight, it's on me.*

My introspection is interrupted as CW2 Jim Steele comes running up to the bird.

"Hey, sir, what're we doin'?" I tell him that all I've gleaned so far is that a convoy is taking enemy fire from high ground. As soon as he's onboard, I give him the eight-digit grid and he begins punching it in while I get the rotors turning. At the same time, a second bird with AC CW3 Steve Beach and CW2 Rebecca Bemis as copilot is running up.

On any other night, our flight to the TIC would've been routine, but knowing that I'm now "the man" must've put a few extra squirts of adrenaline into my system. I am amped. We're blacked out, pushing it fully loaded at 120 knots, 200 feet above the valley floor, using only the infrared navigation lights. Troops on the ground—ours or theirs—might hear us, but without night vision devices, they can't see us.

"You're an AC now. Congrats!" Jim says. "How's it feel?"

I infer that he's probably asking for his own comfort, trying to gauge how confident I am on the stick. "I'll let you know in a few hours," I tell him with a chuckle. Lucky for me, Jim is as good a copilot as we have in the unit, and in my opinion, he should have been upgraded at the same time as I, if not sooner. I am trying to rectify that with upgrade planning.

About five miles out, I can actually begin to see muzzle flashes through my NVGs, right on the coordinates they'd given us. A little closer in, we see tracer fire going upward. It has to be the Americans; experience has taught us the Taliban in this part of the country rarely uses tracer ammunition. When we're almost on top of them, I hit the radio. "Jaguar 2-1, this is Iron 1-6. I think I have your position. Confirm that I'm flying over you right now."

He confirms and efficiently shows us where they're taking fire from by marking it with a laser pointer, which is easy to see on a moonless night. The target he's roping with the laser is about a quarter of the way up the mountain from his position. "Iron 1-6, you're cleared hot."

I coordinate with the other bird, and we roll in, engaging the enemy, primarily using 30 mm gunfire. With the naked eye in the darkness, we see enemy muzzle flash, and then a second later, our fire overpowers it. Each of the exploding rounds looks like those fire-works that initially explode into their normal waterfall display of multiple streams, followed by each of the streams exploding into their own mini banger. Then we hear something unexpected.

"Apache in the vicinity of FOB Naray, this is Bulldog 1-1. We are taking hostile fire and request immediate support."

He must be talking to us, but we're already supporting these guys. Who the heck is this? I key the mic switch. "Bulldog 1-1, this is Iron 1-6. Give us your position."

He provides an eight-digit grid, and while we continue running gun patterns in support of Jaguar, Jim punches it in. "Sir, I think that's on the other side of the valley but not very far away." I glance at my glass display and can see where he's got it plotted. *Not very far from us, less than a mile-and-a-half away on the other side of the valley.*

I come back at him. "Bulldog 1-1, we're currently engaging with Jaguar, but I think we can help both of you at the same time." I give him a different radio frequency. "Bulldog 1-1, go to 58.75 fox mic secure." I switch to the interplane freq that our wingman is on. "After we make the pass over Jaguar's targets, we'll turn our outbound into an inbound for Bulldog. All coms with Bulldog now on 58.75. All coms with Jaguar on 37.25. How copy?"

Steve echoes back, "Copy all." It's surprisingly uncomplicated.

Bulldog also puts lasers on the source of his aggravation, and we begin to light it up, mostly with Jim on the 30 mm, but I throw a few rockets in for good measure. I'm a little surprised that there are no muzzle flashes from the enemy on that gun run. *It's like they knew what we were doing and stopped firing when we turned inbound.*

Then we get help from the technology gods. Some battlefield units had been equipped with Prophet, a near real-time, ground-based, tactical signals intelligence-gathering capability that could intercept enemy radio traffic. Maybe that's the source or maybe it's some other spook system; in any event, Bulldog tells me that according to enemy radio intercepts, the bad guys are saying our last volley hit a little bit above their position.

Jim reacts instantly, telling me he is storing our "shot at" file so it will depict on both our glass displays. On our next inbound, we will be able to slave weapons and sights to that position and then just drop our aim point. "You're the man, Jim!" We make a pass at Jaguar's targets, then come back around, adjust fire off Jim's stored file, and fire for effect, hitting it with 30 and rockets. Through the FLIR, I can see the giant billowing dust cloud obscuring a better part of the mountain face.

A few seconds pass and Bulldog says, "There's no more radio traffic. You must have got 'em!" I'm thinking, *That was interesting; they managed to call an adjust-fire mission on themselves, quite effectively I might add. Thanks, Muhammad! All help gratefully accepted.*

But the bad guys attacking Jaguar haven't given up. Just the opposite. As we roll back across the wide valley, I see the area we had been engaging below the ridgeline, with its sporadic muzzle flashes.

But then my naked eye catches something I never expected to see: the entire ridgeline, maybe half a mile wide, is lit up with muzzle flashes. It looks like what I imagine rock stars see from the stage of a blacked-out arena: thousands of camera flashes.

There are hundreds of dudes up on that ridge, and I'm only seeing the ones who are shooting. Where the heck did they all come from?

Clearly, things have changed. This larger enemy force is up on top, quite a bit higher than the fighters who were attacking Jaguar when we arrived. I'd been able to establish enough situational awareness to understand that because of the way the mountain gently sloped from the top to halfway down, then grew much steeper to the valley floor, it's almost certain that the bad guys on top can't see the convoy below, because they are tucked in close to the base and masked by the terrain above. What takes a second to figure out is that the convoy is no longer the enemy's primary target. They may have been maneuvering to get within line of site of the convoy, but now their focus is on the bragging rights that accompany taking down an Apache. My wingman comes up on the radio, quite animated, "They're shooting at you!"

"I know. Shoot back! Hit my hit!" We're doing a hundred knots, coming at the ridge on a forty-five-degree angle, left to right. I start launching rockets almost as fast as I can pull the trigger. *Pffft! Pffft! Pffft! Pffft! Pffft!* As they leave the rocket pod, one after another, with my naked eye I can see the flames of the booster motors looking like butane torches, starting large and shrinking quickly as they accelerate to the target. Then there's a giant flash, and like lightning in a thunderstorm on a dark night, the clouds and terrain that had been invisible just seconds prior are briefly illuminated. Unlike the guided Hellfire missiles we occasionally carry, once these rockets leave the tube, they're on their own. And it's pointee-shootie. They fly in the exact same direction the helicopter is pointed when I pull the trigger. As we continue to fly by, I repeatedly adjust the target ever so slightly so each impact is to the right of the previous one.

My math is simple. I know the lethal fragment radius of an HEDP (high-explosive, dual purpose) 2.75-inch rocket is fifty meters. Doing it this way, we should annihilate anyone exposed on the hilltop, and if the shrapnel from the rockets doesn't get them, our front-seaters are hitting them on the flyby with the gun as well. The pyrotechnic display is worthy of the Fourth of July on the Capitol Mall in Washington. Even my copilot is impressed. "Dang, sir! You turned the rockets into an automatic weapon."

I fire seventeen rockets on a single pass and Jim empties the 30 mm chain gun of the last of its 300 rounds. We're Winchester on ammo; we stay in formation with Steve for a few more passes until he, too, is Winchester. All we have left in the tubes are three illumination rockets, useless in this situation. Even though after that terrain relocation program, I only see a few random muzzle flashes from the ridgeline, I'm not happy about leaving Jaguar to fend for himself.

Then it hits me. "FOB Naray has a FARP. Let's go! Jaguar, we'll be back. Hang in there."

Minutes later, both birds land, and with rotors still spinning, one of us from each Apache jumps out and begins helping the ground crew rearm us, while the other mans the controls. It's very quick. We jump back in, but before we can take off, BOOM! The entire helicopter shakes. I know that feeling. I key the mic. "Aw crap, was that RPG fire on the ground?"

Jim comes back, "I think that's outgoing from a 155 behind us."

BOOM! BOOM! BOOM!

I feel a bit sheepish and say, "Yep, that makes way more sense. Guess I'm a little jumpy. Cut me some slack. You know it's my cherry flight as an AC."

Jim comes back laughing. "Welcome to the seat, sir."

The good news is that as soon as we're back in the air, Jaguar tells us his situation is resolved and we're free to go. On the way back to

Jbad, I have time to think. *Pretty sure that huge push of Taliban was either on the other side of that ridge when we started or just laying low on top for some reason. Either way, if they had made it down to the convoy, oooh*—I almost involuntarily shudder—*game over, Jaguar. That was an overwhelming ground force for that convoy to repel on its own.*

What I realize is that with the support of a solid copilot and wingman, my learning curve had just gone from a gradual hill climb to a vertical cliff—not ideal for my first flight as an aircraft commander. It took ad libbing and adjusting all along the way, but what a great learning opportunity for me.

In a totally weird way, I'm almost grateful to have faced hundreds of armed men with hate in their heart, spraying 7.62 fire at us, on my first flight as an aircraft commander. Rip that Band-Aid! Little do I know that the chaos we got caught up in tonight was just a JV game. The varsity contests are yet to come.

Barely an hour later, I'm back in my hooch at Jbad, off the clock but on the sat phone. Now nearing my fourth month of deployment, the answers to "Katie, how're you doing?" are no longer a surprise. She'd stopped alternating between "great" and "horrible" a while ago. Now it's inevitably some variation of "My life is horrible. Our marriage is horrible. You don't even love me. I will never be good enough. I'm not sure I want to stick with this."

That cuts deep. Divorce is not something I'd ever thought of; it's not in the LDS playbook. I still believe that any two people can make a marriage work; failure is simply not an option. I'd like to try doing root cause analysis like they taught in undergrad—that's discovering the root causes of problems in order to identify appropriate solutions—but it's tough from eight thousand miles away. Heck, I wasn't nailing it when we were under the same roof back in Arizona.

"So why is it so horrible? What can I do to help you feel loved?" Of course, there is nothing I could do when the problem is internally derived. Clearly, her pain is real. And even though she had family not too far away, she wasn't asking them for help because she didn't want them to know how much she was physically hurting and incapacitated by depression. Even though I knew that talking about anything serious with her would be counterproductive, I had to ask about the shopping she'd been doing. It has been systematically draining eight years' worth of savings, and at this rate, the money is going to run out. Let's just say binge shopping is a not-so-helpful coping mechanism. I'll start with something less in your face. "Hey, were you able to pay the electric bill?"

Big mistake. "That's all you care about..." She hangs up. Well, I guess that's a no.

I really don't feel like calling back now. I know if I don't call back, she will likely send me an email saying the fact I didn't proves I don't care and escalate it, even go as far as threatening to end her life. If I call back, she will scream at me to leave her alone, telling me I am overbearing and controlling. Which one is better? Probably the call. I can take the tongue lashing over worrying if she will actually take her life. I hate this position. I love her and know something in her head isn't right, but no matter what I do...*Maybe I need to do a bunch of push-ups. Too bad it's not poker night. How can it be that dealing with the danger, unknown, and dynamics of the enemy is easier than dealing with the danger, unknown, and dynamics of marriage?* It's a rhetorical question and I have no expectation of a voice from above providing the answer. After my push-ups, I spend some time on my knees before finally finding enough peace to sleep. Tomorrow is a brand-new day.

CHAPTER 7

FIREFLIES ON

The Importance of Listening to Your Inner Voice

Justice will be served and the battle will rage

This big dog will fight when you rattle his cage

And you'll be sorry that you messed with

The U.S. of A.

'Cause we'll put a boot in your ass

It's the American way

—TOBY KEITH, "COURTESY OF THE RED, WHITE, AND BLUE"

https://www.youtube.com/watch?v=ruNrdmjcNTc

FOB Fenty, Jalalabad, April 2007—"Justice will be served and the battle will rage." I keep hearing it repeat and repeat and repeat, complete with twangy guitar.

We were completely surprised when Toby Keith showed up at our forward operating base at Jalalabad and risked life and limb to climb up on a makeshift stage and entertain us.

I've got an earworm, a musical itch that our flight surgeon can't scratch. It's all thanks to Toby Keith, the country music legend who arrived here one afternoon and put on a one-man show for the hundred or so troops who could take time off to enjoy it. It was a real treat because USO shows don't typically come to forward outposts like ours. That man has balls. He stands up on a makeshift stage, putting his head well above the height of the Hesco barriers surrounding the FOB, and sings his butt off for more than an hour. What an outstanding break from our routine, which has been exhausting ever since my check ride a few weeks back.

The only way I can remember the missions is by reviewing the log book. It confirms I've spent a lot of hours in the seat, a conclusion ratified by my lower back. Maybe by the time the next war rolls around, the geniuses at the Pentagon will have given someone who actually has to sit in it eight or nine hours a day approval of its redesign—the seat, not the back. Of course at this point, I'd be okay with a redesign of either.

It's taken some time and email coordination with the bosses at Bagram, but my personnel management plan is beginning to have a positive effect on the fliers. We've now got a regular rotation system to give the guys here at Jbad a break from nonstop flying. I'm not saying that duty at company headquarters at Bagram is R&R, but flying scheduled ring routes and escorts beats our routine lack of routine, of never knowing when you will be sprinting to the helicopter to shoot and get shot at.

Oddly, most of us want to be here at Jbad; we prefer the mission stress over the political stress of being next to the flagpole at Bagram. The new rotation system will allow for all to trade those stressors and get adequate rest.

Through poker games and other recreation, purposeful debriefing, one-on-ones, and more and more combat action, the young and the old are beginning to meld, appreciating each other's contributions to the fight. Not saying it's perfect, but I wasn't expecting perfection.

We got Mike Hersteller back to Bagram just a week or so after he did my check ride. He was clearly showing signs of PTSD following that engagement with the young combatants, but he never complained, not once. Getting him out of here turned out to be good news/bad news. He hadn't been back there for more than a day or two when he got a phone call from the States. His son had been T-boned in a horrible car accident and was in a coma. Just as he hung up after receiving almost the worst kind of news a parent can get, they got a *Gunmetal Go Redcon-1* alert. This is Bagram, where QRF calls are rare. But as luck would have it, they got one, and Mike was on call. He didn't say a word, just ran to the aircraft and flew the mission with CW2 Marco Elsner, knowing as we do with every mission there is a chance he won't return. I am not sure if I could have done that. He never told anyone about his kid until after they'd returned to base. Pfeifer and Pixler, with the aid of Red Cross, managed to get Mike packed up and on his way back to Arizona on the next flight out.

Life is crazy. We are here, in literally one of the most dangerous environments you can be in, and his son is seriously injured back home, where it is relatively safe. *That doesn't seem right. Life back home continues, with its festivities and its travesties, almost completely disconnected from our reality here. Maybe that's why Katie could put such unreasonable demands and guilt trips on me. Her reality and struggles are real and getting worse, and her life didn't stop when I left.*

I acknowledge that she knows little of my life in Afghanistan because I don't tell her. All she understands is that I am a long way from home and unable to be there for her when she wants or needs me. What I really want to say is, "You don't know how good you have it, grocery store around the corner, car you can drive without fear of it blowing up, freedom to go wherever you please, and just plain better quality of life." Would that help? I doubt it because we are on two separate planes of existence at this point. In a way, this way is probably better. I don't think she would thrive or survive on my plane, but the result of this is that there's little room for common ground. *I wonder if I would thrive or survive if I lived in her mental reality.*

Despite the more open dialogue between all pilots, I'm beginning to understand that some of our senior guys—the ones with more flying experience, including some instructors and pilot mentors— are much more comfortable flying their stateside mission sets: that is, training for war rather than really flying in war. It might be the old-dog-new-tricks thing, because these guys are solid dudes, great pilots, great men, but some of them just don't seem to be as malleable or even eager at times. I want to be clear it was just some. I am in no way saying all the senior guys were not hacking it; most were jobbing it the best they knew how.

AH-64 Apache Longbow awaiting the call. Courtesy of Brett Brown.

If Maxwell Smart could see this picture, there's only one thing he'd say: "Missed it by that much!" Two rounds came close to taking out our driveshaft, which would have taken out our tail rotor, which would have taken out—us. Courtesy of Brett Brown.

The most significant personal realization for me is that I'm becoming one with the machine. I know, I know, I sound like a BMW commercial here, but I now understand those sports car ads that use the phrase. The bird just fits me better than it did when I arrived downrange a few months back. It feels more like an extension of my body, almost like I don't have to tell it what to do; it just does it when I think it, as cyborg as that sounds. I mentioned those feelings at our last poker game—by the way, my Monster fund is now in very good shape—and was surprised by the reaction. A couple of the guys knew exactly what I was talking about, and I got blank stares from a few others.

This machine seems to have a personality, one whose driving force is protection for its crew, since it takes a beating with us and for us, staying in the fight. We've all come home with aircraft damaged so badly that we're shocked they still flew as well as they did. And after years of flying the Apache, I still marvel at how it morphs from an object of graceful aerobatic beauty to a snarling, vengeful beast in a nanosecond—seemingly of its own accord. Hollywood should make a movie about it.

I'm also at ease running the missions from the back seat (okay, at ease as you can be when shrapnel and other ordnance are flying at you and you're flinging it back in return), although night flying continues to be a very big challenge. That one-with-the-aircraft stuff hasn't fully translated to night flying yet. We've got dark, dark nights here where the goggles are useless because there's no ambient light whatsoever for them to amplify. How dark? Do this: put on a blindfold and have someone throw a quilt over your head, take you into a room with no windows, turn off the lights, and lock you in the closet. Now you're getting the idea. Absolute dark. Yes, I can pick out muzzle flashes, but that's about it.

I'm learning that FLIR also has its limitations. Forward-looking infrared radar shows us the shape of things by creating and displaying an image of the heat differential that is emitted by them. From training, we're familiar with IR crossover, a certain time of day where so many things on the ground are almost the same temperature, so much so that it's like you're looking at melted film. In Arizona, it seemed as though it lasted about an hour, or if it rained, maybe longer. But I swear, on some nights in Afghanistan it lasts all night. This phenomenon can be more dangerous than the enemy. The saying goes that the probability of a kill when going against terrain is nearly 100 percent—for the terrain. I've had missions where we were flying a slot canyon and I have to ask my copilot if we're looking at a wall, a gap, or water. Bad part is, they often don't even know what I am referring to, which means we are both being bamboozled by the melting film, the proverbial blind leading the blind. It's bad.

I keep thinking, "How do these experienced guys do this comfortably?" and what I conclude is that I'm not at the point yet where my brain can figure it out by itself, with no explicit guidance from me. Eventually, it's not that the FLIR picture will be improved, just that my gray matter will interpret the impulses from my optic nerves better. You know those pictures you stare at to try and find a hidden object? You stare and stare, and finally it pops out... Oh! There it is. It's a T. rex! Once you've trained your mind to see it, it's easy to see it again. I need that to happen with the FLIR image, the sooner the better.

Then there are the rules I've learned to break, like at night when I'm flying with night vision goggles. The problem is that when I move the reticle to the side, I lose a lot of aircraft instrumental symbology that builds situational awareness. So I turn off the FLIR in the monocle and slide that sucker in front of the goggles. That way, I can still see when the "I" symbol goes solid telling me the bird's in constraints to fire rockets, as well as other gems of information such as my bank angle, torque, and trim indication, while at the same time I can still maintain my NVG view of lasers, muzzle flashes, and hopefully of whatever slot canyon we're in. Call it a hybrid. Whenever I mention it during an after-mission chalk talk, some of the guys pooh-pooh it, telling me that it's dangerous to integrate two separate systems, which is why it's not taught in school. Hellooo! It's dangerous not to do it, too. Choose your poison. The solution would be to come up with night vision goggles that could switch to FLIR when needed and always have symbology overlaid on the image. Did you catch that, Santa?

Knowing how to integrate and build a solid picture of the battlefield using the tools available can mean the difference between life and death. Little did I know I was about to learn this lesson in a very sear-it-in-your-mind sort of way.

A few days after the Toby Keith concert, the recorder inside my brain is still stuck on a continuous loop of "Courtesy of the Red, White, and Blue." I'm sure my mom will think it's inappropriate, but there's something about putting a boot up the Taliban's ass that resonates. By mid-afternoon, CW2 Marco Elsner and I had flown a couple of daylight TICs, applying said boot with ruthless precision.

With ulterior motives, we make it a point to refuel and rearm at FOB Asadabad, which is fifty miles northeast of Jbad but just eight miles from the Pakistani border. The FOB there had been built on an old Soviet site, and their KBR chow hall either had a great baker or a secret connection to import the best cream cheese-filled lemon cake to be found in Afghanistan. It had become legendary. As with the poker game, what I'm about to reveal could probably get me sent to Leavenworth if the wrong people learn about it, but I am determined that my guys back at Jbad would not be denied this critical morale booster. While Marco keeps our bird turning, I dart into the chow hall with an empty carton I'd picked up at the FARP, move adroitly past the refrigerated dessert display, and go directly to the 4-by-6 deep freeze behind the serving tables. I open it and remove an entire lemon sheet cake, slip it into the box, and walk out briskly and confidently, as if I'd been sent by someone important to do that. I had partaken of this lemony heaven a week prior and took notice of where they were stored. (Truth be told, if I'd asked, they would have probably given me one, but that's a *probably*. This is a *definitely* and it is way more fun.) On the lookout for imaginary MPs in hot pursuit, I jog back to the FARP, where I deposit the box safely in our storage compartment, and then jump back into the cockpit, gleefully shouting, "I got a *whole* cake. B Company will dessert in style tonight!"

"Of course you did. Things are looking up," my copilot says with a laugh, and he gets us airborne for the twilight flight home while I'm still strapping in.

The loot had been safely delivered to our TOC, and I'd even managed to enjoy a piece—or maybe it was two or more—myself, when the radio on my hip squawked. *Gunmetal, Gunmetal, Gunmetal, Go Redcon-1.* Regretfully, I know there's no point in telling these vultures to save me some for later.

The first word we get over coms immediately after our two birds launch is that it's a TIC support mission in a valley off the Kunar, to the north, probably only twenty minutes away. It's another one of those pitch-black nights—doesn't the moon ever shine on Afghanistan?—and the first terrain change we note as we fly north into that valley is rolling hills, which then begin to give way to steeper, sharper hillsides on the east and west. The farther we fly into the pass, the more mountainous and craggier those hillsides become.

"Hunter, this is Iron 1-6. We're two minutes out."

"Iron 1-6, this is Hunter 0-6 actual. We're taking fire from above our position."

"Hunter 0-6, I need to confirm your position." I'm seeing muzzle flash from lots of different places in this valley and I don't know who's who. "Hunter 0-6, can you turn your firefly on?"

A second later through the goggles, I see the infrared flicker coming from his tiny personal IR beacon and now know precisely where he is. But there's still all sorts of shooting going on, and what's confusing is that I'm seeing tracer fire going both up and down the mountain on the west side. I know American forces nearly always have tracer rounds in their M4 magazines, but it's rare that the Taliban in this part of Afghanistan fire tracers. I'm not saying it doesn't happen, but it's not common.

"Iron 1-6, the fire we're taking is coming almost straight down on us." That's from his perspective. From where we're at, we can see it's not a super-steep hill, but there's a shelf above him where the bad guys have concealment.

"All right, I've got positive ID on your position, pretty sure I know where you are talking about. Do you have a laser?"

He confirms that he does and immediately understands what I need him to do. He lases in the direction of the muzzle flash above him. What we see through the goggles but not the FLIR is a thin lightsaber beam going up the hill. I just need to make sure, so I ask him to rope the target. A second later, the uphill end of the beam starts to make a circle, lassoing the bad guys.

I talk to my wingman. "Iron 2-3, are you seeing what I'm seeing?" He confirms. "Okay, we're going to fly inbound on a heading of 330 and engage that knoll." The plan is that I'll fire rockets and Marco will hit them with 30 mm, with the second bird doing the same thing right behind us. It's a hit-my-hit sequential racetrack attack pattern, pretty vanilla.

I pitch up and gain altitude, then put the aircraft in a slight dive and get in constraints with everything aerodynamically correct for a rocket run. When we're perfectly aligned to hit the intended target, my right index finger begins to apply pressure to the trigger when I get a really strong feeling that something's wrong. I don't know what it is—nothing with the ship—it's just in my gut.

"Iron 2-3, we're breaking off. Follow me and don't shoot. Repeat: don't shoot."

Marco keys his mic. "What is it, sir?" There's obvious concern in his voice.

"Something's not right," I tell him. We can hear radio chatter in the background, so it's obvious there's more than one unit out there—somewhere. We just aren't sure who's where. I reach out to the ground commander. "Hunter 0-6, imperative we confirm the location of all friendlies. We've got you. Where are your other elements?"

"Iron 1-6, you see us here. Our other squad is across the valley." Problem is, there were no muzzle flashes from the east side of the valley.

"Okay, Hunter 0-6, we still need positive ID. We need him to turn on his fireflies." Then a better idea pops into my head. I switch to transmit on the common air-to-ground freq as well as the freq we had been using. "This is Iron 1-6 Apache overhead. Anybody monitoring this freq, turn on your fireflies." We circle and watch.

"Oh, crap! You seeing that?" I ask my copilot. All he does is key the mic. We're looking straight east, at where Hunter said his other element was, and see nothing. But when we swing around to the west, the shelf area we were about to obliterate is flashing like crazy. It's a very dark night and they stand out. There must be a dozen friendlies up there. They'd been shooting at each other. "Hunter 0-6, the location you just roped just lit up with fireflies. I think those are *your* guys." My voice is somber as the image of *what could have been* pulses through me. When rockets impact during daytime, we can see the mayhem. The explosion, then clouds of pulverized rocks, trees, bushes, and particles of whatever—whomever—we were aiming at, all churning through the air. We wouldn't have seen that tonight, except in our minds. Forever.

"You're right, you're right. Cease fire! All elements cease fire!" he responds, sounding desperate. Thankfully, all tracer fire immediately stops.

I'm instantly nauseous, really queasy. We'd come so close to frat-ricide. My finger was putting pressure on the trigger. There was nothing to keep me from firing off a volley of rockets and Marco blazing away with the gun. There was nothing technically or proce-durally to tell me this is a bad shoot. Positively identified by the ground commander with a laser. Muzzle flash and tracers aimed at our troops.

"Holy crap," I say to my wingman, "we just about had a green on green." I taste bile and feel like I'm about to retch that evening's lemon cake across my windscreen. *I almost killed at least twelve of our guys. It was a simple shot and we wouldn't have missed. They wouldn't have found enough body parts to ship home.*

We make another loop and I get on the radio again. "Hunter, there's still muzzle flash coming from up the valley to the north, and I am seeing no fireflies on them. Are those guys friendly? I don't see trac-ers, but are those guys friendly?"

"Iron 1-6, let's hold your fire." He didn't have to tell me. We're not firing until I hear "Cleared hot." Nobody's going to shoot anything until this thing gets figured out. At this juncture, I honestly don't feel like shooting at all, but if the Taliban is fighting, "justice will be served and the battle will rage." It's the earworm again.

"Hunter, how about I shoot an ILUM rocket so everyone can get their bearings?" He agrees. I align forty-five degrees to their position at a hundred knots and pull aft on the cyclic with my right hand, pitch-ing the aircraft nose up about twenty-five degrees. I maintain trim with my feet and add a little power with my left hand. I had already selected the ILUM rocket on the multipurpose display, so I squeeze the trigger and launch a rocket carrying an M278 illumination payload. It reaches apogee quickly, and what's supposed to happen is that an infrared flare under a parachute will release, allowing it to drift down for about three minutes while illuminating a square kilometer below—roughly a thousand yards by a thousand yards— so anyone wearing NVGs can see what's going on. But what does happen is totally unexpected.

Instead of an IR flare, we fired an overt, visible-to-the-naked-eye flare, and this part of the valley now looks like it's lit up for the Super Bowl. Anyone wearing NVGs—including myself—is instantly blinded, which is not a condition Uncle Sam wants his pilots to be in when operating $52 million worth of US government property at high speed in between two large, rocky, narrowly separated mountainsides. Meantime, I'd been moving the Apache so we won't hit the parachute coming down, and for a few seconds, I've got absolutely no SA (situational awareness). *Where's the mountain? Don't know. Where's my wingman? Ditto. Altitude? Attitude? Crap!*

As my vision comes back, I can see our guys on the ground diving for bushes, rocks, anything that'll provide cover. Hunter comes up on the radio. "Iron 1-6, hey, no! No! I thought it was IR."

"Hunter, it was supposed to be. Sorry. Really sorry, man. I have no idea how that happened. We're not even supposed to have those rounds in our inventory."

The good news is that the sudden bright light must have thrown the enemy off their game too, because they'd stopped firing.

A minute or so later—about the time the bad guys start shooting again—Hunter and I get things sorted out. "Hunter, you're now taking fire from the north, farther up the valley. Not from the hillsides east or west. How 'bout we get rid of that for you?"

"Absolutely!"

Since Marco has already stored that area in our targeting system, we know exactly where they are. One pass; problem eliminated. With no more threats to the ground forces, we head back to Jbad.

I'm still queasy when we touch down at the FARP and not much improved as we hover taxi over to our pad and shut things down. My debrief with Major Smith in the 82nd's TOC is mercifully short. I do tell him what almost happened, but he seems unfazed. "Well, you didn't do it. Good job." I head back to my hooch, strip down, put on shorts and sandals, grab a towel and my M9, and walk to the shower unit. I really don't want to talk to anyone.

In the shower, I realize just how important it is to understand all the assets and resources we have available and to make sure I use them when applicable. We used the FLIR, night vision goggles, lasers, radio communication, fireflies, rocket flares, and most importantly for me, divine intuition, which I've taught myself to trust. This is definitely applicable to other aspects of our lives. How often do we have the resources needed but simply don't use them? *For more on this and how it may apply to you, go to www.clearedhot.info/lessons-learned.*

Back in the hooch a few minutes later, I stare for a moment at the laptop on the nearby table, then shake my head. *Not tonight.* Sitting on the edge of my rack, I say my nightly prayer, thanking God for helping me avoid what would have been a devastating event. I still can't quite figure out what caused me to call off the attack. *Maybe I subconsciously computed that it didn't seem right having tracers going in both directions, uphill and downhill. Who knows?* I gratefully give thanks for divine intervention; as far as I am concerned, that played a role, for sure. Knowing how and when to use the tools we'd been given definitely allowed us to reset the battlefield and ensure the right side won tonight. This lesson is now seared in my brain, luckily not with the devastation that could have been.

Sliding into the sleeping bag liner, I simultaneously reach over to switch off the reading lamp. As I rest my head on the pillow, I hear... nothing.

The silence writes the ending to this day. My earworm is gone. So is the lemon cake.

CHAPTER 8

I CALL THAT THE BASEBALL SLIDE

Problem Solving

"Some of the things that were constant were just the very great disadvantages and problems posed by the terrain. You're going to be shot at from across a stream, from another opposite ridgeline, and you're not going to be able to get up there. So there's a lot of long distance firefights and a lot of the use of artillery and airstrikes and mortars to respond to enemy attacks. It was really a war of firepower. It was not so much a war of crawling along on the valley floor, waiting to be struck by an IED."

—**Wes Morgan,** *The Hardest Place: The American Military Adrift in Afghanistan's Pech Valley*

FOB Bella, Pech River Valley, Late April 2007—A war of firepower. Couldn't have said it better myself. And it's Apache they call for most often to deliver that firepower. Never before has the US military wielded a single tactical weapon that can be precisely guided by a human hand/mind/machine meld to target after target after target in real battlefield time, delivering devastating, focused destruction in support of ground troops. The emotion I feel driving this machine that is now part of me—or maybe it's vice versa—is beyond awesome.

But life is definitely not guns and roses for all my fellow pilots. There are clearly some whose short-term goals are less focused on emulating the dudes in the "Be All That You Can Be" commercials and more fixated on solving the complicated equation of "how do I make it out of here alive without letting my guys down or looking like a coward?"

After a couple of months in charge of our detachment at Jbad, I'd slowly become aware that some of our most experienced aircraft commanders may not be cut out to be attack pilots. They're the guys who would gladly take the high position every time when offered the option in a two-bird high-low technique we employ in very tight quarters; same goes when we're in actively trolling-for-fire scenarios. They're quite comfortable to keep circling overhead out of range of small arms fire and never join the fight. In a way, that works well for me and other like-minded guys, since I would rather take the low position every time, because it's most often where the rubber meets the road.

Those overly cautious fliers justify their position, saying that just the appearance of Apaches usually drives the Taliban to cover, forcing them to stop shooting at our ground troops. Ergo: mission accomplished. And that might be true, but unless we find, fix, and kill them, they'll pop back up once we fly away. I don't revel in killing, but I know I get to go back to a hooch behind Hesco barriers, and our ground pounders rarely do. They are out here day after day, and every Taliban sent to the hereafter is one fewer who can fire on them.

I'd actually called out one of my guys during a mission where he was circling so high that he was of no use to us or anyone else. "Yo! Chalk 2, are you up there waiting for your balls to drop? Because it's gonna be a while. The gravitational pull on your wedding tackle doesn't increase with the distance between you and the enemy." It makes me wonder why they chose to fly the Apache instead of where they should be, flying for UPS in civilian life, or maybe here, but in a utility bird, like a CH47 Chinook on milk runs between bases. That's not a hit on the utility pilots; their mission is crucial. But our mindsets are decidedly different.

Long after the war, one of the younger warrants, CW2 Ryan McNeff, a gifted flyer who was a natural fit for the Apache, told me that he'd been a front-seater for veteran aircraft commanders who actually told him they had no intention of shooting anyone. And one of my trusted maintainers recently told me, as I was interviewing him for this book, that he was sure someone had deliberately sabotaged a crucial sensor on the environmental control unit in one of our birds at Jbad in order to get out of flying a big mission. Truth be told, I do remember him telling me something like that when we were downrange, but I naively dismissed it then as being way too conspiratorial. I couldn't have imagined guys doing that.

I don't believe the guys who do that are inherently bad, certainly not criminal, just overwhelmed by the reality of what we are being called upon to do. Most of them would end up finding ways to go back home early and thus self-eliminate. This was probably the best thing for our team as far as effectiveness goes, but it's not as though we had a line of willing replacements standing by to cover down.

Then there's almost the flip side of that personnel problem. A few of my pilots who have been taking it to the enemy hard are showing distinct signs of emotional trauma. "He flew a mission and saw stuff that broke his brain," is how one of their copilots described his AC after a difficult day. I'm not qualified to say whether it's a diagnosable case of PTSD, but what they were going through after engaging in missions where the killing was up close and personal is not only painful but debilitating. Most of them don't want to admit that. Sometimes we could find other medical reasons to send them home.

It's a lot for me to think about, and it all has to get pushed out of mind because we're on a TIC call from a unit that's pinned down from above in one of the steep valleys off the Pech River, somewhere in the vicinity of the generously named FOB Bella. The good news is that it's midday. I've flown those canyons at night and it's scary as hell. Daytime isn't a picnic—and it's easier for the enemy to engage us—but if I do it right, we have a better chance of avoiding terminal interaction with terrain. Frankly, the topography in certain areas is much more menacing than the Taliban, and I am determined not to let it do the Taliban's work for them.

When we first started flying up the Kunar Valley into the Hindu Kush we were glued to the electronic route maps our TACOPS (tactical operations) guys had provided, but this had become almost a regular commute. On this run, we *fly north to Asadabad; take a left at the mouth of the Pech River where it joins the Kunar, then fly twenty miles to the first tributary on the right, turn and enter the Waygal Valley toward FOB Bella.*

Early on, there'd been a time or two when we did enter the wrong valley and had to come back out and go around to the correct one. In case you're wondering why we don't just plug in the Garmin GPS from the golf shop and follow a straight line to our target, consider this: the mountains here top out at more than 14,000 feet. Trying to go over them in a fully loaded Apache is not in the cards.

Even flying our scenic valley-floor route that takes us past FOB Blessing toward Bella, above the river as it winds and twists through an extremely narrow V-shaped valley, is happening at altitudes that are power limiting. Our starting point at Jalalabad is already 1,886 feet above sea level. By the time we reach Asadabad, fifty miles north, we're up to 2,664 feet. Twenty-three miles farther on, as we enter the Waygal Valley, we're a thousand feet higher, and once we're near Bella, we're in the same thin air the Denver Broncos are playing in at Mile High Stadium—and that's at the bottom of the valley. Every day we are poking our noses into what's been described by historians who have studied Alexander the Great's adventures there in 327 BC as "one of the most topographically forbidding operating environments in the world." Let me remind you, old Al wasn't flying helicopters, machines that need air density they can bite.

This is the Waygal Valley, where I had to use "the baseball slide" in order to support our troops. At the valley floor, it wasn't more than one rotor disk wide. Courtesy of Darin Gaub.

As we approach the convoy stopped precisely on the grid coordinates we'd been given at lift-off, we're roughly 300 feet above the
valley floor with maybe—maybe—the equivalent of five rotor disks
from one rocky side to the other—that's about 250 feet. Near the
bottom on one side is a narrow dirt track, big enough for small
vehicles or even camel caravans of Taliban coming in from Pakistan—which we've seen and eliminated in the past—with more of
a melting snow-fed fast-flowing stream than a wide river flowing
down the center. At the valley floor, we're looking at less than a rotor
disk from wall to wall. On the opposite side, we occasionally see a
dwelling. To further complicate our life, there is a saddle just past
the convoy effectively boxing off our route of flight. One alternative
would be to climb higher, but then we wouldn't be able to keep those
ground troops in sight due to the steepness of the valley. Bottom
line: one of us needs to stay closer to the convoy's elevation if this
isn't going to be more than a sightseeing trip.

I know we're vulnerable to small arms fire and RPGs flying this
low, but I can't see any other way to do this. You'd think that with
millions of dollars' worth of target acquisition gear built into the
Apache, we shouldn't have any problem finding the bad guys, but
not here. If they were in vehicles or hardened targets, it wouldn't
be a problem. But we're looking for soft squishies in the vegetation
that pretty much covers the steep sides of this canyon and getting
no help from technology.

"Barracuda 1-6, this is Iron 1-6. We see you on the road. Where are
you receiving fire from?"

"Iron 1-6, it's coming from a cave. Above us."

That's not real helpful. Everything is above them and we don't see
any cave. The canyon sides are too steep and too vegetated for
that. The only way to see the cave would've been to be co-altitude

facing it. Okay, how do we do this? First thing, we've got to stack. So I put our wingman, CW4 Richard Schiffli, 200–600 feet above us. The theory is, it's wider up there and he covers our vulnerable backside while flying circles, which is something we literally can't do at our height above ground level. It also decreases our workload significantly because we don't have to share this tight airspace with another Apache. The expectation is, he pays attention to flying while his copilot watches us, keeping a look out for muzzle flash. Anything that pops up, they nail it—in theory anyway, although the steepness will also limit their ability to identify any points of origin. Oh well, we have to play the cards we've been dealt.

The only way I can turn 180 degrees is to do a pitch-back turn or return to target. (For a technical explanation as to why, see the box at the end of this chapter.) That's where we pitch the nose up, gain some altitude while transferring the energy we lose by slowing down into climbing energy and eventually potential energy as our climb slows, then turn right or left, as though we're rotating around the rotor mast, then transfer that potential energy back into speed by diving. Point is, it's an energy management maneuver utilized to minimize the turn radius significantly. Quite literally, that's the only way we can turn this beast without clipping the walls with our rotor blades.

So keeping us away from terrain is my number one priority. Finding where to shoot is priority two. McNeff can fire off-axis with the 30 mm—we just don't know where to shoot. Just spraying willy-nilly at the side of the mountain isn't going to help, and the memory of the Fireflies On mission is still in the front of my mind.

"Barracuda 1-6, do you have any smoke grenades you can throw in direction of enemy fire so you can adjust us from there?"

"Sorry, Iron 1-6, we are all out. We have had to use a lot of smokes lately."

What I need to do is get some white phosphorus smoke into the rocks above Barracuda's position so he can use it to direct fire for us. That presents the problem of trying to hug the opposite side of the valley, pitch up and turn about the mast with the nose pointed skyward, then let the nose fall back to pointing down so we regain the airspeed we lost on the pitch and are now diving perpendicular to the wall on the opposite side of the valley, get in trim, and fire WP marking rockets without getting dangerously close to the ground troops we're trying to help. But we can't hit too far from them either, or they won't be able to see the smoke due to the incline. Then I need to break the aircraft right prior to impacting the opposite side of the valley, all of which is less than 250 feet of travel. No other way to do it because those rockets only shoot in the direction the Apache is pointing.

Here's another way to wrap your mind around the challenge: an Olympic runner can cover 100 yards—300 feet—in ten seconds. We have slightly less distance to cover, maybe 250 feet across. We do gain a little distance by making that line an angled dive, so let's say 450 feet, but we're going to be moving at 60–100 miles an hour heading straight for a rock wall. I wish we had ten seconds to get it right; if we're lucky, we've got three.

"Barracuda 1-6, I'm going to shoot some white smoke rockets out a couple hundred feet above your position. Will you be able to walk us onto where you believe fire is coming from? Then we can engage it with the 30 mm."

"Wilco, Iron 1-6."

I release the radio mic switch and tell Ryan my plan over the voice-activated intercom. "We're going to get as close as we can to the side of the canyon opposite the convoy. Pitch up. Turn and come back toward the other wall in a dive, hope we get in trim, fire the rockets, and then you cover our break with the 30, hopefully before we hit the other side of the valley."

"Yeah, sir, that sounds like a great plan." And then he snorts, which I take to mean, *So are our wills updated?*

"I think I can do it," I say.

"I am with you, sir," he affirms. "Let's get her done."

I can see on the multifunction display that he's already gone to the weapons page, selected "rockets," and then the zone on the rocket pod that will fire the willie petes.

I wazz *rockets* on my castle switch and fly toward the wall at about 120 knots (138 mph), then pitch up maybe 75–100 feet, bleeding off airspeed as I do, rotate around and dive back toward the other side of the valley, instantly thinking, *Dang, that other side is close,* as we gain airspeed in the dive right toward the wall. I am talking out loud to the bird as well as my hands and feet on the controls. "C'mon trimball, trimball, trimball," waiting for that "I" symbology to turn solid telling me the rockets will fire, and then *pfffft! pfffft!* I don't even look where they go, no time. I just break, feeling the vibrations of the 30 mm as Ryan covers our break. But now we're belly up to the same side of the valley we just shot at, the wheels are thinking about touching down on the rock wall, our rotor disk is vertical like a windmill in an Iowa cornfield, and I have to roll us level quickly to pitch the aircraft up again in order to turn back prior to impact with the box end of this valley, completing a 180-degree turn to head back the other way.

We complete the maneuver and turn, expecting to be able to admire our handiwork. But there's no white phosphorus smoke. We see nothing. Nothing! Son of a gun! *I just did that PhD maneuver and they're duds? We have to do it again? I am not sure I want to, plus we only have one remaining WP rocket. F a duck!*

"Barracuda 1-6, sorry, I guess those were duds."

"No! No! You got it," he shouts over the radio. "Nice shootin'!"

Now I'm totally confused. "I got what?"

"You stuck 'em right in the cave where those guys were shooting from." I hadn't seen a cave. I hadn't seen anything when I pulled the trigger except a rock wall coming at us at sixty to ninety knots.

Bottom line, though, is that Barracuda was no longer receiving fire. Ryan says, "I can't believe that worked."

"What do you mean? You doubted me?"

"Not for a second, sir." Sarcasm noted.

"Yeah, I'm gonna call it the pitch-up rodeo high-dive baseball slide."

"Nah, you'd have to acronym that name. Why not just call it the Baseball Slide?"

Later that afternoon at the debrief, Schiffli tells us, "I didn't know what you were doing. I thought you were going to crash three times—this wall, that wall, then lose your power and hit the bottom. Whatever you did worked, but I don't know how or why you did it."

Why I did it? I thought that was obvious, but therein lies the difference in thinking. Not saying my way is always right—in fact, without a doubt it isn't—but my drive is to help out our guys on the ground. Maybe I do go too bold at times, so perhaps facing questions like "Why?" are actually helpful. Even humbling.

The next day, I head to battalion TOC on one of my regular visits to intel, and Major Smith is holding some pictures. He knew we'd been out to near FOB Bella and was familiar with the details of the engagement. Nevertheless, with a smirk, he asks, "Was this you?" The photos and sit-rep described fourteen Taliban with weapons in that cave, now thoroughly crispified. It was a gruesome sight. They looked like marshmallows that had been roasted over a campfire by a kid who had never done it before. Smith knew we hadn't targeted humans with the WP, since that's a violation of the Geneva Conventions, so no problem, no paperwork. But the photos were definitely unsettling.

What the mission did teach me is that courage combined with capability can create solutions to seemingly unsolvable problems. It also marked one more notch in my confidence belt. This one-with-the-machine stuff actually works; now if I can just get there in my night flying. In a tactical sense, taking those kinds of calculated risks also keeps the enemy guessing. Just when they think they're safe, they're not. The lesson learned is that there are lots of ways to open a can of soup: sometimes you use a can opener, sometimes you use a rock. Either way, you get the soup.

But there's a trap in that too. As in football, an uninterrupted succession of victories can give you a false sense of invulnerability, luring you into taking chances that are well outside of the risk-reward matrix. Hubris has taken hold of you, and almost inevitably catastrophe awaits. If the ending is terminal, that's when folks watching the news in their easy chairs say, "What were they thinking?" To them, it seems like such a *duh* moment. But if we're fortunate enough to survive the event and avoid becoming

a posthumous case study, the hope is that we not only apply the
lessons we've learned and alter our own future behavior but also
teach those lessons to our colleagues.

So far, I'm still on the *invulnerable* side of the scorecard. But the
game's not over and I am about to get a reality check.

Why the Need for the Baseball Slide Maneuver?

If you want to see a video that'll make sense of this maneuver, go to www.clearedhot.info/baseballslide. Otherwise, the
following is a more in-depth look at why we would need to
do what we did.

Readers may wonder why we had to go through all that just
to turn the helicopter around and target the wall. To understand, it helps to know what a helicopter is capable of and
what it isn't. If I could have held the Apache in a hover at the
proper height above the ground, I could have just done a 180
by just using my pedals to increase or decrease the thrust
of the tail rotor. We've all seen hovering helicopters above
their landing pad turn around. But you haven't seen them do
it in mile-high-plus thin air, where they're well above both
sea level and ground level, because the bird doesn't have
the power it needs to hold a hover. (There is an exception,
but that would require a strong headwind coming up or
down the canyon, which would make the helo think it was
moving forward in powered flight making it more efficient.
That wasn't the case here.) One more reason not to sit in a
hover to line up the perfect shot: we'd be a sitting duck for

any Taliban with an RPG or even a simple rock thrown from above through our rotor system.

Then there's the question of actually flying and making a U-turn. Unlike a sports car that can keep all four wheels on the ground in a turn, a helicopter's ability to turn and remain parallel to the ground is limited by altitude, temperature, wind, and gross weight. It has to bank, just the way an airplane does, with one wing tilted up, the other down. Otherwise, it will not bite the air well enough to maintain control. In normal air at lower altitudes, we can put the helo into a steep bank and keep the turning radius tight, just like that Ferrari I keep comparing the Apache to. But up in the thin air of the Hindu Kush Mountains, flying slower, with less responsive controls, it takes a lot more radius to get around. No tight Ferrari turns. And we didn't have enough width in the valley to do a gentle turn. Thus, we have to transfer energy—pitch up, trade airspeed for climb, trade altitude for bank angle, and come around and down trading altitude for airspeed. Hence, the Baseball Slide.

CHAPTER 9

WE ARE BLACK
ON AMMO

The Only Way to Expand your Box
Is to Get Outside of It

Watapur Valley, Kunar Province, July 5, 2007—"Magneto? I hear that's what the maintainers are calling you now." At least Major Smith had a smile on his face as he pulled up a chair and joined me at breakfast in the chow hall.

"You should've heard what they called me a couple months ago, the first time I brought one of their babies home with a Swiss cheese facelift. I guess now they've gotten used to the results of taking it to the Taliban." I had just finished a multi-egg omelet that had more extra veggies in it than I could ever get at Stoney's Desert Inn in Mountain Home. But I still missed the DI's hang-off-the-plate stack of three butter-soaked pancakes and homemade pecan syrup. That was back when carbs had no meaning. Not the case now, hence the omelet... Moment on the lips, lifetime on the hips.

I'd actually had a good night's sleep—no QRF calls—and welcomed the chance to chat with the 82nd's operations officer. He was a man deliberate of both speech and purpose; I am sure he is not just here for idle chitchat. What I really like about him is that he knows how to lead warriors. We know he understands our job is not easy, and he always has our backs when the armchair quarterbacks at HQ begin pontificating.

"I heard through the grapevine that the only way those guys agreed to keep patching up your birds is with a constant resupply of imported lemon cake. That possible? Because there's been some internal messaging from the KBR people that those very same cakes keep disappearing from the chow hall at Asadabad. And it always seems to happen after some Apache pilots pay them a visit." Of course, this is bogus. KBR wouldn't be sending this kind of messaging directly to Major Smith, but obviously the word's out.

"I wouldn't know anything about that, sir," I say, while appearing to concentrate on peeling a fresh orange. "But you did tell me at poker last week how much you enjoyed the lemon cake we had in the TOC. Not sure where it came from. That center layer of creamy, lemony filling is—" I pause, imagining our favorite appropriated dessert, instantly craving a piece "—nothing short of heaven here in the land of angst and turmoil."

"That your reward for dealing with an in-flight emergency last night?" *Aha, this is what he really wants to talk about. See? Deliberate.*

"You heard about that?" I ask, though not really surprised. He is talking about a transmission chip light that came on while we were in the middle of an engagement.

"I heard that. I hear about everything. It's my job. So tell me..." He truly did seem to have a pretty good finger on the pulse of things.

Made me wonder where he was getting his intel and also made me want to post a "Snitches Get Stitches" poster in our TOC.

"We could see muzzle flash on this ridgeline and got a TIC call from a patrol while returning from an escort mission. We'd made a couple of passes and then got the audio warning indicating a caution. When I looked down at the MFD, I saw we had a transmission chip light. The first thought was that we'd been hit somewhere in the transmission. The second thought was that the book says we're supposed to land as soon as possible. *Possible* is a relative term, right? I asked my copilot if he was comfortable finishing the engagement."

"And he said?" asked the major, quizzically.

"'Yeah, sir, I'm as comfortable as I can be knowing that we're about to become a rock.' I figured it this way: It's a twenty-minute flight back home. If the transmission is going to eat itself up, we should get some grinding noises and feedback in the controls before it does." I neglect to tell the major that I'd pulled this theory from my rectal database. Then I continue, "With luck, we can set it down and hope by then we're a good distance away from here when we do, because landing right now would be a terminal event either way. We're over serious bad-guy land, and all we'd have on the ground between the two of us are a pair of 9 mm pistols and a couple of M4s. Then there's the problem of leaving the Apache for them to pick over. We only did one more pass to clean things up, then took it easy flying back to Jbad at a low altitude, so if we had to put it into a landing profile we could do it quick. Trust me, sir, our senses were on full alert for any secondary indications. We did call and let the TOC know what was going on."

"Yeah, that's the call I heard. Something like, 'If we're not back in twenty-minutes, come find us.'"

"Sounds about right. But we made it home, and the maintainers took a look. No damage at all to the transmission. It was an errant indicator. We did have some holes in the tail boom; one round actually hit the hydraulic line and bent it. But the Kevlar did its job, thank goodness. No punctures. That would've been a land-without-delay necessity if it had. 'Take all the time you need; you have thirty seconds of pressure to get it on the ground.'"

"Always good to know when the lowest bidder actually supplies parts that work," the major says.

Our maintainers worked twenty-four hours a day to keep the birds flying, and they never complained when we brought them back shot up. These guys monitored the radios when we were flying and were always anxious when we got into it. Courtesy of Brett Brown.

I am on a roll talking about the maintainers and feel the need to keep going. They do amazing work in the trenches and deserve to have their praises sung before the boss. "Before breakfast, I took a look out there. Our maintainers out here get it. They're fully invested in the mission. We talk with them when we come back, and they really understand that what they do is crucial to keeping our ground pounders alive, not to mention us. You should've seen one of them this morning. There was just this black-and-brown blob moving underneath the bird, doing whatever it is they do. His pants were worn out, held together by grease and oil. I swear his butt cheeks were just flapping in the wind, but it all looked like a greasy blob."

"Who was it?"

"A guy who actually flew to Bagram with me and the Apaches. Staff Sergeant Sidney Aaron. He truly has a connection with these birds. The other day, I came out of the TOC and he'd had one of the aircraft towed so the tail boom is next to a building, and he's directing another one of our guys who is up on the roof doing the splits—one foot on the building, the other on a tail strut, doing something with the rotor. Field expedient yoga maintenance. Unky Sam didn't think we needed a jack stand. Guess he was right."

"Whatever works. You on call this morning?" asks the major as he stands up to leave.

"In about an hour. We'll see what the day brings."

* * *

I'd just finished an email to Capt. Pfeifer in Bagram about crew reassignments when the alarm went off. The voice on my hip had barely gotten the third *Gunmetal* out of his mouth when I hit the TOC doorway. By the time the voice was saying *Go Redcon-1*, I was picking my way through the rocks to the concrete pad. CW4 Brett Brown, one of the best hands in our guard unit who got sent to Jbad as punishment for not properly puckering up to kiss the battalion commander's backside, arrived just as I grabbed my vest off the rocket pylon. We both finished suiting up and climbed in. Four minutes later, we were airborne, just ahead of Chalk 2.

At the same time, an HH-60 Black Hawk Dustoff bird was lifting off the pad just beyond ours. "Dustoff 1-1, Iron 1-6. Please don't do anything stupid today, sir. I need your money in the pot at Saturday's game." Capt. Dave Horn is flying this mission. I like flying with him. He's a gutsy pilot, willfully flying into hot LZs (landing zones) others wouldn't go near, but he has the hands to back it up. Their standing orders acknowledge that they fly into dangerous LZs, but they are "not to take unnecessary risks." The way that got briefed is, "If you can't get there and back, there's no point in getting there." Horn's response was something like, "Tell that to the ground troops trying to save their buddies' lives." And that's how he flies.

This TIC is in the Watapur Valley sixty miles north of Jalalabad, about a twenty-five-minute flight for us. Word from Able 6-2 is they have three casualties, "one expectant [likely to die], two critical."

"Hey, Able 6-2. Iron 1-6 inbound with medevac for you. What's your situation?"

"Iron 1-6, we are pinned down in a saddle between two spurs off the ridgeline. Taking effective fire from above." He was noticeably out of breath.

"Roger, Able. Understand the LZ is cherry?"

"Affirmative, it's cherry red. Hot as hell."

"Okay, Able. Where do we have to start shooting to cool it off?"

The voice that came back was clearly desperate. "Anywhere on the ridgeline. You can shoot anywhere. All friendlies are down here in this saddle."

We could see now that the entire area was heavily forested; no one—good or bad—was out in the open. The landing zone was sort of obvious; it looked like a brown postage stamp in the middle of green. Even though he tells us they're taking fire, we can't see any muzzle flash in the bright daylight, not to mention I am sure the bad guys are in the trees and rocks, so they're nearly impossible to identify.

"Iron 1-6, this is Dustoff. I'm going in." It was Horn, chomping at the bit as usual. Not wanting to wait for us to cool things down. Definitely not a good move.

"Dustoff, hold off on that run. Let us at least throw out some suppressive fire to get their heads down before you head in there. Roger?"

"Iron 1-6, let's hear the plan?"

"Both Apaches are going to fly a race track directly above the LZ, laying down some 30 mm into the tree line. Dustoff, you come in to land from the valley below us, so you are terrain masked until the last second. Able 6-2, have those casualties ready to be loaded quickly. We don't want that bullet magnet on the ground any longer than needed."

Both Dustoff and Able confirm.

"Iron 1-6 in hot." Brett begins turning pine trees into toothpicks with the 30, which forces the Taliban to hunker down, giving Horn the opportunity to sneak in and land. Thirty seconds later, he lifts off, and we can see fire directed at him from the ridgeline of the next spur.

"Dustoff, break right down the valley. I am going to hit those dudes that think your red crosses are targets."

"Breaking right. They're all yours, man."

On the intercom to me, Brett says, "I wouldn't want to have to put it down there in this ship. Hardly any room and no power."

"Couldn't agree more. Glad Horn's flying it, not us." I didn't know it then, but later in the day, this statement would come back on me.

As we exit the Watapur Valley, the ground commander says, "Hey, Iron 1-6, will you please relay to higher we're black on ammo? Luckily, these ragheads don't know it because we're just spacing our shots out to keep them at bay. But they could overrun us. We need ammo and water ASAP!"

Crap! Black on ammo means they got nothing. "Able, I'll pass the word on at Abad and request a speedball for you and tell them to put a kick-it-in-the-butt clause in the request." I know it sounds a bit grim, but units typically used body bags—they call them speedballs—to drop an emergency ammo or water resupply to ground pounders in dire straits. Doing it that way lets them avoid the extremely vulnerable state of landing under fire, yet still resupply. It's not an ideal delivery system—quite often, half the load is destroyed by the impact.

Just minutes later, we land at Abad and rearm and refuel so we can make the long escort run to the hospital at Bagram with Horn. I contact Abad TOC by radio and tell them about the desperate need for ammunition and water using the exact phrasing I told Able. They assure me it'll be relayed and taken care of. I'm having an "if I were in their shoes" moment. *Man, I would hate to be those guys pinned down out of ammo.* I wanted to go back to Watapur and stay overhead, but we were tasked to stay with Dustoff all the way to Bagram.

We make the nearly hourlong flight to the main American base in Afghanistan on the tail of the Dustoff. At Bagram, we hover over to the FARP and refuel. I take an extra minute to run to the shopette to grab as many cans of Monster as I can. But they're out of stock. Crap! I redirect to the chow hall, where I have to settle for the illegitimate child of energy drinks, the KBR-provided Rip It. I also take the opportunity to pee standing up; the piddle-packs in the cockpit are useful but not ideal, if you get my drift. And then there's the disposal problem.

Climbing back in, I'm figuring on an unexciting flight home. Bad figuring. Halfway to Jalalabad, we get another TIC call. It's routine. We pick up our wingman; we roll in; the enemy hides. We leave, again heading to Jbad, where we refuel, and almost immediately get another Dustoff escort call to a valley just north of Naray. Then it's back to Jbad. By the time we land, we're going on seven and a half hours of flight time.

It's been a busy day, but it ain't over yet. Jbad assigns us yet another medevac escort mission, telling us to hook up with Dustoff and a second Apache at Asadabad. That's going to put us past eight hours, which we can't do without an extension. So I radio the request, and it gets immediate approval at company level. I also send along a second extension request, since I know we'll inevitably push past nine hours as well. That one gets approved by Major Smith at battalion level.

As we're approaching the FOB at Asadabad, we hear from Capt. Horn. "They've got two KIA now, one wounded. They're just picking these guys off." I can hear the pain in his voice. Dustoff pilots like Horn often get up close and personal with fallen angels. It's got to be difficult.

"Then let's go get 'em," we say. Without landing, we begin heading in the direction of the Watapur, the other two birds joining us in a flight of three.

Brett and I talk on the intercom a bit. Because it's almost dusk, the FLIR isn't too reliable due to temperature differentials not being ideal, and it's not dark enough to use night vision goggles. The only good news is now it's easier to make out muzzle flash.

On the radio from Chalk 2, a crew augmenting out of FOB Salerno, I hear, "Holy shit, there's muzzle flash."

"Yeah, when it's not friendly, you shoot at it." Clearly someone in that other Apache is new to the fight. First time?

It's déjà vu all over again. We start engaging, blowing stuff up. Big trees are falling, the ridgeline is peppered with exploding rounds, but this time we can see a lot of flickers even with the tree cover. It's obvious there is a decent contingent of abadabas down there. Horn races in, picks up the casualties, and flies out. Just then, our radio crackles. "This is Able 6-2. Is this the same Iron 1-6 that was here this morning?"

"Roger that. How you guys doing?"

"We never got our ammo."

I'm dumbfounded. *How could that be?* "Dude, I passed that message up. I promise, I did. I will get on it and stick with it until you get something, I promise."

"Iron 1-6, we've got nothing left. Since you left this morning, there've been two more Dustoffs in here to pick up my wounded. One of them brought us a little unofficial help, but we're done. These guys are going to overrun us." I'm not quite nauseous but getting there. *This isn't supposed to happen. Don't those rear echelon types at Bagram give a crap about our guys? I guarantee someone dropped the ball, or at least I hope that's the case. If someone deliberately decided not to send these guys aid in their situation? Well, let's just say there is a throat punch waiting for them.*

I say to Brett, "This is freakin' unbelievable. Abad is ten miles away, just around the corner. It's got a FARP—that A stands for arming. Why are they in a stupidly bad situation?"

Our three birds talk. Horn has to land first to refuel, and there's only room for two helicopters at a time at the Abad forward arming and refueling point. I tell Chalk 2 to land next to Horn and then escort the Dustoff to Bagram. I also pass the word to launch or retask another Apache in our direction. The way that LZ is being lit up by the Taliban, going back in there cannot be a one-bird mission. *What the heck can we do, right now, to help?*

Meantime, while we're circling, I contact the Abad TOC. "Abad, this is Iron 1-6. What happened to that speedball of ammo I requested this morning for the TIC in Watapur?"

The response spikes my blood pressure. Nobody knows anything or seems terribly concerned. *I need to calm down; yelling right now isn't going to help.* "Look, Abad. Their situation is dire. You need to get with Bagram and get them help immediately. This is what I need to know ASAP. When can you get it to them? I need an ETA. How quick are they going to lift off? Are they even tasked?" I know the guy I am talking to is just the relay man, but I want to punch someone so bad right now, and he's first in line. It's probably a good thing I'm in the air.

An eternity goes by, maybe two minutes, and I get my answer. "The soonest they can get somebody out there is forty-five minutes to an hour, and that's a maybe." *Really? They're enjoying dinner and don't want to be rushed? You can't tell me every Black Hawk and Chinook in this part of Afghanistan is tasked out right now. This has got to be one of those situations where dudes drop what they're doing and make it happen. Damn! I'm pretty sure the flight crews would be going balls to the wall if they knew, but the bosses must be getting the word out with smoke signals. How do we fix this?*

I immediately realize that the game of radio tag we're playing won't resolve the situation; something is being lost in translation or transmission, because for some freakin' reason these rear echelon types in their air-conditioned TOC at Bagram just don't get the urgency. They must not understand the picture. But I do have that crazy contingency plan that's been plowing circles through the back of my mind, almost not daring to say it out loud. Probably because I am not sure if it will even work. But we've reached that decision point where you opt to do nothing or you do out-of-the-box, first-time-for-everything stuff. "Do you guys have small arms ammo at this FOB that I can take?"

They answer in the affirmative, saying their guys were aware of the firefight and have spent several hours loading rounds into M4 magazines. By this time, both Dustoff and Chalk 2 have lifted off. As I prepare to land, I say to Brett, "We're going to fill our storage bins on both sides with everything they've got, and we're gonna take it around the corner and deliver those poor suckers some ammo."

"I'm with you, boss. Buuuutttt I don't think we're going to have the power margin to take off from here, let alone land on that hill. Dustoff could do it, but he's not carrying guns, ammo, or external pods. He has the power margins to do that; we don't. Also, sir, not that I care, but we have busted our extension already."

That I can fix. Or at least I think I can. "Abad TOC, this is Iron 1-6. I need you to relay Able 6-2's situation in detail to the highest-ranking dude you can get on the horn. I repeat, you need to emphasize

Able's urgency of need, an hour wait won't cut it. Then tell them Iron 1-6 has a plan but needs an additional two-hour extension in order to make it happen."

Easier asked than done. The problem is, we had already received two extensions. Two more requires the approval of the two-star commanding general of the 82nd Airborne Division, call-sign All-American 0-6. Standing orders require that only he can approve this. I've never heard of that happening, but as I said, it's that first-time-for-everything type of night.

"Brett, I'm figuring we're gonna get this extension. But either way, we're doing it. You with me?"

"Well, LT, I am just happy to be here and away from the flagpole, so you know I'm on board."

From where I sit in the AC's cockpit, all I can see is the back of his head. But I can picture his face, with his ever-present unlit cigar clamped in a corner of his mouth, grinning at the anticipation of this mission, while at the same time not believing it's going to work.

"Besides, you're the boss. I'm just your lowly copilot. Let's roll." Brett has an interesting history. He's got thousands of hours but got busted down to copilot because he was perceived as a bit of an airshow-type guy and because he didn't get along with our organic battalion commander Desert Hawk 0-6. Probably more of the latter. Brett had been exiled from Salerno, where our organic Arizona Guard head shed ruled the AO, to Bagram, with the directive that he not be allowed to fly. When I heard about it, I immediately asked Pfeifer to send him to Jbad, adding, "He's definitely going to fly even if you need to plead ignorance."

We were short pilots, and no one is going to tell me we sit on a dude who can outfly most of us because some commander got his ego bruised. That's stupid. I'll put him in my front seat. Right about now, I am glad I did.

On the ground at Abad, Brett stays on the sticks with rotors turning, and I jump out, pop open the storage lockers, and with the help of some ground guys, load several black plastic garbage bags they'd already filled with loaded thirty-round magazines. As soon as both side bins are stuffed, I jump back in and confront the first reality facing us: the ten-foot-tall Hesco barrier filled with sand, rocks, and broken concrete and then bonded together with a concrete slurry. With both engines maxed, we're having a hard time holding a foot-high hover. We hover as far away as we can get from the barrier, turn around making sure the wind is at our face, then slowly nose the aircraft forward, gaining speed in an attempt to make it through ETL. (Time for brief tech/nerd talk. Effective translational lift is when the lift generated by the rotor disk is more efficient due to increased aircraft speed. Try this: take an index finger and push your glasses upward while scrunching up your nose. ETL is the term used to describe the airspeed at which the entire rotor system realizes the benefit of the horizontal flow of air. To make this happen, the rotor disk must move completely out of its own downwash and into undisturbed air.) In Slade-speak, we need some speed to be able to fly.

We are slowly speeding up with our wheels bouncing off the ground here and there, but I'm not sure we are going to clear that barrier. *It doesn't matter. We are all-in committed at this point. Don't think I've ever made a helicopter skip before.* I clench my teeth because I'm pretty sure we are at least going to take some concertina wire with us. I give the collective a quick pop downward, smacking the wheels into the ground, then immediately pull everything we've got, maximizing any advantage we receive from the bounce and the in-ground effect. I give a little aft cyclic as we climb, and almost to my surprise, our nose barely pops up over the top of the Hesco. It's like a little porpoise jump and dive—the nose pops up and over, I immediately force it down, which causes the tail to pop up and avoid the concertina. We immediately take advantage of the quick terrain drop-off on the other side to build airspeed, and then slowly climb up to about 700 feet, where we pick up our new Chalk 2, piloted again by CW3 Steve Beach with 2nd Lt. Christine Thomas in the front seat.

"Iron 1-6, this is Iron 2-2. I have you in sight. We are on your six."

"Iron 2-2, welcome to the fight. We're headed back to the Watapur. Here's the deal. There's a lot of bad dudes up there and our guys are black on ammo. Higher should have resupplied them hours ago, but they must've had other priorities."

At this point, it would have been nice to give everyone my plan, but the truth is, I don't have one yet. "Steve, somehow I'm gonna put this bird down on that same spot the Dustoffs have been landing. All I know right now is that we're gonna be super vulnerable."

"No worries, sir. We're full up on ammo and we're not afraid to use it."

"Brett, here's what I'm thinking. We've got no choice but to come right over the top of the bad guys, then slowly toboggan down the spur just above the trees. Well, mostly above the trees. We'll probably knock the tops off a few because we've got to stay low enough that the entire ride down is in ground effect. We need that air cushion, and luckily that plan is into the wind, which should help. Then we break away from the trees and set it down. What do you think?"

"I think it's stupid, but I'm with you. If you're set on going in, I don't see another way to do it. You definitely won't have power to do it coming up from the valley. This way? Maybe."

"Iron 2-2, we need you to shoot behind us, blast the crap out of that ridgeline. Anything you can do to keep their heads down. Just shoot."

Then a thought crosses my mind. "Brett, can you grease 'em with the 30 as we're going down?"

"I don't think so, LT. The gun won't depress enough to be effective." Duh, I knew that, but my mind was racing trying to think of anything that might help. I even think of jettisoning our two rocket pods, which would have dropped about 600 pounds and given us about 3 percent more power margin, but conclude that's a last and very unappealing resort.

"Iron 1-6, this is Abad control. Be advised your extension has been approved by All American 0-6." That would be Major General David M. Rodriguez.

"Copy." *Uh, okay, good to know.* "Okay, here we go. Probably only going to get one shot at this."

As we come over the ridgeline, we can see muzzle flash firing downhill on our patrol. *As soon as we're past the bad guys, they're going to redirect that fire at our backside.* Now we're down almost into the treetops, taking that toboggan ride downhill no more than fifty feet AGL to keep that cushion of air under us. I pull slight aft on the cyclic, bringing the nose up to try and slow us to just above ETL but careful not to slow below it until we can trade efficiencies. I am carrying a little more smash than I had expected and have every bit of power applied at this point. Now it's a finesse game. As we slow below ETL, we're decreasing that efficiency while simultaneously getting as low to the ground as possible to increase our in-ground-effect efficiency. I'd pull up harder, but the engines are right at limiting; any more and the rotors will droop, in which case we'll lose lift and fall. I see fire coming up through the trees all around us. *I was wrong. The*

Taliban aren't waiting for us to pass them to shoot. This might not have been a great, or even a good, idea. We're going to come in hard. No other "survivable" way to do it.

I'm not sure if I'm holding my breath, but if I am, the landing knocks it out of me. I know Brett can hear my OOOOFF! over the voice-activated intercom. It isn't a crash, but it's definitely not a landing my instructors at Rucker would be happy with. I can almost hear them saying, "Lieutenant, are you *trying* to break my helicopter?" And that's what's going through my head: *Did I break it? Are we gonna be able to fly out of here? I know this wasn't a good idea, but it's the only idea we had. A Hobson's choice. If we don't do it, these guys are gonna wait another hour or more for ammo. How many of them will die in the interim?*

Brett is sarcastically complimentary. "Well, it worked. Uuuugly but it worked."

"Able 6-2, we've got ammo for you. Come and get it."

As several of these dudes break out of the wood line, stumbling toward the left side of our bird—where most of the enemy fire is coming from—others continue pointing their empty weapons uphill, and I can see one still trying to make it uphill to this saddle from down below. He's dragging a wounded buddy, while firing his M4. All of them are exhausted; it's clear they've got nothing left. The camo on their faces is streaked with dirt, their uniforms are soaking wet. *These guys are completely whooped. They look like death. They've been in a firefight and getting their butts kicked. All freakin' day. They look like zombies, emotionally spent. How long have they been fighting their way up this mountain? These guys don't even have enough energy to look scared. Pinned down, black on ammo, and resupply doesn't show up all day?* I don't have time to be angry right now, but it'll come.

"Oh, crap!" I say it aloud, suddenly realizing that they can't figure out how to open up the freakin' compartments. They're repeatedly banging on the lower fuselage to no effect. I can see Brett in the front seat, frantically pointing at the compartment they should be trying to open. I even hear him shout, "No, that's the wrong compartment." But of course, they can't hear him.

"Brett," I shout, as I pop open my canopy, "they can't figure it out. I'm getting out!"

"Oh, hell no. I've got this." And before I can respond, he rips off his helmet and contorts his way out of the forward cockpit, Cuban cigar firmly clenched between his teeth. The second he hits the ground, he darts around the nose of the Apache to the left side and pops open the correct storage locker. All the while, incoming rounds are literally puffing up dirt all around us. He reaches in and pulls out a black garbage bag filled with loaded magazines, and it splits open, spilling half the load back into the compartment. One of the infantrymen takes the bag, as others come up to grab as many loose magazines as they can carry.

Brett is working like a madman to empty that compartment. Another garbage bag breaks and the routine continues, but by now there's a ragtag bucket brigade, passing magazines up to the guys waiting in the tree line, who immediately lock and load and begin returning fire. I can see that there's this huge, crazy-eyed grin on Brett's face. It's like I can almost hear him doing an Oprah giveaway: "You get ammo, and you get ammo, and you get ammo." But then a sobering thought strikes me: *If he gets hit...if that happens we're screwed. How long have we been sitting here? Way too long.* Rounds continue to come in. *They want to destroy this helo.* I imagine Brett going down, knowing that I'd have only two choices, both bad. *I couldn't leave him. I'd have to get out of the cockpit, muscle him back into the front seat, and position him so he can't foul up the controls—hands or feet.*

I see him point to the open locker, urging the guys to keep unloading it, and then watch him run around the nose of the bird and crack open the locker on the other side. I can't talk to him because he's taken off his helmet, but I actually shout, "Look out!" after a bullet strikes the ground right in front of him, probably missing his crotch by mere inches. It makes me flinch. He reacts to the flying dirt by stopping in his tracks and then turns and gives me two thumbs-up. I shake my head. I can see his cigar has taken a real beating. *Holy crap! He's fifty freakin' years old and acting like a kid in a messed-up candy shop.*

CW4 Brett Brown was rarely seen without a Cuban cigar securely clamped between his teeth. Fortunately for me, he used more modern weaponry when we were out doing crazy stuff.

Sitting on the ground, we are able to hear our wingman pouring all the firepower they can expend on the ridge above us, to the right of us and to the left of us. Although I can't feel them, I'm sure we're taking hits from the Taliban's 7.62 Kalashnikovs as we sit here. *We need to crap and get off this pot. Please, God, no RPGs today,* I think, with one eye on the engine page of the display, just waiting for something to go red.

Several of the ground pounders who followed Brett around the nose of the bird join him in emptying the starboard compartment. When it's empty, he closes it, slams that compartment shut, climbs up, and shimmies back in. But I have no intention of waiting for him to plug in before we lift off. There's now a song playing in my head and it's from another era. I chomp a new wad of gum while singing along with The Animals, "We gotta get out of this place, if it's the last thing we ever do."

The first words I hear from Brett as soon as he plugs back in are something about being good to go. "No master caution lights."

I pick up, sensing through the controls that we've got a little more power margin now that we've dropped all that weight and burned a little fuel. Although I don't feel it, I'm certain Brett is shadowing me on the sticks. Immediate problem is, there's low bushes and then trees in front of me, but it's downhill. I pull as much power as I possibly can, we split the trees—well, actually our wheels and the belly of the bird probably scrape through them—then dive down the descending terrain and we're flying.

"You do know that they were shooting at you?" I ask, ready to poke some fun.

"You're wrong, college boy. They were shooting at you. I was just closer to them." *Uh-huh.*

"Now," I say to Brett, "you ready to blow some stuff up? I know I am!"

It feels personal.

We gain altitude, then light up the mountainside above the patrol, pivoting from a bird bringing salvation to one ensuring damnation. It doesn't matter how hard you pull the trigger, the impact will be the same. But as I said, this one feels personal, so my trigger squeezes are with purpose, my head jerking forward with each squeeze, unleashing the fury of rockets unceasingly on the mountainside and its hidden villains. Brett is dotting all the exclamation points with 30 mm, and together, our fury blends the elements of rock, wood, and dirt into fifty-foot-high clouds of dust and debris, obscuring the contours until both Apaches are Winchester. Glad I didn't jettison our ordnance or we wouldn't have been able to add that stamp on our opus.

"Iron 1-6, this is Able. You guys are awesome! Thank you so much for your help today."

"Sorry you lost some guys today, Able. Truly sorry." *How many were avoidable?*

The after-action debrief back in the TOC is fairly predictable. The maintainers give us lots of sarcastic lip about the holes we've put in their baby. Brett, chomping on a new cigar, turns on me with a smile, telling the guys, "You should've seen the landing. Hardest we could have had and not collapse the struts. I'm not filling out no paperwork. I wasn't flying it. The LT gets the bill for this one."

That's when it hit me. Why the heck didn't I have him fly it? In the heat of the moment, it never crossed my mind. He's got ten times as many hours as I do.

The reflection causes a barely noticeable pause before I respond to the ribbing. "Hey, you said you wouldn't tell."

My logbook at Jalalabad reflects the pace of our flight operations.

Three Apache crews had been involved in the Watapur mission, and then there were the Dustoff guys. When Capt. Horn stopped by, I gave him a huge ration of crap, wrapping love in sarcasm and chastisement—at least as much as a first lieutenant can give to a captain. "Hey, Cap, you gotta rein it in. All balls and no brains is gonna get you killed. I don't want to have to call a Dustoff to come pick up a Dustoff. That means the likelihood of missing my lunch would increase." Horn actually looks a bit sheepish. Nevertheless, I continue, "You know those things you don't have? What do you call 'em? Oh, yeah, guns. Well, turns out we do have them. Next time, give us thirty seconds to use 'em. We'll make your life easier. Hell, we'll make your life, life."

Before he can respond, I add, "Able 6-2 said something about a Dustoff providing some unofficial help. So I'm guessing he's saying there was more than water bottles in those body bags you dumped off?" The Geneva Conventions, which the United States insists its soldiers scrupulously follow, no matter what the enemy does, forbid medical helicopters—the ones with the red crosses—to ferry weapons and ammunition. The Taliban, of course, are not signatories.

"I haven't the slightest idea what you're talking about, Lieutenant. I've had my Geneva Convention PowerPoint briefing just like you, and I review it every night before I go to bed. Religiously."

"I know you do, sir, but from me to you, I know it was you and I love you for it." I turn away before he can see that I've choked up with emotion. Too many fallen angels today.

Sunset at Jalalabad, with a sandstorm on the horizon.

My conversation a bit later with Major Smith isn't high on humor. I'm pissed. "Where's the disconnect, sir? Black on ammo is black on ammo; these guys were pinned down and getting picked off with no way to return fire. That kind of stuff can't happen. We're just setting them up to fail, terminally so. We have got to be better than that! We've got Black Hawks just sitting on the ground; you got others flying ring routes. Reroute them; wake somebody up. If a FOB doesn't get their Little Debbies today, that's okay. Not getting ammo? Not okay."

He listens but doesn't respond until my rant has run its course. Then pointedly he says, "I'll fix it." I so badly want a better answer than that; I want to know someone will be held accountable. Ultimately, that isn't my job, though; that is his. Luckily, he is one I trust. He says he will address it. I believe him. That has to be good enough for now.

Two hours later, after a decent meal and a shower, I'm back in my hooch and have time alone to reflect. *Sixteen-hour day, 11.7 hours of flight and this wasn't our mission to fly. No reason we should have had to do that. But if not us, who? If not now, when? Yeah, it was a lot of risk but for a lot of reward. Sort of golden rule time. If I'd been on the ground*—I shake my head in mid-thought—*they were really helpless, taking fire from three sides. And the enemy had figured out that they had the upper hand. Bad guys were ten times more aggressive the second time we came in there. We had to do it.*

Then my mind switched to what I'd personally learned from the experience. How'd the commitment, courage, capability, confidence thing work out? *Focus, be deliberate, and keep thinking outside the box.* That's my main takeaway. *Affect what you can affect.*

I'd gotten wrapped up in how others weren't doing their job and my blood had begun to boil, but time didn't allow for me to stew. Once I committed to the goal, understanding the unknown was no longer important right then. It had to be trumped by the needs of the moment, so the onus was solely on us if we were going to get it done. On the technical side of the equation, my actual capability was definitely increased. I know more about the aerodynamics of flying in mountains than I could have ever learned in Arizona. Heck, I know I can fly through trees—sorta. What was it that instructor said at Rucker? Think of these things as learning events. If you can walk away from them, they're successful. Bottom line: we made a difference today. And we even flew away.

Time to give God some credit, for watching over me, for guiding me. My theory: you can never give Him enough credit; even things that might have been me are His accomplishment as well.

Oh yeah, and finally that fourth of my four Cs, confidence. Mine had been enhanced, but what I am about to learn is that it's a two-edged sword and it can swing both ways.

To hear Brett's perspective on this adventure, you can watch the two of us relive it at www.clearedhot.info/blackonammo.

CHAPTER 10

MORE BALLS THAN BRAINS

Be Bold, but Mind the Indicators
Telling You When to Rein It In

Korengal Outpost, Kunar Province, July 10, 2007—All of a sudden, I hear the master caution audio wailing in my ear. What's that? I look down at the display and it shows my stabilator—the horizontal wing on the tail of the aircraft that lets us smoothly adjust our flight path—is driving to the down position, pitching our nose down. WTF? It doesn't dawn on me that we've just been hit, only that something is drastically wrong with the stabilator and we need to fly out of this thing. I pitch the already downward pitched helicopter forward and ask Brett to see if he can manually slew the thing back up. No dice. That's when Patriot cuts back in. "Iron 1-6, you're taking fire. We can hear it. They've fired an RPG at you too."

Let's back up to earlier that day. I hadn't called Katie the night we took that toboggan ride down the ridgeline in the Watapur; in fact,

I hadn't actually spoken with her in more than a week. There'd been some email exchanges, none of which led me to believe that my mid-tour, two-week home leave coming up in a matter of days was going to be lollipops and roses. Nevertheless, I decided I had to call. Sort of a pre-leave recon. I hoped we could set some goals and take advantage of the time together to reset our table.

Just getting ready to dial her number on the satellite phone takes an odd kind of courage—sort of like flying into a valley where we pretty much know there'll be a hostile welcome. There's an oxymoron for you. I usually don't tell her about our confrontations with the enemy, offer no details, just generalities. I think it's something most troops at war have always done with their wives or husbands, kids, and parents. We feel a need to protect them. We can take it, but they're not able to.

I'm in a bit of a different situation, though. As I have mentioned before, part of me wants to tell her what's really going on in hopes that it might cause a paradigm shift where she starts seeing a bigger picture than the myopic, depressing reality she is living, and how sitting there in America, blessed to have a comfy home in Arizona and a husband who truly does care for and love her, is not so bad a place to be. Maybe that will alleviate some of her hurt.

But then I analyze it and see that there are only two outcomes to that approach, both bad. She'll either lay a guilt trip on me—"You're just trying to make me feel like a horrible wife"—or she'll worry incessantly, adding to the laundry list of stuff that's already messing with her mind. Likely both. Fact is, her pains are real to her, even if by my scope they are unwarranted. It took me a while to believe that could be possible. I love her and always have, but what happened to the laughs and truly enjoying each other's company? What happened to her drive and ambition, the charisma that drew me to her in the first place? What happened to mutual support? Saying "I do" seemed to dissolve all that in an instant. But I know it's there, it's got to be, buried under hurt and an altered reality.

There was one conversation we had with a different twist. I can remember it almost word for word. "Katie, how come you never ask if I'm safe?"

She says, "I don't worry about you. It's you; you'll win." For this deployment, I'm thinking, *Thank my maker she's been right so far.* I know in her mind, I always have won. Maybe that's even where a lot of her animosity comes from. She sees her struggles and feels I don't have any. She assumes life is easy for me and resents me for it. If she only knew the turmoil our estrangement causes me. Ironically, as I said, sharing any of the challenges I face daily—and I'm not even talking about the time spent in the air—would only make it worse.

Sure, my confidence as a combat pilot has increased with each mission. But being successful in the air doesn't moderate the reality that I'm exhausted, working sixteen hours a day, dealing with leadership issues and a third world existence, all the while struggling to compartmentalize my domestic relationship so I can keep it all together.

Understand, I'm not unique among deployed married military, or even unmarried for that matter. If every one of us with serious domestic problems saw the chaplain, the line would stretch from Abad to Jbad. And that wouldn't be good for the mission.

All that notwithstanding, I am getting better at my job; my skills as a leader and confidence level as a combat aviator have grown with each sortie. On the flip side, as I gain confidence in some areas, it actually highlights other areas I need to work on. I don't actually *know* the right way to handle a lot of things; I'm just making educated guesses. So much of combat flying is on-the-job training, especially when most of my mentors are in the same boat as I am—this is their first combat experience too. I didn't see that coming.

I do know that as a team, we have grown to believe there is almost nothing we can't do if we hang it out there working together. With that black-on-ammo mission, I'd come close to convincing myself that even the craziest plans executed assertively would work. Sound cocky? Well, the line between bravery and arrogance is so thin that sometimes it's imperceptible. I really don't want to sound smug, but I do really want to maximize my effect in this war by the way I lead my guys and the way we all fly this remarkable machine. The circular logic at work here was once noted by the Duke of Wellington, who wrote, "You will never have confidence in yourself until others have confidence in you." I don't know if I fully agree with the duke. I think you can have self-confidence regardless of how others feel, but I definitely see how others' confidence in you helps your own confidence grow. In fact, I would say the circular part is simply confidence begets confidence in all involved.

But there's just a sliver of a wish buried in my brain somewhere that someone would tell me when I've gone too far. Kind of like Rich Schiffli did when I executed the baseball slide. "Not sure why you did that," he said. I felt my *why* was justified in that instance, but I like the sanity check. It's certainly preferable to the terminal sanity check Johnny Taliban is capable of dishing out.

Speaking of confidence building, my boss at Bagram had just sent me a message. I was being considered for command of one of our battalion's companies, and Capt. Pfeifer wanted me to pack all my stuff and leave it at Bagram when I head to the States on mid-tour leave. There was going to be a round of interviews for the position, and he wanted me to stay close to company HQ when I returned.

I was using some downtime to begin packing when the radio on my hip went off. *Gunmetal! Gunmetal! Gunmetal! Go Redcon-1.* Four minutes later, Brett Brown and I are both strapped in and learning that we're about to pay a visit to the Korengal Valley. The Korengal runs for six miles north to south, off the west-to-east flowing Pech River. For us, Waygal is a right turn off the Pech. So is Watapur. To get to Korengal, we fly to Asadabad, take a left, and then another left where we see the flashing neon sign that states, "This way to Hell."

To the uninitiated, one valley in the Hindu Kush may seem just like another. Unfortunately, we've already been initiated. Like most of the valleys, the Korengal is both steep and high, and even though the map says it's less than a kilometer wide, mostly covered with cedar forests, the walls seem really craggy, more up-and-down canyon-like than gently rising valley. That's just the geography, which has a big vote here. Then there's the enemy. Whereas our ground troops can move around for days in other valleys in Kunar without getting engaged, on any move into the Korengal they always manage to find people willing to shoot at them. But it's even more intense than that, because the fighters in the Korengal are not usually imported Taliban or al-Qaeda but Korengalis themselves. Again, it's difficult from cockpit perspective to sort out which bunch of abadabas is more of a threat, but intel briefers always make the point that the ones in the Korengal are experienced fighters who seem to be able to scamper up and down cliffsides as though they're mountain goats, and they have a well-earned reputation for inflicting more casualties on American forces than enemy fighters elsewhere in Afghanistan.

Finding, fixing, and killing them is a huge challenge. Even more so than in other valleys, when the Apaches fly over, these fighters cover up and just wait with infinite patience for us to leave. Other helicopters? Chinooks, Black Hawks, Dustoffs—they shoot at. They only fire at us when our backs are turned on the way out. Bottom line for us: the Korengal offers pretty much the usual challenge, but for the guys calling for help, our support is often less effective than it is elsewhere, making it definitely a riskier place for them to be than other areas in the Pech River Valley. Maybe that's why US forces call Korengal the "Valley of Death."

As we take that left turn into the Korengal, I just seem to feel it; hair rises on my neck, and I get a little bit of a gut-cringe that, to this point, I've never felt anywhere else. You know the feeling you get if you go down an unfamiliar alley at night, or you accidentally find yourself in a bad neighborhood? You may not see anything, but that feeling is real. Maybe it's because I think the stakes are higher for our ground pounders from the 10th Mountain Division who drew the unlucky straw and got sent to KOP, Korengal Outpost, which was built a year earlier by the 1st battalion 3rd Marines in an abandoned lumberyard. Or maybe it's God telling me, "You need to focus, son, this isn't your normal playground."

"Patriot 2-7, this is Iron 1-6 inbound to your position. Two Apaches each carrying 330 rounds 30 mm, 19 HEPD rockets. Two-plus-30 playtime. What is your situation?"

"Iron 1-6, we've been taking it all day long from several azimuths. Like usual, they stopped about five minutes before you got here." I can hear the exasperation in his voice. The enemy has a system of lookouts along our normal routes who would radio-relay a warning that mosquitos—that's what they call us—are on their way. End result: the attackers harassing the KOP would stop shooting early enough that the infantry wouldn't be able to designate legitimate targets once we were overhead. "Iron 1-6, since everybody's getting fussy about PID, I can't clear you to just light up the place, though I would love to."

PID—positive identification of the enemy before we can engage with firepower—is developing into very limiting, very frustrating handcuffs. The fobbits in their air-conditioned TOCs at Bagram are so worried about negative news stories focusing on collateral damage that they are actually putting us at more risk by limiting our abilities to fight, insisting that if the ground commander can't precisely identify the source of the incoming, or if we don't have our own eyes on muzzle flash, we can't pull the trigger. The policy naively gives a decisive edge to our enemy.

This game is getting old, but it's the only one we can play under the current rules of engagement. So for several minutes, we fly around in circles, trying to see if someone will take a shot at us or our infantry so we can fix a location. But Korengalis don't play that. Next idea?

"Patriot, here's what I have in mind. We're both going to leave the valley the same way we came in. Then we're gonna go around the corner and take the next valley that parallels this one like we're going to another FOB. Break." I release the mic switch long enough for Patriot to tell us if he isn't receiving. No response, so I continue.

"We will get that Taliban telephone to report we are outta here. Then we will fly south till we can climb up and over. Break.

"In the meantime, you're gonna start taking fire again, I guarantee it, and we need you to radio us grid coordinates where it's coming from. Break.

"Then we'll come screaming in from the south—where they've never seen us come from before, so they likely won't have their tattle-tail train set up in that direction. Break.

"We will pop up over the ridge, slave our weapons to your co-ords, and reduce your varmint population. It's important you let us know if you or any other friendlies change location as well. How copy, Patriot?"

"Iron 1-6, copy all. Sounds like a plan if you can get over the top."

My thought exactly. I really didn't know how high we'd have to climb to make it up and over. But I'm thinking like the Little Engine That Could. *I think I can, I think I can, I think.* It's all about confidence and the fact we have some good canyon winds today that we can use to our advantage in helping us climb.

Mark Spangler is the Chalk 2 AC, and he chimes in. "I'm not sure we can make the climb, but I do like the idea of screaming in from a different direction."

"We won't know until we try. Follow me, Mark."

"Roger that." Our two ships turn to leave the Korengal. *See you soon, Hell.*

The climb up the backside is more spiral staircase than escalator, but we get there with a minimum of huffing and puffing. During the climb, I tell Mark that we need a theme song, especially for this cockamamie plan. He says that he'll work on it, which catches me off guard, because Mark's nature is usually subdued—just the opposite of Brett's, who is in my front seat and already setting up to program the gun.

As promised, Patriot delivers a pair of solid grid coordinates to some caves, which gives us PID if we hurry, so we do. I put our Apache into a dive over the top, then—because we'd promised to come screaming in—I offered a full-throated yell over the interflight radio that would have made Geronimo proud. As I finish, Mark comes in. "You been telling us for months that we're the A-Team, so here y'go." And he begins an ear-splitting version of the theme song for the show that made Mr. T famous. It was awesome! (It was also the ring tone on my phone. Readers are advised to Google the A-Team theme song while reading the rest of this chapter for full effect.)

Our birds are line-abreast diving in from altitude, and we've each got one of the targets on our acquisition system with weapons slaved. "L-T, I'm giving them a fifty-round burst. Ten won't cut it for these bastards."

"Roger that." The instant Brett sees on the tactical acquisition display that the target is in the crosshairs, he pulls the trigger, causing the aircraft to shake with rhythmic gyrations from the gun recoil. The cave is probably history with the first twenty rounds, but the bullets just keep going as we dive closer and closer to the target.

"LT, hoooold this course."

I restrain myself from pulling out of the dive until the gun stops firing, by which time we are actually entering the gigantic dirt cloud caused by the cascade of these 30 mm grenade-type rounds. "Woooohooo!" I cheer as if we just made a game-winning touchdown. To this point in my tour, I hadn't yet experienced a fifty-round volley. That much gun kick without a break gets you amped. It was a lesson in focused 30 mm firepower that would prove to be applicable later.

"Iron 1-6, you guys nailed the targets!" *Patriot sounds excited.*

"I love it when a plan comes together." It's a catchphrase from the A-Team that I transmit to Mark, knowing that Brett should have been the one to say it, since he actually resembles the Hannibal character on the show, complete with the ever-present unlit cigar.

Our euphoric mood is instantly broken, however, by the voice from KOP again. This time, bad news. "Iron 1-6, we're taking fire now from one of those compounds directly across the valley."

It's sort of dumbfounding really. Usually, these guys duck and cover when we come in. This time, we did manage to slip in the backdoor and surprise them, but another bunch has apparently decided they'll stick it out. It's the Korengali way. On the cliffside across from KOP, we can see dwellings on stilts, built at various levels terraced all the way up from the valley floor like a giant layer cake. I now have to identify one compound out of—I don't know—fifty?

"Patriot, can you pinpoint the area any closer for us?"

"Iron 1-6, workin' it." I can hear gunshots in the background when he keys the mic. We're not sure if it's his guys shooting or the incoming rounds, but by the sound of his transmission, they're still taking fire. "Iron 1-6, about midway up the terraces there is a compound with a green wall. See it?"

Green wall, green wall, green wall. Aha! "Yes, I see it. Verify between two brown two-story compounds?"

"That's it. I think that is where we are taking fire from, but I'm not sure." *Well, crap, that doesn't fit our handcuff criteria, does it?*

I get on the interplane. "Mark, you see it?"

"I do."

"Let's fly closer and see if we can catch any bad guys making bad decisions." We buzz past it a few times but see nothing.

I try the KOP once more. "Patriot, any more fidelity on that point of origin?"

"Sorry, Iron 1-6. Pretty sure the POO is that green-walled compound but not certain."

I need to figure this out, and the game clock is running. *So how do I get this foe to show his hand to the destroying angels flying overhead? Idea! We have a strong wind coming up the valley about forty knots. Which means I can fly very slowly—maybe as slow as twenty knots, almost an out-of-ground-effect hover, and dare these lead slingers to take a shot at us.*

Back on the interplane freq. "Hey, Mark, cover me from above. I am going to do a slow drive-by at co-altitude with that compound and entice this sucker to shoot." I take the gun from Brett and slave it to my reticle. My plan is to just crawl along adjacent to the compound, stare at it—that is, my 30 will stare at it—and the moment I see his muzzle flash, I will respond with a thunderous amount of firepower.

"Copy, I'll cover you from above."

Remember that sliver of hope I talked about? That at the right time someone would ask if what I'm about to do is a good idea? Nobody does. Both birds are all-in; we got this. Why wouldn't we? We always win. Brett and I have actually had this conversation before. Because we've taunted the enemy before, together and separately. He says it's like a six-foot-five guy just dying for this little smartass five-foot guy to hit him. "Yeah, you can hit me. But I'm gonna hit you back and you're done. The fight's over. I'm gonna kill you."

Right. How dare these man-dress-wearing warriors shoot at me? Brett calls it invincibility ignorance. "Never been shot down before. Can't be scared of something that hasn't happened." It sounds like something a drill instructor in basic might have once said to him, and it stuck.

I am amped. Time to go mano a mano with evil. I pull into this slow crawl. The bird is flying comfortably into the wind, just like I figured it would. I line up my reticle and virtually shout, "I'm right here. Shoot me. You know you want to. You can't resist this big juicy target, can you?" *I know the aircraft can take it, right? We win; you lose, big time.* In theory. There we sit, waiting, when all of a sudden, I hear the master caution audio wailing in my ear. *What's that?* Brett and I both look down at our displays. The master caution light is on, showing several different faults. And the airspeed read-out is now in a rounded box, telling us that a sensor has been hit and our Doppler flight management computer system is getting bad information.

"Keep flying," shouts Brett. "I'll look it up." Just seconds later, he comes back with, "Stabilator's failed. Doesn't know what airspeed it's at."

I now look down at the display and it shows our stabilator—the horizontal wing on the tail of the aircraft that lets us smoothly adjust our flight path—is driving to the down position, pitching our nose down. It doesn't dawn on me that we've been hit, just that something is drastically wrong with the stabilator and we need to fly out of this thing.

That's when Patriot cuts back in. "Iron 1-6, you're taking fire. We can hear it. They've fired an RPG at you too."

"Keep flying," Brett says again, then he reads off a laundry list of all the things that have failed. "This is just an airspeed indicator problem that shouldn't mess us up."

"Oh, it shouldn't mess us up? How fortuitous," I say sarcastically.

All I hear back is a derisive "Know-it-all college kid."

Aside from the nose pitching down, we never felt or heard a thing, which means whatever hit us didn't hit the frame, just the aluminum skin of the stabilator and apparently an actuator that controls its movement. And the shot had to come from beneath us. Go figure. I trolled slowly over populated terraces, Mohammad stepped out of his dirt-floored yet nicely carpeted living room and said, "Thank you, Allah, for providing me this big juicy target right over my BBQ pit," and then pointed his RPG straight up, shouted "Insha'Allah," and pulled the trigger. Allah must've been listening but not carefully.

Twenty minutes later, we make a delicate landing at Asadabad, the nearest place where it's safe to touch down. With Brett on the sticks, I get out to assess the damage. "Yeah, we do have battle damage on the stabilator." It's blasted up, looks like it got hit with AK in the actuator and RPG fragged the skin pretty good. But with the rotors spinning, it's hard to see the tail rotor, so we decide to shut it down.

When everything stops moving, I begin a slow climb up the vertical stabilator, using little pop-out steps. On the way up, I notice more shrapnel damage to the skin, but when I get all the way up, I can't see anything wrong with the tail rotors themselves, the pitch-change links, or the hydraulic lines. The abadaba who fired that RPG probably has no idea how close he came to winning the Apache takedown lottery. Destroy the tail rotor at our power setting, in an above-ground hover, and it's game over. That is absolutely the worst position to be in and one of the most difficult emergency procedures for a pilot to implement. I should probably add, least successful. We avoided it by the slimmest of margins, and yet my thoughts are mostly just frustration that we didn't get the guy, not on the vulnerability of the position we were in. The position I put us in.

We climb back in, no longer singing the A-Team theme. I'm actually quietly somber. The best I can do on the short flight back to

Jalalabad is agree with Brett when he says, "Those suckers. I'm glad we got some of them."

Before their buddies got us, I think.

What is this? My first time? But I'm not laughing.

CHAPTER 11

THOUGHTS WHILE IN THE ACT

Step Out of the Problem in Order to See It Clearly

Arizona, USA, July 7, 2007—It's like a scene out of Hitchcock's North by *Northwest,* only in this movie, I've got the Cary Grant role, and instead of dropping me off in the afternoon on a highway near a cornfield in Indiana, the Greyhound bus from Phoenix has left me at dusk in the parking lot of a windswept truck stop off I-10 in the desert near Casa Grande, not quite halfway to Tucson. I'd left Bagram seventy-two hours ago, with orders that gave me two weeks of mid-tour leave. The good news is that they don't start counting until I'm boots on the ground in the United States and also that I've got a free travel voucher I can use on any commercial airline that will get me where I want to go—once I manage to get to the States.

The bad news is that getting from Bagram, Afghanistan, to CONUS flying military space available requires more than travel orders. It requires lying, cheating, acting, conniving, begging, bragging, and occasionally making veiled threats, which coming from a mere lieutenant do very little. The NCOs of the Military Air Transport Command have heard it all, and they're uniformly unimpressed.

You don't just walk up to a counter and expect them to put you on the next outbound nonstop back to the world. There's a list of departing flight times and destinations, both of which can change with very little notice. After several hours of failing to make the cut, I figure my best shot at making it home in this decade is to abandon any notion of hopping a C-17 to Germany with a connection across the Atlantic, and board the first plane that will carry me anywhere out of Afghanistan.

Hello, cramped C-130.

Welcome to Doha, Qatar.

"I need to get to Phoenix. Yes, Arizona."

"We don't have anything going to Phoenix. Our rotators go to Baltimore and Atlanta."

"Okay, I'll go to Atlanta. I can get a nonstop to Phoenix from there."

"We don't have any space on the Atlanta flights today."

"Tomorrow?"

"No flight tomorrow."

By this time, in my head I'm writing parody lyrics to John Denver's "Leaving on a Jet Plane."

I'm leaving on a jet plane

But can't seem to get outta Afghani-stane

These fools, can't get me back again

It's my newest earworm. I'm figuring with the time and subject matter I have to work with, I'm good for about a dozen more refrains. *We've been rotating troops home from here for five years or more, and they still don't have this figured out?* I can only shake my head and chuckle as I utter under my breath, "First time?"

"What about Baltimore?"

"We can get you on a flight."

"Great."

"Tomorrow night."

"Fine."

"Thank you for your service."

Hmm. Maybe twenty more refrains. Or thirty. Maybe I can get everyone to sing. We're leavin' on a jet plane...

I suddenly understood why they don't start counting our fourteen days until we actually set foot in America. You ever spend a day and a half at a military PAX terminal in the Middle East, looking forward to an almost fifteen-hour nonstop flight in coach aboard a military charter? Hooah!!

I gained seven hours on the flight to BWI, only to discover that I've got to wait until 1:00 p.m. for a three-plus-hour flight to Dallas, where I'll layover for two hours and then get to spend another two and a half hours on a plane to Phoenix. John Denver would continue:

The dawn is breaking, it's early morn

No taxi waiting, or blowing its horn.

I'm so stinky, I smell like a homeless guy.

The drive from our home in Coolidge to Sky Harbor Airport normally takes about an hour. But *normal* is not currently in the Slade family playbook. Expecting Katie to pull herself together to pick me up would just be setting her up to disappoint me, so I opt to leave the driving to Greyhound and catch the last bus leaving downtown for Tucson. Now the question in my mind is, *How long will I have to wait for her at the Casa Grande truck stop?* I had called from Dallas to give her my ETA, but she hadn't picked up. She did answer when I called from Sky Harbor and told her the bus would drop me around 7:30 p.m. Now it's 8:30 p.m. and I'm getting really annoyed. Sitting on my duffel in shorts and a wrinkled T-shirt, looking like some down-on-his-luck drifter, is not my idea of time well spent. After three hours, there is a pile of empty Monster cans beside me, and she still hasn't shown. Her phone goes right to voicemail. I'm caught in a trap: I can't try hitching a ride because as soon as I get one and leave, she'll show up. Then it'll be my fault. So I wait. I take a moment to stare up at the stars and appreciate the fact that I am in the United States of America. Suddenly, I can wait.

Around eleven o'clock, she pulls into the lot, parks, jumps out of the car, and wraps her arms around me. My head is swimming. Okay, don't judge me here; keep in mind I have been gone for six months, so as much as I am looking forward to America and interacting with my wife on many different levels, the first thing that hits me is her physical appearance. That in no way means that was the most important thing on my mind. It does mean I am a guy. *Katie looks amazing! A complete surprise.* She's wearing a white T-shirt with the sleeves rolled up and the hem tied at her waist, above jean shorts. *Holy crap! I never expected this. She's got a six pack, a great tan; she is shredded. Has she had work done?* I know I sound superficial, but this really takes me by surprise.

"You been working out?"

"I have. For you." Only later would I learn that she's been exercising. It's actually become her newest compulsion—a surprisingly healthy one—but unfortunately, she's also become bulimic. Although I certainly appreciated her efforts in the gym, a little voice in my head couldn't help but wish she put as much effort into tuning up our communication and our emotional relationship. I will take what I can get, though, and be grateful for the effort she's put forth.

The last time we'd spoken on the phone, we agreed to start fresh. Nevertheless, our drive home is a little uncomfortable. After so much time apart, we're just not familiar with each other the way a married couple should be. And in the back of my mind, I'm still thinking, *Let's start fresh isn't going to erase six months of roller-coaster rides.* Suddenly, here we are. I opt to reaffirm our agreement head-on— well, maybe not so head-on, more like obliquely. "Honey, let's make these two weeks great. Let's commit to being positive. No talk about serious stuff, like finances, for now."

We'd never taken a real honeymoon, which was one of the recurring sources of her proof that I did not love her the way she expected to be loved. I'd promised her when my deployment was over, we would. But she'd been hinting about going to a spa and it seemed reasonable, so I booked five days at the Wyndham Resort at The Buttes in Tempe.

Talk about cultural whiplash! I'd been living on a bare-bones FOB in a plywood B-hut for six months—which feels like six years—and now I've got a plush mattress, fluffy towels, a Jacuzzi tub, and whatever I want to eat, whenever I want it. And she is looking good; more importantly, she has been all smiles, no blow-ups or breakdowns. It is more like when we first dated. I love it.

Perhaps this is TMI, but we were actually somewhere between hanky and panky when this absolute disparity of life and lifestyle hits me like a two-by-four to the cranium. *I've spent six months killing people and having people try to kill me. Was that on another planet? Things are so good right now. Everything is great. Flashback! I'm gonna sacrifice all this just to get a guy behind a green wall in the Korengal? Who cares about him? Yeah, he wants to kill me, but he's wanted to kill any outsider who dared to show up for a thousand years. Come to a hover in a hostile environment exposing myself and my copilot recklessly, for what? My life for his? Am I nuts? Why would I give this up?* And I feast my eyes on my surroundings and the blessings that abound.

Yes, I want to do what we went there to do. Osama definitely needs termination. The world needs to see that we will deliver retribution to anybody who dares attack our homeland. Our ground guys need our support, so I definitely want to provide that. But I'm no longer sure there's a legitimate purpose to what I, myself, am doing over there other than protecting my brothers who are also there for what? What's the strategic plan? I want to protect the ground guys. But taking stupid risks? That's just dumb.

"What's wrong, honey? You're shaking." Katie's question brings me back to the present. She can sense that my mind has taken a strange turn. And it has. I'm definitely no longer in the moment. *What's just run through my head is a huge paradigm shift for me. How did I get to the point where I'm taking stupid risks? My first engagement with an experienced mentor, we were hovering slow, right over bad guys.*

Very aggressive, dangerous, high-risk/medium-reward-type flying. They almost got us with RPGs too. I noted that at the time and decided to not hang it out there quite as much as he was doing. Yet I just put myself in nearly an identical scenario in the Korengal. I got too comfortable being an aircraft commander; do some things outside the box, things nobody else is willing to do. And I'm having success doing them, right? I'm invincible, right? I'm always gonna win; they're always gonna lose.

Not right! Wrong as hell. I'm setting it up for them to win by my sheer foolhardiness. Of course, I know they could shoot us down, but that's not my reality. I begin replaying engagements in my head, just like I do in my hooch at Jbad when I crawl in bed. But my paradigm has seriously shifted from where it was just a week ago. *Dude, why didn't you just see that that's stupid? I'm just like a meth addict. The first time you do it and succeed, it feels good. After a while, you don't realize you're addicted. That's the point I've gotten to—it's the point most of the younger pilots have gotten to. Maybe the old guys have it right? Maybe we can't even see that we're taking needless risks because we feel like we're not gonna get hurt? Can I possibly be that stupid?*

Katie has dozed off. I look around the luxurious room, feel the clean, soft sheets on the king-size bed, and inhale the exotic scent of the woman beside me. *This woman is my wife! My future. What was I thinking? I've got to go back there. Army cot in a wooden hovel. Sleeping bag. Incoming. Abadabas just waiting for me to pull a Tarzan move and beat my chest long enough for them to have an Insha'Allah moment through my tail rotor. Is that MY flag-draped casket coming off the plane at Dover? Yeah, Katie and I have issues; she is definitely not stable. But what we're doing here is part of a life with a future attached; what I do over there is definitely not. It will come to an end one way or another and I have to stop thinking it's a given we come home.*

As I said, a paradigm shift. *But it's my job. I took an oath; I am still going to take it to the enemy, just in a more risk-reward manner.*

How did Chaucer know, back in about 1374, that "there is an end to everything, to good things as well"? Just because he said it, does it have to be so in 2007? If we can fly to the moon, why can't we make good things last? Obviously, that's rhetorical. Also obviously, my good thing with Katie ends about the same time her key card to the resort's spa stopped working.

Not sure if it was on the way back to our home in Coolidge from The Buttes or a day later, but we were talking in the car, and when I stopped at a stop sign, she jumped out and just walked on the side of the road in the middle of nowhere at night. We weren't even fighting, just disagreeing. A counselor explained much later that it's one of those things that people with borderline personality disorder do to manipulate, because now, you have to follow them if you care. You can't just leave a woman you love in the desert. It's as though they're testing you, to find out if you'll stick around, to test how much you really care. Ironically, they are risking damaging the very thing they are testing in order to see if you have staying power.

It had happened more than once in our marriage, sometimes in town, sometimes in the middle of nowhere, and I found myself following her, awkwardly sitting in parking lots and watching, moving when she moved, like a frickin' stalker. I have no desire to be this guy, but what else am I supposed to do? Eventually, she'd get back in the car, usually several hours later, and we'd drive home. Then she'd either tell me that I didn't love her, or she would apologize profusely, in a torrent of tears, saying she knew she overreacted and she didn't deserve me.

I truly feel trapped. Always damned if I do, damned if I don't. I care about her so much, but I don't even know where half of the heartache is coming from. How long do I wait for an epiphany like the one I had about taking risks in the war?

I have identified several areas where I felt I was being unwise with Katie and worked on them. She's also suggested a few more, and I didn't argue. I've worked on them. But I'm still waiting for that *aha* moment. I keep praying for it to come, for the tumblers to fall into place. Smiles will resume, and we will work through disagreements like adults, not whatever it is we are doing now. All I can do now is continue to pray.

With only a few more days in the land of the free, I decide to focus on the fact that we have had a few very good days where we got along, and that obviously had an impact on her. She had put in a lot of work in order to meet me as sexy and cheerful as she could when I first arrived. That effort meant a lot. I'm thinking, *Okay, I'll take what I can get, and I will choose to be appreciative of it.*

Not so fast. It's as though the anti-relationship fairies heard my decision to focus on the good, and decided to mess with me. About two days before I was due to go back to Afghanistan, she drops the bomb on me. "There's some new credit cards...but I've got a job, and I'm going to pay them off." What new credit cards? That's when she shows me the bills for three different cards that she'd taken out in my name, on my good credit, totaling about twenty grand, all for clothes she's bought online and apparently hidden at her parents' house so I wouldn't see them. More betrayal.

"I got a new job as a respiratory therapist, and I'm gonna pay it all off. I promise."

Brian, don't get angry. She got a job. That is a good thing. Focus on the positive. Don't rip her head off. Stay calm.

"Katie, I don't want you paying a little here and a little there; you can't pay the minimums. Your whole paycheck has to go to this until they're paid off." I was thinking quickly. "Here's what you're going to do. You'll deposit your paychecks into our savings account, and I'll pay off the credit cards. That way, I know it's being done."

To my surprise, she agrees. What she doesn't know is that my plan is to pay them off immediately; paying 19 percent interest is dumb. Besides, doing it this way doesn't tank my credit score if she fails to make the payments on time. But I'm not just going to bail her out. This kind of behind-the-back stuff is killing me, and that hurt is doing its best to come out as rage. Then it hits me: if I have a scheme to pay the cards and am not telling her about it, am I betraying her confidence too? I'm doing it in hopes that she'll learn some valuable lessons and, of course, to minimize the potential for damage. But I am her husband, not her parent. They're in my name; isn't that justification? Or am I overthinking this?

"And we're cutting up those cards." Then the anger gets to me. "You know you committed fraud? Yeah, we're married, but that doesn't mean you can take out credit in my name, with my Social Security number, my credit. You ever heard of identity theft?" Shocker. That didn't go over so well. But we manage to talk it through, and I commit to leaving on a good note. Kiss-and-make-up time.

But remember those anti-relationship fairies? They never seem to take a day off. On my last day at home, she tells me about one of the guys who was a friend of ours—a married guy, with kids, whom we've had barbecues with—who comes over to check on her periodically while I'm deployed. Do I really have to tell you the rest?

Among our friends, Zach was a guy I trusted implicitly and the only one I asked to check on Katie while I was gone. Trent was in the mix of friends and a guy I more or less trusted but not enough to ask him to check on Katie. He took that up on his own. He was LDS, went to our church, but there was just something off.

"What happened?"

"Trent came over one night and asked if we could go for a walk." I wait. "And then he tried to kiss me. But I pushed him away and said, 'No!'"

Uh-huh. Knowing Katie, that's likely not the whole story. I'm furious at him, and I'm furious at her for waiting until my last day at home to tell me, because she knew if I had the time, I would pay a visit to Trent. I can't believe it. My life had just become the cliché the drill sergeants in basic training warned me about.

Ain't no use in going back,

Jody's ballin' in your shack.

Jody's got somethin' you ain't got,

It's been so long, you almost forgot.

Your baby was lonely, lonely as can be,

Till Jody provided the company.

Ain't it great to have a pal,

Who works so hard, keepin' up morale?

You ain't got nothin' to complain about,

He'll keep her happy till you get out.

An' you won't get home till the end of the war,

In two thousand twenty four.

And that's the baggage I'm bringing with me on the rotator back to Afghanistan. That, and my new paradigm, the one that may help me ensure I make it back alive. But I can't help but wonder, *What's going to help me recover from this?* When she told me, I felt like I'd been knee-capped. Even my bowels reacted. My skin got cold and clammy; my mouth went dry. Shock.

Isn't this the ultimate betrayal by a person I truly love? Dealing with Trent when I come back home won't be a problem. Dealing with Katie? I just don't know.

Sometimes, in order to gain perspective on what's actually going on, we need to take a big step back. People in the throes of depression often can only see what's right in front of them—with devastating results. *For a discussion of this, check out the video at www.clearedhot. info/perspective.*

CHAPTER 12

LANDSLIDE

Be the First to Act and Effect Change
for Those Who Follow

Bagram Air Base and COP Kamu, Nuristan Province, Late July
2007—"Lieutenant Slade, upon taking command of a company, what
is required for acknowledgment of responsibility for unit assigned
equipment?" The voice coming from the speakerphone in the small
conference room at our Bagram HQ was that of the Arizona Guard
battalion commander at FOB Salerno. I'm in the middle of my interview for promotion to company command. *Promotion* may not be
quite the right word, but I don't know what else to call it. If I ace the
interview, my rank and pay will stay the same, but my responsibilities will more than double. So whatever you call that, that's what I'm
being interviewed for.

"That's an excellent question, sir." I need to stall a bit while I scan
the three uniformed men and one woman seated around me, each
with a large whiteboard. It's the senior sergeant from supply I see
scribbling quickly. I begin my response while she's still writing.
"Sir, army command-supply discipline as stated in AR-710-2 as

transmitted by the Quartermaster Corps requires that the officer assuming command personally inspect and sign for all unit property—which means all property not already signed for by individual soldiers—ranging from fifty-dollar canteens to fifty-million-dollar Apaches." And on and on and on.

In the middle of my answer, the door opens and Captain Pfeifer walks in, takes a look around the room, sees the top sergeants from intelligence, maintenance, and supply, plus Lt. Pixler for admin minutiae, and with a bemused grin shakes his head. He knows exactly what I am doing. Then I get a look that pretty much says, "It's what I'd expect from Slade."

I'm sure some of you are judging me, thinking that I'm violating some sort of sacred honor code and cheating on the interview. Sorry, you're wrong. I'm exercising one of the essential leadership skills I learned way back in ROTC at Utah State: use all assets available to accomplish the mission. The team I assembled with the whiteboards are my assets. My mission is to ace the interview. This is not a calculus test at West Point where the honor code applies. Still, I am truly grateful this is simply a telephone interview with no video, because then I would have to worry about strategically placing my subject matter experts outside of the camera's view.

To my surprise, I learn a day later that I'm going to be upgraded to company commander very soon. There are several captains in our battalion who have not yet had command, so I figured they'd get the nod over me and other hopeful first lieutenants. Even more of a surprise, I learn from one of the officers who had been quizzing me on that call that I had been selected for the assignment even before the test. "Then why the test?" I asked him.

"We're jumping you over several captains who are senior to you, but they're not up to the challenge you're going to face at Kandahar."

Well, that answers that question. The interview was CYA. It keeps them straight in case someone files an IG complaint.

Kandahar. That's our Alpha Company. I'd heard crazy stories, including a couple of fratricide incidents where they'd fired on allied forces by mistake. I'm guessing that their CO is being relieved of command. How soon? No one can tell me. Meantime, I'm still on the flight rotation and know I'm going to be flying escort on a ring route going north later this morning.

In the nearly three weeks I'd been gone, the positive ID rules had been tightened once again. I'm thoroughly appalled. We hadn't been blowing up people just for the hell of it. Sure, there'd been occasional ambiguity—I'm not going to BS you. But in that terrain, you can't be absolutely sure. You see a flicker in an area identified by the ground commander, and you know it's not good guys who are shooting at you. So you obliterate it. We know it's a good shoot. So does the grateful ground commander. No cowboy stuff. But with the new refinements to our rules of engagement, that might not be a righteous shoot.

They're practically telling us we need a personal email from the enemy inviting us to the party, informing us that he's going to shoot, with the map coordinates and exact time. What are they going to ask for next? That we take Haji's fingerprints before we send him to heaven? Used to be when friendlies tell us they're taking fire from the east—there's no friendlies there—we could throw some rounds out to keep the bad guys down. It's called suppressive fire and a very basic tenet of warfare. Can't do that now. They really have handcuffed us, and it's making it more dangerous for everyone.

Personally, I've quietly made the decision that I will still engage if I believe it is beneficial for friendlies. If later on intel questions us, it's, "Well, sorry, the gun camera didn't record. Technology. What can I say?" At the end of the day, I have to be able to sleep, and not helping out friendly forces in life-or-death situations because of ridiculous requirements would not allow me to do that. If I have to stand tall in front of the man, so be it. Besides, I am coloring within the lines of the ROE (rules of engagement), not truly breaking any rules. I'm just refusing to add more lines to the coloring book. What these guys are doing is making up their own definitions for already defined engagement criteria. *If you want to learn more about ROE, check out the video at www.clearedhot.info/ROE.*

Talking with some of the other pilots, I learn the Taliban's tactics have become more brazen as we've backed off. Go figure; it's not rocket science. Even a small guy in the ring with a roided-out giant who won't swing will eventually realize it and get up the gumption to attack. They're blasting away at Black Hawks and Chinooks when they're most vulnerable—on approaches to landings—and they don't seem to care that an Apache is with them. The Apache is now the passive, roided-out giant, and that's not good.

This long list of new rules is roiling my brain as we fly through the narrow winding canyons fairly close to Pakistan on our route to Combat Outpost Kamu in Naray Province. It's the northernmost stop on this particular ring route. Flying up there almost always means a six-hour day in the cockpit. Less than a week ago, a Black Hawk attempting a landing at Kamu drew enemy fire that came way too close. An RPG round actually went through both open side doors, without actually hitting anything, but the flame streaming from the rocket set some fires. One soldier was burned badly and the interior suffered damage. You'll never guess the call sign for that bird. Would you believe Hardluck? We'd escorted this particular pilot many times before I went home on mid-tour, a cool guy who'd given us a radio frequency and then plugged an iPod into the system and fed us his rock-and-roll playlist, which was awesome. Definitely a healthy break from our usual game of Kiss, Marry, or Kill. (Look it up. Yeah, I know: disgusting. You try to keep from going stir crazy during the 90 percent of the time when nothing is happening on a ring route.)

That's me in the cockpit, showing the Helmet Mounted Display with the reticle fixed over my right eye.

Just two days ago, one of our own Apaches got lit up in Kamu, losing an engine while in an overwatch position. When I heard about it, I wanted to jump in a helicopter and immediately head up there to send a message loud and clear: no more pot shots will be tolerated! Don't care where you are hiding. It really got under my skin and drove home the point that this new look-a- man-in-the-eye-and-count-his-eyelashes-before-you-fire ROE is going to get a lot of good guys killed. CW2 Ben Kuntz and 1st Lt. Brendon Libby were the crew on that bird. Fortunately, they flew it out of Kamu single engine but had to stagger back to FOB Naray, where they made a rolling landing outside the wire and then ran to the FOB.

So it's understandable why we're on high alert coming into Kamu. In addition to the enemy, the terrain is inhospitable. The walls are at least 1,000 feet high and it's only about a quarter- to half-mile wide at the top, just a bit less at the floor where some geniuses decided to put an outpost. On one side at the top is an even smaller fortified observation position. Why they thought the enemy would fear that dinky outpost is beyond my pay grade.

Two minutes out, I get on the radio to the Black Hawk. "Everybody, keep your head on a swivel. If you see anything identifiable as enemy fire, you need to talk me onto that target instantly with bearing, range, and azimuth. Don't think about it."

"Kamu, this is Iron 1-6 inbound to your location with your resupply bird. Looking for a sit-rep."

"Iron 1-6, we took fire from the east wall about fifteen minutes ago. Quiet right now."

"Hey, if you start taking fire as we approach, you need to define where it's coming from; give me clock positions and distance using the east side of your FOB as twelve o'clock. How copy?"

"Kamu copies all. Wilco."

Less than a minute later, as the Black Hawk flares for a landing, we can see dirt puffs around the ship. "Iron 1-6, this is Kamu. They're taking fire from the wall on the other side of the river."

"Kamu, I need clock position and distance."

"Iron 1-6, unable to locate. We can hear the gunfire. They are still shooting."

It's a huge freakin' wall. There's gotta be 500 caves or crevices the abad-abas could be shooting from. "From where, Kamu? I need a good POO."

"Sorry, Iron 1-6, we're unable to identify point of origin."

That sucks. The new PID rules suck. But knowing that doesn't help the Black Hawk on the ground. It's going to take them a couple of minutes to unload cargo, disembark troops, and embark others waiting for a ride back to Bagram. I'm still seeing *poof! poof!* as Taliban rounds keep impacting the ground. *I know the bird has got to be taking rounds. Just hope they'll be able to fly out of there. We gotta do something.* I try 3-D geometry and triangulate the angle of the shots hitting the landing pad back to the cliff face in order to figure where they're coming from. Maybe that works on Looney Tunes but not from an orbiting Apache. Next plan?

"Kamu, Iron 1-6. Confirm there are zero friendlies on that side of the cliff."

"Oh, yeah, there are no friendlies. We have friendlies here in Kamu and the OP above us."

"Copy that, Kamu. To your knowledge, any civilians on that cliffside?" I think the guy on the radio knows exactly where I'm going with this.

"Nope, Iron 1-6, no civilians! Never! No goat herders ever. There's never goat herders up there."

That's clearly BS. But he knows what's going on and my scan hasn't seen anyone—meaning everyone on this side is probably staying out of sight on purpose. Brett did real damage with the fifty-round burst in the

Korengal a few weeks ago—or was it months? It's all blending together.
On the intercom, I tell my copilot, "I know a fifty-round burst left a
violent impression on the Korengalis. Let's select ALL and see what
it does."

"All? Uh, okay."

With that, I take control of the chain gun, slave it to my reticle so
it's aimed wherever I look, and select ALL under *GUN BURST* on the
multifunctional display page, so that now it will fire all 330 rounds
with just one pull on the trigger. I begin moving the Apache toward
the wall at about sixty knots. When we get within 100 yards and
about 350 feet above the canyon floor, I bank to the right, bringing us
parallel to the rock face. The plan is to start at the top, then move my
head in a Z-motion, back and forth, all the way down to near ground
level. My trigger finger slowly pulls back until the gun reacts. We feel
every round leaving the barrel, which is aimed off-axis to our left.
Gutgutugutgutgut! without stopping. The repetitive recoil is buzzing
my adrenal glands and amping me up. AC/DC's "Thunderstruck" is
playing in my head. You know, the part that says, *Dununt-naaa-na-na-
na-naah THUNDER! Dununt-naaa-na-na-na-naah THUNDER!*

I know I'm only about fifteen seconds into it, but the chain gun is
still firing and I feel like I pulled the trigger an hour ago. *Gutgutugutgutgut! Damn, this is taking a long time.* Adrenaline gives way to
reason. AC/DC gives way to *Maybe this was overkill?*

With the rounds still going out, still shaking us, I have to do a shallow
right bank away from the target because the cloud of dust, pulverized rocks and whatever, is beginning to envelop us. At first, watching a granite wall disintegrate before my eyes—more precisely, my
left eye; the right is seeing the crosshairs through the reticle—I feel
exhilarated. But as the gun finally runs out of ammo, even with both
engines roaring, it suddenly seems dead quiet, if that makes any

sense. And the excitement is gone. I'm now experiencing a disquieting mood change. Watching tons of rock still falling from the wall,
I'm overcome with foreboding. It's as though we've unleashed hellfire and damnation of biblical proportion. The Kunar River tributary
below us is blocked by a mini mountain of our creation, forcing the
water to create a new channel. I flash back to my mission in Brazil,
where I read Scripture three hours a day. "Behold, the whole face of
the land was changed, because of the tempest and the whirlwinds,
and the thunderings and the lightnings, and the exceedingly great
quaking of the whole earth."

It's a voice on the radio that brings me back to the present. "Iron 1-6,
this is Kamu. That was the coolest thing I have ever seen! Did you
see the enemy?"

"Yessir!"

"That was awesome! How many rounds did you fire? What kind of
gun is that?" He was like a twelve-year-old kid.

Then the Black Hawk comes back to us. "Hey, Iron 1-6, we're no
longer taking fire." I can hear the grin and sarcasm in his voice, with
an undertone of relief.

That's certainly good news. But I tell my copilot, "There's no way
we're getting away with that."

"They were taking hostile fire; we engaged the enemy. No more
hostile fire. What's the problem, LT?" he responds, pretty much as I
expected he would.

"Someone is going to say something. That Black Hawk is out of
Bagram. Guarantee that'll be water cooler talk for a while. It's not
gonna be like, 'Nothing happened today.' More like, 'Dude, they

made new contour lines. We gotta redo the maps of that place.' And Kamu's gotta do a daily sit-rep for task force HQ. You think it'll just say 'Apache engaged'?"

I knew my own after-action report filed with intel would be accurate—just not very detailed. "Kamu was taking hostile fire; positively identified as enemy; we engaged and neutralized target." I never say how many rounds we fired, mostly because I didn't actually know. This time, I know. But the answer, if they ask, will be, "Enough."

I think about what I'd really like to say in my report. *Something had to be done, which means somebody had to have the stones to do it. Might as well be us.*

In the chow hall back at Bagram, I tell Pixler and Pfeifer that they shouldn't have a problem with Kamu anymore. I skirt the details but once more register my disagreement with incorrect interpretation of the rules. They totally agree and share in my frustration. "We have to punch first and punch hard. If you do that, you send a message and you don't have to punch often, and not as many punches will go the way of the guys we are protecting either."

I know that I'm preaching to the choir. The three of us have had this discussion before. I'm sure most of the deployed troops recognize the problem in OEF. We're always pulling our punches. This is American military history repeating itself. These people don't want to be who we are trying to make them be. But we're taking unnecessary risk when we get sent out with orders to pull our punches. I don't revel in violence, but I understand the big-kid-on-the-block rules. If you send a message every now and then, things are safer overall.

They have no answers. I don't expect them to. Here's where my new post-R&R paradigm shift takes hold. No unnecessary risks, yet do what's necessary to preserve lives. Use those things hanging off both sides of the Apache to preserve the lives of as many as you can, even if it means someone's panties are going to get in a twist. But doing stupid stuff is off the table, or at least I will try my best to keep it off the table.

To my utter surprise, nothing negative ever came of that engagement. I was totally prepared to stand before the man and respectfully call him out, if need be, emphasizing how American lives are absolutely being needlessly exposed to death by their crazy interpretation of the rules of engagement. But there was never any backfire. No email, no knock on the door by a messenger saying the task force commander would like to speak with me. Nothing. I realized there were a lot of folks who had to file reports about the engagement at Kamu, and they all must have been very circumspect. That tells me that everyone out on the tip of the spear is tired of what's been happening, they appreciate what we did, and they had no problem going into CYA mode on this one.

This would be my last engagement in RC-North, the largest of the coalition's six regional commands, prior to taking command down south. Turned out to be one heck of a goodbye to the enemy I have learned to respect. By the way, it's worth noting that no one took fire at Kamu for a long time after that day.

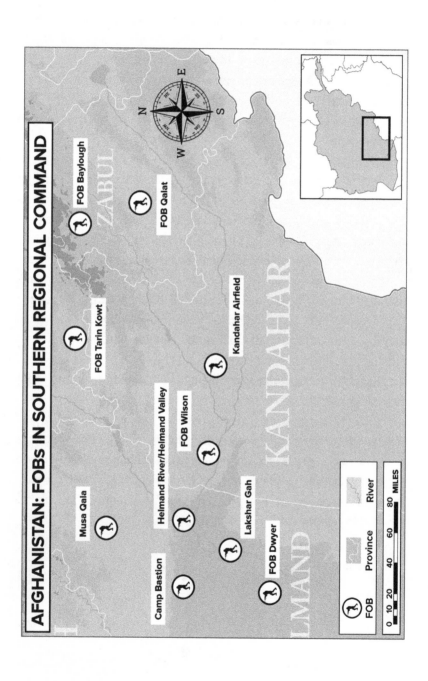

AFGHANISTAN: FOBs IN SOUTHERN REGIONAL COMMAND

FOB Baylough

FOB Qalat

ZABUL

FOB Tarin Kowt

Kandahar Airfield

KANDAHAR

Helmand River/Helmand Valley

FOB Wilson

Musa Qala

Lakshar Gah

Camp Bastion

FOB Dwyer

HELMAND

FOB   Province   River

0 10 20   40   60   80 MILES

CHAPTER 13

ALL POLICIES AND PROCEDURES REMAIN IN EFFECT

Embrace and Move Forward; Don't Dwell on the Past

Kandahar, August 2, 2007—Here's the good news about my new assignment as commanding officer of Alpha Company at Kandahar Airfield: there's no way I can do worse than the jerk I'm replacing. The bar is that low. The bad news? The captain, henceforth known as Teflon Don, TD, for reasons that I'll shortly make clear, has left me with a demoralized company to reconstitute into an effective Apache fighting force in the Helmand District, where the Taliban regularly wreak havoc in much more organized ways than up north.

Lots of things are different down here compared to Jalalabad. For starters, the terrain isn't enemy number one. Helicopters are not as power limited by altitude as we were in the Hindu Kush. On the other hand, much of the fighting is in urban, heavily populated areas, where the risk of collateral damage is greater. On the ground, I'm sure given my predecessor's checkered performance, I'll be under much closer scrutiny by the brass, which now is just down the road at the 82nd Airborne Division's Aviation Task Force Corsair headquarters.

On the plus side, living facilities are much more civilized here—the air-conditioned quarters I inherited are so large that I chose to share them with one of my platoon leaders, and full bathroom facilities are actually just down the hall inside a real building with concrete floors. That may not sound like a big deal, but it obviates the need to flip-flop down a dirt road to a shower tent a block away, with M9 and towel slung over my shoulder. One more plus—my own personal refrigerator to keep Monsters cold.

Teflon Don—who earned the nickname because he always seemed to shed blame for his screw-ups, which included a fratricide incident where he pulled the trigger—hadn't actually been formally relieved of command. He was just being "transferred." Why? Primarily because our Arizona National Guard leadership at FOB Salerno didn't have the spine required to follow through with what needed to be done. They just knew they had to get him out of there before his behavior reflected poorly on them or because he got the wrong people killed. I know that order doesn't make sense, but unfortunately, that is often the way our head shed prioritizes things. (Of note: whenever I vent about leadership in this book, do not assume I vented the same way with those who worked for me; only peers and up get venting, never down.)

For four days, TD and I are both in the TOC. It's necessary but uncomfortable given the nature of his departure. Part of the process requires the incoming CO to put eyeballs on every piece of military gear being signed for. Remember that question on my promotion interview back at Bagram? Here it is, live and in person, with TD telling me to ignore the fact that items are missing and "just sign on the dotted line" to make things easy. "Lieutenant, you've got to sign this. It will all show up or be cleaned up upon redeployment as combat loss."

"No, I don't. I'll sign the form, no problem, as long as all items missing are annotated as such."

"You can't do that."

"I absolutely can. I am not just going to take your 'iron clad' word for it. I'm not trying to make this a hostile takeover, but I'm not signing for it unless I see it, and neither would you." I knew I was on solid ground with the conditional signature; that was one of the regs the supply sergeant had quoted to me on the whiteboard during my promotion interview. What's more, my new supply sergeant showed zero loyalty to his outgoing boss. As long as he wasn't in earshot of TD whom he feared, he was more than happy to make sure I knew the right way to make the liability land where it should. When the sergeant offered that guidance, I reassured him. I had his back; he wouldn't be made a scapegoat. We both know what kind of dude the outgoing commander is.

If I needed concrete proof that TD was shifty, it came while I was doing an inventory in the TOC and discovered an Air Mission Planning Computer with classified files on it that had gone missing from Bravo Company back at Fort Hood. We'd torn the place apart looking for that laptop but never found it. There were suspicions that TD had pilfered it. Capt. Pfeifer even asked ol' Teflon directly, but he adamantly denied any involvement, indignant that something so nefarious would even be hinted at. Imagine Pfeifer's surprise when I reached him at Bagram. "Hey, you know that AMPS computer that went missing? It's not missing anymore. Guess who had it?"

"I knew that sucker stole it!"

In between these inventory Easter egg hunts, I have brief conversations with members of the company, some of whom I had known back in Arizona and at Fort Hood. It was apparent they were all hungry for change. But even though they would hint at things, most weren't ready to unload their full list of grievances until TD was physically out of the TOC. What's more, they had no idea whether I'd be change or more of the same.

Turns out the captain was a bully, much like the senior pilot I had to deal with at Bagram when I arrived in country. The difference here is that he was in charge. The CO is the one who's supposed to protect his troops from abusive higher-ups, excessive taskings, or anything else that unnecessarily makes life more difficult than it already is in combat. And the complaints weren't minor. TD's leadership style was caustic. He also judged his pilots on their body count. Support of friendlies was collateral to that, not the other way around. The consequence had been a tendency to open fire before knowing precisely where all friendly forces were situated. The adverse results weren't surprising: two fratricide incidents, one of them with TD himself pulling the trigger. At this point, I don't know how many close calls there had been.

I felt for the guys. I saw how Prepotente at Bagram was a tumor negatively affecting B Company and observed the immediate healing that took place once he was cut out. Here at Kandahar, this tumor was in charge, and they had to continue with the mission despite all his questionable requests and narcissistic rants. They were beaten down, almost reminding me of those infantry guys who were black on ammo up in the mountains. These guardsmen had a desire to do their jobs well, but the resources were not afforded them, and that lack of support drained the life out of them.

Before I formally take command, I have my first meeting at Corsair Task Force headquarters with the commander, Lt. Col. Jayson A. Altieri, and his XO, Maj. Craig T. Alia, both of whom are Black Hawk pilots. They don't mince words, telling me that my soon-to-be-predecessor has been a cowboy who has lost the trust of his troops. "If it was our call, he would have been relieved for cause, not reassigned," Major Alia says, point blank. (Several months later, Altieri even put it in my Officer Evaluation Report, saying I took over for a commander who should have been relieved of command.) They also express concern that a first lieutenant is being given command of a company, something that isn't done in the 82nd, and tell me they intend to pull strings to get captain's bars pinned on me sooner than it was scheduled to happen. Alia says, "You can't be in meetings where you're calling your peers 'sir.' You have to be able to engage on even ground since they are at your same level of command." (Pinning on the next-higher rank—it's called frocking—before the promotion is official happens occasionally if it serves a unit's needs.)

It's what Lt. Col. Altieri says next that really has impact. "This is your company; you run it as you see fit. We trust you with it until you break that trust. If we ask you why you're doing something, have an answer. We may not agree, but we'll let you run with it as long as it isn't unlawful or carry with it excessive risk." I appreciate that he acknowledges risk is a given; it's excessive, needless risk that should be avoided.

He goes on, saying, "We are not attack pilots. That makes you the subject matter expert in your arena. Therefore, your input regarding your role and capability will be weighed heavily."

Major Alia puts it more colorfully when he says, "We're going to give you plenty of rope. Just use it to make a lasso, not a noose to hang yourself."

Actually, I am astonished by the entire conversation. Given my predecessor's track record, I was expecting them to micromanage, not empower me. I'd never seen commanders at that level offer that kind of support, not to mention the humility it takes to acknowledge they do not know our mission as well as we do.

After the meeting, I track down TD and let him know I'd like to address the company, suggesting he make himself scarce until the change-of-command ceremony the next day. Since he was grounded as a result of the fratricide incident and couldn't be on the flight schedule, he had no problem disappearing.

Word must have spread quickly that the captain was gone and the coast was now clear, because I could have used a revolving door on my office that afternoon to accommodate the number of guys coming in to unburden themselves. I'd had no doubts that Teflon Don was a scuzzball, and these conversations confirmed it in spades.

At changeover from day to night shift that evening, I bring the whole company into the TOC and formally introduce myself.

"I've known and been friends with a lot of you before this, starting back in Arizona, and I'm looking forward to getting to know the rest of you. I don't know everything that's been going on here for the last eight or nine months. Truth is, I can't change what's happened. What I will do is move forward with you guys from this point. What I will do is take the steps to ensure we can do great things as a company. What I will do is look out for every one of you and defend you when need be. What I will do is deal with issues quickly and decisively, cutting out any cancers.

"I've already spoken with many of you and realize some things need to change, and they will, not necessarily to everybody's liking. My test for effective change is simple: Is it good for the company? I will need everyone's help with this. Many of you know me as an easygoing guy who likes to joke around, but right now, we do have work to do. How we tackle that work together will be completely up to you. We can be friends and I prefer that, but it's not a requirement. Let's all work together to get this thing fixed up."

The Company A "Archers" at Kandahar.

Although I wasn't precisely certain how to proceed when I delivered that speech, I knew they needed to believe I had a plan. My leadership learning curve is about to take the same cliff climb my pilot learning curve did the night of my first flight as an aircraft commander.

Interviewed for this book, now Lt. Col. Jack H. Denton, the platoon leader who had been my roommate at Kandahar, says that line about "being friends isn't a requirement" was seared into his brain. "Our company was pretty broken. Morale was in the toilet.

We all trusted that you were there to lead us, to get us through the rest of the deployment. We just needed someone to be that leader at that time."

What Lt. Denton told me when I arrived at Kandahar is that the four lieutenants were having a tough time balancing being loyal to an abusive commander with the need to do damage control, especially with the warrant officers/pilots. Put simply, the junior officers can't badmouth the boss, yet they need to acknowledge his failings in order to let their subordinates know their complaints are being heard and that help is on the way.

Or as Jack put it in our recent conversation, "We had to bandage it together until the point you came down."

On my seventh day at Kandahar, the task force command held a formal change-of-command ceremony in front of their headquarters. Shocked the heck out of me. We were in combat. I figured it would be a very simple ritual—sign things over, and bada-bing, bada-boom, done! But they set up bleachers, assembled all available personnel, and even shut down operations for an hour to make it happen, music and all. Teflon Don gives a very slick departure speech, eloquently saying all the right words about the unit's accomplishments *under his leadership*, but the troops see through it. What they hear is, "I did it myself—you were just along for the ride." Pretty much everyone in Alpha is thinking, *Don't let the door hit you on the way out. Leave already.*

When it's my turn to speak, I make it brief. I can remember being in formations, miserably sweating out many change-of-command ceremonies in the Arizona desert, listening to the brass pontificate. The Kandahar heat is worse, so I keep it short and to the point. "I'm glad to be here. Humbled by the opportunity. All policies and procedures will remain in effect. Let's get to it." That was that, and now I am 1st Lt. Brian Slade. Commander. Alpha Company, call sign Arrow 0-6.

One of the first situations I have to deal with is the aftermath of a fratricide incident that occurred three months earlier during a nighttime battle in an urban area with two of our Apaches supporting troops in contact. The company's senior pilot, CW4 Kalashnikov, mirrored TD's attitude in that he always knew his alleged kill number and made certain it was always larger than anyone else's. Lucky for me, he had already been transferred out of the company. On the night in question, however, he was living up to his reputation as a "shoot first, ask questions later" type of guy; he saw a flash from the ground, assumed it was an enemy RPG, and without determining where all the friendlies were positioned, fired a ten-round burst from his 30 mm gun directly at the British ground unit. Seconds later, they heard an urgent call to "Cease fire, cease fire!" on the radio frequency reserved for fire coordination throughout the area.

Shortly after that, the Brits radioed to the Arrow helicopters that three of their soldiers had been hit *and actually provided their names.* What Kalashnikov thought was the flash of an enemy RPG round fired at him had actually been the firing flash of an M203 rifle grenade fired by friendly forces at a wall.

Hearing the names of the wounded soldiers so unnerved CW2 Cassable, the aircraft commander of the second Apache, that he froze. His front-seater, relative newbie 1st Lt. Stephen Gladish, says hearing those names "really did something to him. I started talking to him, and he wasn't responding. Finally Cassable said, 'You take the controls,' and he went unresponsive again."

It turned out that the pilot had actually removed his helmet after he began having problems breathing, which was ultimately determined to have been part of an emotional response to the fratricide.

With the aircraft under his control, Gladish informed Kalashnikov, "My pilot isn't responding. My ability to effectively cover you is essentially gone. Due to a malfunction, I cannot use the weapons system effectively from the back seat." Then he regretfully told the infantry troops who were still in contact with the enemy, "We now have to break station and leave you guys."

As the ranking officer, Gladish led the two-bird sortie back to the nearest coalition airfield where they could refuel, Camp Bastion, the British army base about seventy-five miles west of Kandahar near the Helmand River. About five minutes out, Cassable put his helmet back on and took control, landing the Apache. They shut down, and Gladish went into the TOC to explain the unscheduled shutdown, describe what had occurred, and inquire about the status of the casualties. At that point, the TOC was unable to confirm that a fratricide incident had occurred. Meantime, Cassable insisted he was feeling much better.

The pilot who had been emotionally disabled for about ten minutes was one of our trusted aircraft commanders. We meet, and I tell him I've reviewed the file, interviewed others involved, and the inevitable result of his flight evaluation board will likely be the loss of his flight wings. His career as an army pilot is over. He tries explaining the situation, but his justifications fall on deaf ears. I feel for him, but I can't fight for him on this one. He wasn't there when he needed to be; he froze, and good guy or not, we can't have an attack pilot freeze. I tell him, "There's no buts here. I'm not arguing whether or not you're a decent pilot; you just can't fly combat. I don't care if your front-seater's head explodes and pieces of his brain are obscuring your vision; you keep aviating, communicating, and navigating as required. You may be meant to be a pilot, but it's for UPS, not for the US Army."

Shortly after that conversation, I hold a meeting for all personnel and lay down a few new points of order. The first and foremost is, body count is no longer the way we measure success. I didn't want to hear numbers of bad guys killed. "Stop counting. Our goal should be to support the ground troops, to support the crews whose aircraft we're assigned to escort. To support the good guys. We often do that by blowing up the bad guys. That is often what's needed. But if we keep in mind that our primary goal is to support coalition forces, then we certainly aren't going to pull triggers until we know where they're at. And once we know that, I will support *smart* aggressive interaction with the enemy. I'll give you latitude to do that, and we will work together to continue to build our tactics, techniques, and procedures [TTP] based not only on what you have all already learned fighting down here but adjusting for any changes the enemy makes in their own TTP. Please don't get me wrong. I want us to be aggressive. I want us to be nimble, adjust to the enemy and give them hell, but I want to do it anchored to the principle that our purpose is to support our team."

I can tell from the head nods that this is not going to be a hard shift. These guys want this; they want to be solid warriors and do it the right way. They just needed someone to truly support and empower them in that endeavor.

Then I set to work sorting out the personalities who are now in my charge. I rely on advice from a few trusted agents right off the bat. Lieutenants Denton and Gladish, my platoon leaders, as well as CW4 Jim Skillman are men I consider professional and forthcoming one-on-one. Frankly, they give me a heads-up on both the problem children in the company and the go-getters. Until I could personally interview everyone in Alpha, what they offer gives me a place to start reshaping things.

Then there's my personal life. I'm still struggling to discover a paradigm that will lead to a positive outcome with Katie. Although I am confident that I've got the team needed to successfully rebuild Alpha Company, I find myself thinking that I could really use some trusted professionals with this dilemma as well and for the first time in my life seriously think that maybe consulting a therapist wouldn't be such a bad idea.

As I ponder my interactions with Katie and how I can fix them, I have an epiphany: my reality is not something she would be able to relate to, but that doesn't make it any less real *for me*. Therefore, even if Katie's reality doesn't make sense to me, it's real *to her*. Not so profound, actually. In fact, I had already acknowledged it was real to her but not given weight to what that means. Why couldn't I see that before? If the stuff she says is real to her, of course she's a mess. Who wouldn't be?

I truly care about her. So if I care about her, what is important to her needs to matter to me as well. Also not terribly profound. Why has this been so hard for me to comprehend?

Yes, she is broken. But my trying to fix her from thousands of miles away is not working, and it's definitely not helpful. What I have to do instead is solely focus on trying to be loving and supportive. Easier said than done, but the difference is, this one's on me alone. I've already taken off her plate all of the financial responsibilities that I can possibly manage from Afghanistan. I won't put those back on her plate for now. If she continues her online buying sprees and we go broke, we go broke. I'm confident I can rectify that later. Right now, I have to accept the situation for what it is, just listen to her, and keep our interactions loving.

After several weeks at Kandahar with relatively easy access to satellite phones, I have had a number of conversations with Katie. One indication that things are improving a bit—she's been answering the phone more often than before. For the most part, applying my new mantra has resulted in neutral to positive exchanges, and I'm encouraged that she's managed to keep her job as a respiratory therapist.

What keeps gnawing at me in a way that I can't force myself to ignore is her flirtation with Trent. I was absolutely sucker punched by it and assume it went further than a kiss, but it hurts too much to consider beyond that. I can't think of another time in my life where anyone has betrayed me like that.

Remember when I first arrived in country and I was confident in my ability to compartmentalize? To not let my domestic problems interfere with my military duties? With this Trent thing, I've come to realize that compartmentalization isn't enough. I've got to bury it completely for now. Maybe by incinerating it first. I have things that require my full attention here.

For more insight on application of lessons already learned and how I was able to draw upon them in my new role as company commander, go to www.clearedhot.info/lessonslearned.

CHAPTER 14

CLEARED HOT ON ANYTHING SOUTH OF THE AEROSTAT

Empower and Learn from Those Who Have Been There

Helmand Valley, August 10, 2007—"Hey, Arrow 0-6, you wanna come fight with us?" The voice on the cockpit radio is CW4 Kevin Eaton's, and even though he said it with a jovial tone, I can tell he isn't kidding. We'd both just landed from separate missions, coming into the FARP at Camp Bastion to refuel and rearm. Being parked side by side, I could see him as we were talking. That's actually never happened to me before. It reminds me of those scenes in World War II movies where the pilots are looking at each other while they have a cleverly choreographed conversation about how they are going to kick butt and take names. You can see their heads bobbing as they talk, and it gives you the feeling that you're watching a normal face-to-face conversation.

Do I wanna come fight? What kind of question is that? Before I can formulate a response, he elaborates. "I can't carry enough ammunition. We escorted a resupply convoy into FOB Dwyer. Now we've got to get them out." I must have had my visor up because Kevin recounts seeing my eyes get big after his last statement.

Even though we were supposed to be done for the day, I'm thinking, *This is going to be a good one.* "We're in. What's the situation?" The "we" is me and my copilot, 1st Lt. Sean Maiolo. Eaton tells us that he'd been on the receiving end of considerable fire escorting the convoy into Dwyer. And he'd gone Winchester returning the favor. He'd even seen the Brit JTAC (Joint Terminal Attack Controller) running full force down a hill toward the outpost, with rounds kicking up the dirt ten feet behind him.

I'm pretty certain that whatever we get into, it won't be anything like the missions I'd flown in the mountains up north. I hadn't been in a real engagement since moving to Kandahar. We'd flown some basic escort missions, including the one just completed that brought us to Bastion to refuel, but no shooting other than some test firing and some low-key suppressive fire into tree lines. Oh, yeah, they let us do that here. The brass has figured out that we really are in a war. Same rules of engagement, just accurate interpretation and more empowering leadership.

Immediately after arriving at Kandahar, I'd put myself on the regular rotation, knowing that I had a lot to learn about the area the Taliban owned in the Helmand River Valley. Just from talking with other pilots, I discerned that the nature of the terrain alone—red sand desert, wasteland, and a narrow green zone along the river that the bad guys occupied—requires a significant change from the tactics I'd used flying out of Bagram and Jalalabad.

The Green Zone showing the dry riverbed. If we were looking for trouble, we deliberately flew over this area, knowing that's where the Taliban infiltrated troops. Courtesy of Kevin Eaton.

The enemy here is much more organized than the guerillas we battled in the mountains. These guys set up air ambushes, and they definitely do linear attacks on ground troops using flanking maneuvers and other infantry tactics. Mountain fighters did some of this too, but *linear* has a different meaning in the mountains than it does in the populated cities that are interspersed with marijuana and opium poppy farms in the Helmand Valley. These fields actually remind me of home—not the specific drug crops but because I grew up working in and around farms. Every time I see suspicious-looking characters down here, I say, "Check out these guys. They better get to farmin' real quick." The phrase has become a running joke when we are evaluating unknowns.

I'm very fortunate to have spent considerable time being briefed by the guy flying in my front seat today. Maiolo is a total intel nerd. He'd get so deep into the weeds when he'd brief me or anyone else that it could drive us crazy. But he's given me a graduate course on what the Taliban had been doing, how they communicate, where they mass, why they mass, and their battle tactics. Sean is able to paint a great picture, and it's helped me formulate ideas on how we can engage the enemy, which I practice during chair flying sessions at night in my quarters.

Maiolo and others had also warned me to take added care when flying at night over the red desert because depth perception goes to hell in a low-light, very-low-contrast environment. It's so bad, they warned, that it's difficult to tell where sky ends and ground begins, which I've always thought is fairly important for a pilot to know, at least until they invent an aircraft that can fly through both. One crew had been out on a night mission and Murphy's Law was definitely in play (if it can go wrong, it will, at the worst possible time). Their radar altimeter went out, and the FLIR was acting up. That left them just using night vision goggles that offer little in the way of detailed imagery on a very dark night. Bottom line: they had no clue what altitude they were at because the instrumentation that should tell them that was out to lunch. End result was that they inadvertently hit the ground at more than a hundred knots. Yep, that experience will turn coal into diamonds if placed anywhere near your sphincter. Miracle of miracles, they bounced and popped back up into the air. But when they impacted the desert floor, they had collapsed one of the landing gears, so when they got back to Kandahar in the middle of the night, they needed help to land. One of our maintainers, Sgt. Sam Shope, threw a jack stand in the back of the Gator ATV and raced down to the pad. He walked up to the hovering helo, plugged in his communication cord, and casually asked the pilot, CW4 Jim Skillman, "How's it going, sir?"

Shining a light on the undercarriage, he confirmed that the landing gear was collapsed, then ran back to the Gator and got the jack stand. Shope crawled underneath the hovering bird, put the stand in place, and gave the pilot instructions over the intercom, telling him which way to move. "Come left, now come right, now down." End of problem.

That crew was incredibly lucky. They could have just as easily somersaulted when they struck the ground, and that would've been all, she wrote. As it turned out, aside from the collapsed landing gear, the only problem they had to deal with, I am willing to bet, was paying extra for special service when they sent their skivvies to the laundry.

As we lift off from the British army base at Camp Bastion at dusk, I find myself dwelling on the unique challenges of this new battlespace. Frankly, I'm looking forward to the fight because it'll help me earn my street cred with the pilots I now command. Sure, they're aware that I've expended more than my share of ammo in the mountains up north, but fighting in the Helmand is very different, and getting into it down here is the most significant way I can let the guys know I understand what they're up against. I also realize that having been in engagements here in the south of Afghanistan will give me more credibility when I'm requesting additional support from higher-ups. It goes back to lessons learned in football and boot camp, as well as up north. Lead by example and don't ask them to do anything you aren't willing to do yourself. When you do it, go full throttle and they will gladly follow.

That analysis doesn't have much time to ferment on the relatively short flight to FOB Dwyer, where our mission is to keep the Taliban from harassing the convoy on its way back to Bastion.

"Kevin, you're the air mission commander on this one. You guys know what's going on here better than I do." There's no place for ego here. I'm the frickin' new guy.

"Wilco, boss."

As we approach the Aerostat, Kevin checks in with the JTAC on the ground. "Widow 1-1, this is Arrow 2-3 and Arrow 0-6. We're two AH-64, each carrying 32 rockets and 330 rounds of 30 mm, with 1-plus-30 minutes of playtime."

This particular Aerostat is being used by the US Customs Service in New Mexico, but it's the same kind that was flown in many parts of Afghanistan. The helicopter gives you an idea of the massive size of these tethered balloons. US Customs Service Photo.

"Roger that, Arrow. I've got nobody in the stack—you're out here all alone. You're going to come in on a north-to-south run-in. Do not fire prior to the Aerostat. You're cleared hot on anything south of the Aerostat."

I already was aware that intel types there operate an Aerostat, a tethered 117-foot-long helium-filled blimp-shaped balloon that floats up to 1,500 feet high. It carries the Persistent Threat Detection System, which Lockheed-Martin claims is capable of gathering audio and video intelligence from one hundred miles in every direction.

Flying missions in the vicinity of an Aerostat requires constant vigilance to avoid making contact with the cable tethering the giant balloon to the ground. The problem is that when you're engaging the enemy while taking fire and multitasking at one-hundred-plus knots, things happen quickly. A relatively thin cable extending from the ground up more than 1,000 feet is difficult to spot in daytime. At night, it's nearly impossible to see.

What really strikes me is not that there is an Aerostat or the added vigilance required to fly around one but rather the fact that Widow said, "You're cleared hot on anything south of the Aerostat."

That's a *huh?* moment. "Sean, did he just say cleared hot on anything south of the Aerostat?"

"Yes, sir," he says, chuckling. My copilot has played this game before.

All I can see past the balloon is a very populated area. It's actually a city of mostly different kinds of mud huts in walled compounds, packed in tight. It's maybe a half mile to a mile wide and goes on as far as my unaided eye can see. There's hundreds—maybe even thousands—of these compounds. I'd previously been told that these urban areas are all bad guys, that any non-Taliban sympathizers long ago made the choice to move out, knowing they'd be murdered in sadistic fashion if they stayed. *But what's this JTAC talking about? He can't clear us hot onto the better part of a town? Or can he?* Just as I'm about to get on the radio and ask for more clarity because I don't believe I can just start shooting, I begin to see lights flickering in lots of windows. Lots of lights. I hear Kevin say, "Arrow 23 in hot."

That *huh?* moment quickly changes into a HOLY CRAP! moment. We are taking fire from nearly *everywhere* south of the Aerostat. I guess that clearance does make sense. It's not quite nighttime, but it's dark enough that the muzzle flashes show up pretty good. And they're throwing everything they have at us. *So the JTAC isn't a warmonger; he knows what he's doing after all.* One of my slow-learner moments. Both Apaches come in significantly lower than the Aerostat, and we just begin flinging rockets. It's so easy that I don't even have to aim at anything. Just pull the trigger and we're guaranteed to hit a compound that's contributing to the flickering light show. They are all fair game.

We shoot rockets and 30 mm until we've flown beyond the forward line of enemy lead-flingers, then break away and come around for another run on a different vector. *Now I understand why Kevin said he couldn't carry enough ammo.* The only time I'd seen this much muzzle flash was on that mountain ridge back in the Hindu Kush on my cherry AC flight, but this is something else entirely—a flat, easy-to-shoot city, where the flashes are coming from windows, doorways, and alleys, rather than from rocks, tree lines, and caves.

I remembered duck hunting when I was a kid. There were a few times we'd sneak over the berm of a pond that was chock-full of ducks, and once we made our presence known, the whole pond would erupt with the sounds of wings, splashing, and quacking. No aiming was necessary. Just shoot, and we'd get our limit. That's sort of what this feels like. We're just reducing their manpower.

After the second pass, I get the sense that there is a definite line of friendlies and a definite line of massed enemy forces. Not something I was used to at all; it was more like conventional warfare. There were two fronts with a no-man's-land in between. With this setup, the engagement feels simple and relatively safe. After all, I'm not doing pitch-back turns in a slot canyon. But on one of our run-ins, the JTAC reminds us just how vulnerable we are.

"Arrow, you are taking fire, both small arms and RPGs, from directly beneath your positions on your run-ins." I can tell by his tone of voice he isn't referring to sporadic potshots but effective fire. That is an abrupt wake-up call. I guess all the abadabas aren't shooting at us as we turn in. Some have the discipline to wait until they have a higher percentage shot with us directly overhead. Then it hits me. *I don't believe what these guys have been doing for the past five-plus minutes is accidental. They've deliberately baited us with massive displays of muzzle flash into thinking their main fighting force is farther into the city. We took the bait and flew directly over concealed fighters more than once in order to engage where the muzzle flash is coming from. Now we're sitting ducks right above them—or would be if we weren't moving at 120 knots. I'd never flown into an ambush like this one. Time to change tactics.*

We break off that attack, go around, and start engaging from much farther away than our original firing line, which actually puts us much closer to the JTAC on the ground, who is in duck-and-cover mode. Now he wants us to eliminate enemy positions closer to the FOB. He's either seeing them through binoculars or with the high-tech cameras on the Aerostat. His guidance is precise. "Arrow, I see enemy 500 meters northwest from walls you obliterated on your last run." I'm not accustomed to getting that kind of fidelity on target follow-up and adjust-fire directives, but I love it.

On our third pass, Kevin comes in right behind us, breaks left for his outbound, and gets busy evading enemy fire—AK rounds mixed with RPGs, and at least one heavy machine gun, probably an old Soviet-era DShK firing a 50 cal equivalent. In the midst of evading fire, he is also resetting the sequence for rocket fire on the tactical display in his cockpit, preparing for his next run, so he almost doesn't absorb the elevated voice over the intercom from his copilot, 1st Lt. Sean Randall. "Oh, you're pretty close to that wire!" Kevin looks up just in time to see the Aerostat cable zip past them on the left side of the cockpit, no more than a rotor disk away—that's fifty feet. That's way too close for comfort.

Now it's Kevin warning me. "Hey, Arrow 0-6, watch out for the Aerostat cable!"

"Wilco." I can tell by the inflection in his voice that was seconds-old experience talking.

The Apaches, like the majority of military and even civilian helicopters, are equipped with a Wire Strike Protection System that has a number of V-shaped metal devices positioned around the aircraft that extend out from the fuselage. Imagine open alligator mouths facing outward, with the gaping jaws designed to catch a wire and guide it to the waiting blades at the base of the V where it's attached to the fuselage. They're even located at the base of the rotors. If they work as advertised, the cable slides down and gets cut; that's good for the helicopter and crew, maybe not so good for the Aerostat, which then becomes an unguided, uncontrollable $8.9 million surveillance balloon for a while, until it deflates and wrecks on the desert floor or a mountain peak.

The Army Safety Center at Fort Rucker claims 90 percent survivability in a single-wire strike, but I personally knew a few folks who have hit wires, and only one is still alive to talk about it, so that high percentage seems optimistic to me.

While we'd been keeping the abadabas busy, the convoy of ten or so vehicles had managed to emerge from the FOB about one-half mile away and get back on the road to Bastion unmolested. We both went Winchester making this happen.

As a side note: on this one mission, when you consider that each of the 2.75-inch rockets we fired costs the US taxpayer $2,800, and each of the 660 rounds of 30 mm costs $100, that action south of the Aerostat rang up just about $300,000 in ammo costs. To put it another way: we bought a nice house in a good neighborhood. But to give you a bit more perspective, if we'd fired four racks of four Hellfire missiles from each Apache, at $75,000 per, that would have cost about $2.4 million. That's a much nicer house in a much better neighborhood.

My transition into the role of company commander has been relatively easy—the troops quickly figured out my style was way different than Teflon Don's and responded positively. They are an amazing bunch of guys who are very diverse in their talents, which makes for a solid team. They've already seen that I'm not pulling rank by cherry-picking missions on the flight schedule; they've noticed that I'm flying both nights and days, just like the rest of the aviators. Early on, I redesignated the company truck, making it available to everyone who might need it, rather than having it sit around for the sole use of the commander. Most importantly, they know that when I engage with them after missions, it's a positive interaction. Unlike Teflon Don, who wanted to demean them for not firing enough ammo or killing a sufficient number of bad guys, I'm trying to understand what they're dealing with and figure out ways to make our jobs more efficient, if not easier.

I did have one pilot whose lack of will to fight was causing concern and even resentment among some of the guys. Before I arrived, he had gotten into at least two combat engagements that really shook him up. After that, he did everything possible to avoid flying missions. He was on mid-tour leave in the States when I took command, and when he returned, I thought I could help him avoid combat, yet still perform an important function for the company. He was a qualified maintenance test pilot, so my plan was to have him be the guy who flies all the maintenance test flights, which is a task most pilots disdain.

But it quickly became apparent that he was going to be a seagull— you know, the birds you have to throw rocks at to make them fly. He didn't want to fly at all. Immediately upon return from his mid-tour leave, he put one arm in a sling and claimed he had a sprain of some sort. I insisted he be examined by the doc and get a timeline to recovery mapped out. He did, and right about the time his sprain should have been healed, he started complaining about insomnia. That could have been credible. Sticking to the schedules we were on and having those adrenaline-charged moments sandwiched between hours of flight scouring for the enemy, insomnia goes with the job. I hadn't slept well since Jalalabad. But he wasn't flying.

Whether he was really suffering from sleeplessness or malingering, it became obvious he was killing the morale of his teammates who were having to pick up the slack. I had several conversations with him trying to urge him to come back to work and be part of things. He responded by saying some of the right things, but it became obvious I was trying to push a wet noodle. The time investment that would be required to maybe get him back in the saddle wasn't worth the damage it was doing to the rest of his team. Eventually, it became clear that he was never going to get back to flying combat missions, and we sent him home for medical reasons. Cost-benefit analysis 101. I had promised my guys I would deal with issues swiftly and decisively, so I owed them that.

As I write this book with the benefit of twenty-twenty hindsight, I see his situation a little less black and white. This man went home on leave back to Arizona, where he spent time with his wife and three young daughters. I'd bet money that he went through some of the same rethinking that I went through on my mid-tour leave—a sudden realization that my overaggressive style could very easily result in my death and ensure a return home to my family in a flag-draped box. When it happened to me, I only had my wife and things weren't roses there. Now I have an incredible nine-year-old son, Axel. If I'd gone on mid-tour leave and spent time with him, it's very possible it would have radically changed my approach to the job when I returned to Afghanistan. That pilot had three young daughters. He'd been in at least two difficult combat missions. Even though I still believe he took the wrong approach by malingering, I believe I now understand.

CHAPTER 15

CHOKE POINT

Lessons Learned Are Only Useful
If Applied

Helmand Valley, September 9, 2007—We're on our way to FOB
Qalat, where Flipper 1-2, the Chinook we are escorting, will pick
up a 105 mm Howitzer, sling it beneath the fuselage on a trio of
cables, and then transport it over a mountain ridgeline to FOB
Baylough in a valley on the other side. We turn north at Qalat once
the Chinook has attached to its payload. Instead of farmland below
us on this night escort mission, the landscape on our route east of
Kandahar is very rocky, with the valleys between low mountains
strewn with boulders, much like Goblin Valley State Park in my
native Utah.

A couple of minutes out of Baylough, actually as soon as I can make
radio contact given the terrain, I do our routine check-in and request
a sit-rep. We get an immediate response. "Arrow 0-6, we've been
taking small arms and IDF fire on and off all day long. We believe

it's from a cave located at—" and they give us a grid that my copilot, Sean Maiolo, quickly punches into our computer. "We believe that there's a weapons cache in that cave as well." As it turns out, it's not actually a cave but a large hole in the ground probably originally dug as a well to get and store water.

Since it's nighttime, we should be seeing muzzle flash if they are shooting small arms. If they're launching mortars, I would expect to see dudes out milling around for no apparent good reason. But we're not seeing any of that. "Flipper 1-2, hold just north of the ridgeline until we clear you. Possible enemy firing position." The last thing I want is a Chinook slinging a Howitzer coming under fire when they're most vulnerable. I get back on the radio to the FOB. "Can you confirm that you're taking fire now?"

Their radio operator comes back with, "No, nothing for the last twenty minutes, but we periodically get targeted and we believe it is from that cave." So even though we've now got grid coordinates programmed on the target acquisition display and eyes on said "cave," under the rules of engagement, we can't fire. What to do? "Baylough control, what we can do is test fire our weapons." That's allowed under the ROE, as long as there are no friendlies in the area.

"You're cleared for test fire near that grid point. No friendlies."

Now I'm comfortable clearing the Chinook in to drop its load while we attend to the suspect cave. "Flipper 1-2, you are cleared in, approach from the west. We will be in a blocking pattern east of the FOB executing a test fire."

"Copy all, Arrow. Wilco."

As I wazz up rockets, I think back to my first experiences firing them at Fort Hood, where any impact within fifty yards of the target was considered a hit, most likely because their significant blast radius means an off-target hit is close enough for government work. I'd gotten a lot better using them in Afghanistan, even though I still don't like using the symbology in the reticle over my right eye because it simplicates the entire process. (That's my word for making a simple process complicated.) You have to line up crosshairs and fidget with the pedals until this dashed "I" symbol goes solid and then make sure it is overlaid on the correct position with relation to attitude indicator and other symbology. Even when I get it all lined up and pull the trigger, it's not as accurate for me as when I use a sight-picture method I developed here in OEF that's good enough to put rockets through windows on diving passes. That's something I didn't think would ever be possible.

To do it, my sight-picture is the frame of the Apache's windshield and my copilot's helmet in front of me. I actually use the little slider that brings the visor down on the top of his helmet as my front rifle sight. Then just a slight dive, remain in trim, and no muss, no complications.

Immediately after Baylough clears us to test fire, we come around and begin a dive onto the target. We're more than 1,000 meters out when I have it lined up in my improvised sights and fire. Unfortunately, I realize too late that Sean is considerably shorter than my other front-seaters, and the first rocket hits short of the hole. I make a quick sight-picture adjustment and fire again. The time between shots is infinitesimal. It sounds like *Pfffft! Pfffft!* This second one hits closer but just above. Too much correction. By now, we're screaming in on the target, less than 600 meters away, maybe 150 feet above the ground at 130 knots in a dive. One more shot. I make a very slight adjustment in our pitch and pull the trigger.

Yahtzee! This one goes in the hole. Since there's no enemy fire aimed our way, I stay on course to fly directly over the target, but when we're about a hundred meters away, a giant dragon-breath blowtorch of flame comes jetting out of the ground. It's a *Star Wars* death-star moment requiring immediate departure from the area, just as in the movie. There's a huge secondary explosion. Baylough was right; there were a lot of explosives hidden in that hole. I immediately break right for fear of getting scorched if we were to fly through that blowtorch, or worse, getting hit in our vitals by shrapnel or anything else launched from that hole.

Just then, we get a call from the FOB. "Hey, are you guys in a fight?"

If we were, it was a one-punch knockout. "Nope. I think we just confirmed your assessment of the weapons cache was correct. Test fire complete. Our weapons system works just fine."

The next day, we get word to prepare for a major convoy escort mission that will involve two pairs of Apache gunships based at Kandahar and flying relief for each other, and a pair of British Apaches based at Bastion yo-yoing with two Dutch Apaches out of FOB Tarin Kowt near the convoy's destination, which is adjacent to the capital city of Uruzgan Province, seventy-five miles to the north. The area is strategically important to the NATO coalition because it's been a Taliban stronghold for years. The group's founder, Mullah Omar, was born there, and one-time Afghan president Hamid Karzai has called it the "heart of the Taliban." Some intel experts believe that Osama bin Laden had at one time been hiding in nearby mountain caves, and it's still thought that the majority of Taliban fighters are living in the mountains between Tarin Kowt and the Pakistan border.

A cockpit view of the area near FOB Tarin Kowt. Courtesy of Kevin Eaton.

In 2004, a combat engineer task force from the Louisiana and New York National Guard began work on the first two-lane leg of a paved highway from Kandahar to Tarin Kowt. Jon R. Anderson, a *Stars and Stripes* reporter, wrote a vivid description of the existing road.

> At places little more than a goat trail, the tire-shredding, bone-jarring seventy-five-mile stretch of road is currently a full day's marathon in only the most hardy four-wheel drive vehicle. Ranging over narrow, mile-high mountain passes, through ancient medieval villages and across rocky desert moonscapes covered in inches of thick dust, the road runs through territory that is treacherous in more ways than one.

Three years later, the Army Corps of Engineers is still paving and building bridges on the northern portion of the road but warn that there are places subject to washouts. As we fly north from Kandahar Airfield, thankfully leaving behind the ever-present aroma of the poo ponds—affectionately dubbed Lake Shittycaca—we can see just about every kind of military vehicle used by coalition forces getting on the road. There are old Humvees, up-armored Humvees, MRAPs (mine-resistant ambush-protected vehicles), Land Rovers, trucks, and Romanian Geckos, eight-wheeled troop-carrying extended all-terrain vehicles.

The plan is to get them all up to Tarin Kowt in one push. The danger is that if they spread out, the vehicles become juicy targets of opportunity for the Taliban. Our specific task is to fly ahead of the convoy looking for trouble. If we see anything, we'll radio back to the convoy commander, who will either ask us to deal with it while they wait or have the recon forces positioned ahead of the main convoy check it out.

About an hour into the flight, we reach the point where the road starts into the mountains. The terrain is very rocky, with multiple hairpin turns that slow the vehicles down as they begin the climb to the nearly mile-high pass. I'm not nervous, but I'll admit to butter-fly-type feelings in my gut and apprehension in my mind. If I were planning a hit, this is where I'd do it. The turns minimize how much effective fire follow-on vehicles could provide, and they also increase the difficulty of our own firing solutions. It's not a long leap for me to wonder, *Is this where the abadabas are waiting?*

As we fly around one of the turns, we see a narrow two-lane bridge over an almost dry riverbed. From the air, we also can see that the locals had been bypassing the bridge, taking a dirt path down the bank, then driving across the riverbed and back up the bank on the other side. *Why are they doing that?* That's when we spot a mid-size pickup truck just sitting on the bridge. *We're well ahead of the convoy; the truck will probably leave before the lead vehicles get here.*

We make a couple of passes over the wider area, but the truck still doesn't move. Time to take a closer look. I drop down to about twenty feet off the riverbed and keep my speed around eighty knots. It's slow enough to see well but fast enough to keep my energy state where it should be in case a quick move is required. I am basically at co-altitude with the truck, looking right into the cabin. *This isn't right. There's nobody inside it and no one around it.* We see a tarp covering whatever is in the bed of the truck and note that it's riding low, as it would with a lot of weight back there.

Prior to deploying, we watched a lot of corny videos describing what to look for in order to spot an IED. They didn't cover this particular situation, but I'm going to suggest that they add it. The hairs on the back of my neck are standing up; maybe not as good a bomb detector as a dog but almost as reliable. Then we see something else that indicates trouble. I key the radio and talk to my front-seater Ben Smith and our wingman Jeff Lynch. "Get a look at what's in the tree line." There's probably fifteen dudes in black man-jammies with red turbans—surely some mullah's battle dress uniform—all on or next to motorcycles, just sitting there watching the truck on a bridge that is a sure-as-hell choke point for our convoy.

"Badger 1-1, this is Arrow 0-6, about one mile ahead of your position. I have a loaded pickup on a bridge with multiple MAMs [military-aged males] in the tree line."

"Copy that, Arrow. You are cleared to engage as necessary to clear our path."

Jeff comes back, "Let's blow it in place."

I respond, "If we blow it there, you think the convoy will still be able to get by?"

"I think so, but it'll be tight. Let's just stick a Hellfire on it. That's the kind of target they're made for."

The byplay has given me a few seconds to think. "But, Jeff, if we stick a Hellfire in that thing, we might just blow up the whole bridge. I don't want to do the Taliban's work for them."

"Good point," he says, but I can hear disappointment in his voice. We're always excited for the opportunity to use our biggest weapon, and we've been having more and more opportunities as of late, often using thermobaric Hellfires in caves and on compounds, but we don't often get to deploy them against targets like tanks, trucks, cars, even bridges.

"I'm going to make a close-in pass and hit it with 30s." But once again, something causes me to stop. It's the memory of yesterday's death-star-like secondary explosion out of the hole near FOB Baylough that nearly singed our biscuits. "Change of plans. We're going to blow it but from a distance." I bring our bird back around, and from about 1,200 meters away, Ben hits the truck with a ten-round burst from the 30 mm chain gun. The reaction is instantaneous. With a loud bang that we can feel more than we can hear over the roar of our engines, the truck goes up into the air on a trajectory that carries it way off the bridge, finally landing in a flaming wreck on the riverbed. Two points for the good guys. Spielberg and Lucas would be proud.

A second after the truck blows, all the abadabas in the tree line jump on their motorcycles and race away. We foiled their ambush. Not the show they were hoping for but pretty cool for us. Opting not to stick around and admire our handiwork, we take off after the squad of bikers, quickly catch up, and fly right over them. Ben's ready with the 30 mm, but they aren't aiming the weapons they have slung over their backs at us. They're not actually doing

anything hostile, so under our rules of engagement, we can't eliminate them. "Better get to farmin', fellas!" I say over interplane. Best
we can do is punch a few flares in their direction, making sure they
know that the gig is up, and if they even look as though they're
going to cause trouble for the convoy, they will be dispatched to
abadaba heaven forthwith.

Next, I get on the radio and contact the convoy commander. "Badger,
this is Arrow 0-6. I've got good news and bad news. The good news
is, that truck we told you about is no longer parked on the bridge.
The bad news is that I'm not sure that the bridge will now support
your vehicles. Consider taking the path around it that the locals
have been using, but make sure you check it for mines."

Thirty minutes later, the strung-out convoy is still navigating that
turn when the two other Kandahar-based US Apaches that we were
yo-yoing with, Arrow 21 flight, announce their arrival. We give them
a sit-rep handover brief. "Of course we get here just after something
happens!"

"Yeah, but keep your head on a swivel. This may just be the first of
many setups. By the way, wait until you see the video. Ben made a
truck fly."

That night, back in my hooch at Kandahar, I lie down on the bed
and reflect on my journey so far. It's been the better part of a year at
this point, but it feels as though I've spent a lifetime in Afghanistan.
I've managed to stick with my plan to be supportive of Katie, laying
off the inquisition of task accomplishments and certainly avoiding anger. That's been tough. She lost her respiratory therapist job
because she didn't keep up with the required certifications. And, of
course, she blamed it on the HR folks for not reminding her. But I
didn't engage. I'm getting the bills paid; I'll deal with any financial
fallout when I'm back in the world.

On the battlefield, I'm still running into surprises, but I've also developed the ability to quickly apply, during decision-making moments, the lessons I've learned in combat. I think they call that wisdom, right? I am truly grateful that all those experiences have been ones we have been able to walk away from. Early on, that fortuitous result was due to sheer luck. Then it morphed into some luck, paired with my increasing ability to wield the menacing lethality that is the Apache. As we get further and further on this journey, however, I believe the luck-to-skill ratio has shifted. Now luck is just a bonus. We are all refining our skills as warrior aviators and fighting with experience-built skillsets that none of us had prior to this deployment.

I am enjoying leading these men. Initially, I was confident but wasn't exactly sure what the best plan of attack would be. I had been successful in building teams since I was a kid, but this was a unique scenario. I knew it was my job to turn morale around and figured focusing on empowering guys to do the mission the right way would be a good place to start. The recipe for that was not unlike the "meet me at the ball" tactic I used back in football. Have the commitment to lead by example, have the courage to empower guys, synergize talents to increase our capability, and enjoy the result of a collective increase in confidence and better job performance.

As it turns out, executing the mission in that way also bleeds over into overall increase in morale and unit cohesion. Go figure: job satisfaction and a good work environment improve morale. Although morale and mission success were rockin' steady, I felt we needed an off-duty diversion, something we can do as a group that has nothing to do with our jobs. Every army unit has its scrounger—Cpl. Radar O'Reilly on M*A*S*H or Sgt. Ernie Bilko even before that. We have CW2 Ben Smith. We need movies to show at night in the TOC. Ben takes requests. I don't ask where the DVDs come from. I am sure if I task him to throw a barbecue, days later Ben will have a company-sized grill, the steaks to go on it, and all the fixings. Just the other day, he said something to me in passing about a swimming pool he is building. I just nodded and smiled as I walked away.

Yep, this is going to happen. Now with visions of rare beef, cold drinks, and a swimming pool filled with clear, cool water, I close my eyes and fall asleep.

CHAPTER 16

SOMETIMES A MOSQUE NEEDS TO BE BLOWN UP

Never Act Out of Hate but Don't Be Restrained by Fear

Kandahar Air Base, October 12, 2007—Today is going to be a good day. How do I know? Because the abadabas took a shot at me a few minutes ago, and I'm still here to talk about it. Not only that, but I got to Timmy Ho's—that's Canadian for Tim Horton's—while the doughnuts were still hot. It's amazing. I'm in Kandahar Af-freakin-ghanistan, where people I don't even know and didn't personally piss off are trying to kill me, and I'm eating real doughnuts like back home. Okay, so maybe I did upset a few of them on our last mission. But hey, we just gave their elders gold. They can stroke their beards at the village council and say, "Let me tell you about the time the infidels' war mosquitos made a Nissan truck fly."

About that shot they took at me. I walked out of the chow hall with a guy from the 82nd, stopped for my morning doughnut, and then cut across the open area known as the quad, taking a shortcut to the TOC. The Canadians had laid out a dirt soccer field and, in a salute to their heritage, had also constructed a concrete roller hockey rink. The quad is surrounded by a covered wooden board-walk with little shops side by side, where locals sew on patches and tailor custom clothing, sell knickknacks and souvenirs, and make their foot bread—naan-e-Afghani. As we started across the open quad, the warning sirens went off. It's a big, loud, warbling WAAAWAAAWAAAWAAA! that lets you know they've detected incoming indirect fire (IDF).

We're supposed to duck into these huge concrete tube shelters they've placed throughout the base and wait for the all clear. Since I was in the middle of the soccer field and it was a long run to a shel-ter, I opted to ignore the warning. After ten months in country, I'd pretty much become a fatalist: if they get me, they get me. What I do every day is more dangerous than this. Except for this time. We suddenly hear a whistling noise and a loud thud, followed by a heavy Whoooosh! of air pressure I can feel all over my body. I can actually see an artillery round hit the field about forty feet from us, causing a huge dirt cloud. But there's no explosion. The round just slams into the ground, then comes flying up, spinning end over end making an eerie sound almost like a giant cat purring aggressively. It spins right through the walls of a couple of those shops lining the board-walk, leaving a two-foot hole, just slightly larger than the round. But it never blows up, fortunately. If it hadn't been a dud, I'd no longer be in a place where I could read, much less write, a book.

This is how war changes your perspective. Prior to my deployment, this event would have qualified as a once-in-a-lifetime near-death occurrence that begs to be shared. Here, I just call it "Wednes-day." Aside from the initial wide eyes at the realization of what just happened, we both just laugh and continue our stroll, talk for a minute about how cool that was—"Never saw an arty round in action like that"—and then switch subjects. Nothing more than if we'd seen something funny on the way to work back home. You may remember to share it with your coworkers, but you just as easily might not.

Most likely, the Taliban were firing munitions that were left over from their conflict with the Soviets, using makeshift tubes. Sometimes they work; sometimes they don't. Was it just dumb luck that saved me? They keep throwing those rounds into this big area populated by us infidels, and nobody gets hurt, even when they do blow up.

This is not the first time it's happened. Up north one day at FOB Naray, all the FOB head shed had just gone to the chow hall, leaving a junior lieutenant to man the TOC. He stepped out for a smoke just as a round hit. The LT earned his Purple Heart Forrest Gump style for a small piece of shrapnel in the butt-ocks—one of the rare cases when smoking was good for a guy's health. Had the round struck a few moments earlier, the leadership would have been wiped out.

My near brush with death is quickly forgotten once I get to the battalion TOC for the operations meeting with Task Force Corsair leadership and all the company commanders. The main agenda item is the operation that's been rumored for months—the takedown of the major Taliban stronghold in Musa Qala, a city of 20,000 that hasn't been targeted in recent years. The Taliban there claim a fighting force of at least 2,000 men. I hear through the grapevine that although it's going to be an American-heavy mission, politics dictate that the Afghan army forces, along with the Brits based out of FOB Bastion, will get the credit. That stuff is above my pay grade. All I can do is wait until they tell me where my guys have to be and when.

If it does go down, this will be a big one. But our time in country is waning. If they don't make a decision soon, it may end up being my successor's mission to execute. That would be a mistake. We've got just under a year's worth of experience fighting here. To my mind, it makes no sense to send in newbies, but it wouldn't be the first time the generals made an unwise decision for what I believe are political reasons.

As I leave the meeting, I hear someone calling, "Capt. Slade! Capt. Slade." I look back over my shoulder to see Capt. Nervous (okay, that's not his real name, but it is for the book), the commander of our supply company. He's the beans and bullets guy, and he's upset with me. "Capt. Slade, you guys are shooting way too many rockets and Hellfires. We are running low on inventory."

"Is that so?" I'm trying not to roll my eyes. "Dang it. Well, just how many rockets and Hellfires would you have us shoot, Nervous?"

"I don't know, less?"

"Then you've got to tell me which bad guys we should let go. Which convoy asking for help should we tell, 'Sorry, not today. We've fired our quota'? Which patrols should we tell, 'Just hold tight and things will work out'?" Obviously, he didn't have an answer, and he'd annoyed me by even broaching the notion that conserving ammo as a war-fighting strategy is a responsible idea.

"Dude, look around. How much money have we sunk into this war?" Yes, I get that the dollar amount spent on ordnance is staggering, but you have to look at it as casino chips. "I am not telling my guys to pull punches and not protect the infantry for fear of depleting our inventories. Rockets and Hellfires are like Doritos. We can crunch all we want; they'll make more."

Capt. Nervous wasn't giving up. "Just try to be more judicious, please." Honestly, I don't think it's even the dollar amount he cares about. He just wants his inventory slide Chiclets to be green so he can report full inventory in meetings. This kind of myopic perspective gripes me, but I don't have the inclination or time to waste right now arguing with this whiner.

"Copy all, Capt. Nervous. Thanks for your support."

A few hours later, my number comes up to fly a one-ship mission to escort a Dustoff going out to pick up casualties at FOB Wilson, twenty-five miles to the east, on the outskirts of suburban Kandahar. It's a beautiful blue-sky day, and my front-seater, 1st Lt. Josh Daniels, an augmentee from Charlie Company at FOB Salerno, and I are actually enjoying the relatively stress-free twenty-minute flight. From a distance, we can see the fifteen- to twenty-foot-tall Hesco barriers that surround the base. FOB Wilson is one of the few forward operating bases we have with a large gravel area that's just big enough for us to pull off a rolling landing if needed. I'd actually been out here a few weeks earlier to practice that maneuver, just in case our bird ever gets crippled and can't do a normal landing to a hover.

Time to check in. "Hey, FOB Wilson, this is Arrow 0-6, inbound with a Dustoff for patient pickup. What's your sit-rep?"

"Good to hear from you, Arrow 0-6. We've been taking small arms and intermittent 50 cal all day. They're actually impacting buildings in the center of the FOB. And that Dustoff will likely be a target when it comes in."

"Wilson, any idea where that fire is coming from? It's daylight and we're not picking up muzzle flash."

"No idea, Arrow. Our casualties are CAT Alpha, though, and we need to clear that Dustoff ASAP, if you can make it happen."

Daniels and I are scanning in every direction, trying to figure out where the bad guys could be. On the intercom I say, "If those rounds are hitting ground at the center of the FOB, they've got to be coming from somewhere elevated that can fire down over those Hescos. There could be abadabas in the grassy berm just outside the base, but they can't make the shot from there. And there's no higher ground around here." It is relatively flat for miles.

I begin trying to do basic geometry, figuring how high the gun has to be to shoot over the wall at the landing Black Hawk. Given the status of the patients, I'd cleared it to land, hoping that just having us in the air nearby would deter the enemy long enough to pick up the wounded. We quickly conclude that the likely source of the fire is the spire of a mosque less than half a mile away, just on the edge of the city. "I think it's coming from the mosque," I tell Daniels. "It has to be. There's nothing else around tall enough to make that shot."

"That's not good. We can't shoot a mosque."

"We can if they're shooting at us from it." We both knew from past missions that firing anywhere near a mosque, much less right at it, would result in the Spanish inquisition. Everyone in higher headquarters who has never flown a gunship would get a crack at playing Torquemada. Of course, Daniels was coming from Salerno, where the leadership was in your cockpit micromanaging, much like my experience at Bagram. I tell him the bosses here at Kandahar empower, instead of hinder. If it's a righteous mission within the definition of the ROE, I have faith our task force leadership will defend us rather than throw us under the bus. Word here had always been, if you're taking fire from near a mosque, just don't hit the *mosque*. Hypotheticals had been thrown out like, if you're actually taking fire from the mosque, technically you can shoot it, but it was always said through gritted teeth with questioning eyes.

But Daniels wasn't buying it. "I'm asking you, Captain, are you sure you want to shoot a mosque?"

"I'm pretty dang sure." I know that's not quite as firm a response as I'd given him just moments earlier. But now that shooting the mosque has become more reality than theory, I'm not quite as confident. I can handle political trouble, but I'm not pigheaded enough to go out of my way to look for it. Maybe there's a better plan. I don't have to pull the trigger this second.

"Hey, Wilson, any way you can get optics on that mosque? What're you seeing right now?" Some of my other front-seaters would have had that mosque locked up in the tactical acquisition display in a minute, but Daniels was a little slower. Rather than give him the controls and me try to do it from the back where the controls aren't set up to be as user friendly, I figure the FOB could put eyes on quickly. It was a workaround but something I would talk to Daniels about later when we had a little more time.

"We're taking fire again. Dustoff is ready to load casualties and rounds are striking the ground. They're walking them in."

At this point, we're down to 100 feet, maintaining about 130 knots so we can avoid giving the shooters an easy target as we come screaming over a stand of trees. We're both looking for bad guys but see nothing. We turn and make a run directly at the mosque, which consists of a rectangular flat-topped building with a single blue-topped phallic-shaped spire in one corner. And right there on that flat roof, we've suddenly got military-aged men running in all directions, but no one is firing a rifle.

That's when Wilson comes back in on the radio. "It is confirmed. We are taking 50 cal from the top of that mosque right now."

That's good news/bad news. "Okay, we understand it's confirmed. You're taking fire from the mosque." I don't want to say I'm feeling tentative, but I'm truly conflicted. And Daniels isn't helping. It is very possible for us to just suppress enemy fire until the medics get the Dustoff loaded and out of here, but that will leave the FOB vulnerable to gunmen in the spire who can target the next inbound aircraft or anyone walking in the open with heavy machine-gun fire.

Daniels is voting to leave the mosque alone. "Boss, it's not worth the trouble. Let's just annoy and distract them with the gun."

"Man, these guys got an angle and they're walking them in on the helicopter. Eventually, they're going to hit it or the next one in." We buzz past the spire heading back toward the FOB but see no muzzle flash, quickly figuring the enemy is being judicious with the machine-gun fire to keep us from pinpointing their location.

That's when Wilson comes back up on the radio. "Arrow 0-6, you're taking fire from the mosque tower. So are we."

I recognize that they must have opened up with the 50 as soon as our backs were turned. Even now, Daniels, who is competent but not a lean-forward type, still isn't onboard with the notion that we obliterate the mosque. He might be my voice of reason. "I don't know. I don't think we can shoot this mosque."

"Yeah, we can shoot it. If it fits the ROE. If it's shooting at us or friendlies, or we're defending ourselves or friendlies, we can shoot the mosque." Why? Because at that point, it is not a religious building anymore; it is an enemy military stronghold. I'd actually chalk-talked this scenario with intel and even chair-flown it before. "That's what they say," Daniels tells me, "But you know what's going to happen. We hit this mosque, there's going to be huge blowback. The Taliban will claim there was no fire coming from there, and we just blew up the mosque because we hate Muslims."

I'm thinking, *He's not wrong.* But what I say is, "Maybe so, but we've literally been cleared onto the mosque by Wilson, which is the definition of PID [positive identification], right? And sometimes, a mosque simply needs to be blown up."

"Then let's do it. A Hellfire?"

Finally, he's onboard. "Wilson, we're going to engage that mosque."

"You guys are going to engage the mosque?" The voice sounds a little surprised, even though it's the same guy who'd been begging us to suppress the hostile fire.

Unlike up in the mountains where we rarely were armed with Hellfire missiles, on most flights out of Kandahar we carry some on a rack because there is a call for them down here. We're not as power limited at this lower altitude and we have the ability to handle the extra weight, so it's better to carry a variety of ordnance allowing us to better match the tool to the job.

Hellfires are guided missiles, unlike the rockets we carry which are pointie-shootie—yes, that's a technical term. Hey, I understand it; you should too. With a Hellfire, the front-seater locks the missile onto the target before launch in our tactical acquisition display. Then he pulls the trigger to squirt an invisible coded laser beam at the target, as we both watch our displays to see the dashed box turn into a solid symbol. That tells us two things: brains in the missile have followed the laser beam and locked onto the target, and the aircraft is within specified constraints for a firing solution.

My job is to keep the Apache in those shooting constraints while making certain we're no closer than 500 meters from the target when we shoot. I'm waiting to confirm that Daniels has it aimed at the base of the spire, knowing that a direct hit there will take care of anyone shooting from any level within the sixty-foot structure. In two seconds, the symbology box turns solid, and I tell him, "Okay, you're good. Go ahead."

Daniels pulls the trigger. The missile flies off the rails and immediately climbs into a rainbow-type arch. They are designed to do this so when they hit the target, the missile is pointing down. If the target were a tank, that would allow it to penetrate the top, where the armor is the thinnest. A few seconds later, we see the explosion. It's an awesome sight. The missile doesn't blow on impact but is programmed to wait until it's actually inside the structure (or tank, or bunker, or whatever). So we actually see it hit and make a hole in the spire with some debris flying off the structure due to impact, then a fraction of a second later, everything shakes. Parts of the building expand, others crumble.

The spire doesn't fall over; it just sort of disintegrates on itself. And as we watch, dozens of squirters come running out of the rubble. Are they bad guys? Worshippers who happened to be in the wrong place at the wrong time? No way to know. If you spin your wheels thinking about all the possibilities regarding collateral damage, I have found it gets you nowhere fast. The questions that need answering are: Was it within the ROE? Yes. Did it save or potentially save friendly forces' lives? Yes. As a matter of self-preservation, if those answers are both yes, I am content and I stop asking myself questions. In this case, they were definitely both yes; it was a good shoot, but I can't resist teasing my copilot on the intercom. "Man, you just blew up a mosque. What were you thinking?"

That's when FOB Wilson comes up on the radio again. "Yeah, we're not taking fire anymore. I think you got it." I always love those affirmations, even if in this case that's a *duh!* statement.

On our next pass alongside the FOB, we can see the Dustoff has loaded all the casualties and is ready to lift off, when we get another call from Wilson. "Arrow 0-6, can you hit the tree line one hundred meters to our west? That's where we're taking fire from now." It's the bad guys' last-ditch effort to hit this Dustoff on takeoff. *Ballsy move. I mean, we just proved we would shoot a mosque. You think you are safe in the tree line?*

It's easy-peasy. We suppress the fire, then fall in behind the Dustoff, trying to keep up as they rush the severe casualties back to the hospital at Kandahar Airfield.

When we land, I head to the 82nd TOC alone to do the debrief. Lieutenant Daniels is very clear. "I ain't going." *Wuss.*

"It'll be fine, you know. This is Kandahar, not Salerno, not Bagram. They actually understand we're in a war here. Sure, we're under the same ROE, but these guys actually read Sun Tzu. We're not handcuffed."

A few minutes later, alone, I confidently tell the 82nd intel guys the story. I can see the eyes widening, but I continue, adding, "You might get some pushback, but we had 100 percent PID on the shooter, confirmed by the firebase."

"Wait a sec," says the S-2, "you blew up a mosque?" The silence is deafening.

For a brief second, I'm not sure which way he's going to go. *Did I make a huge mistake? I mean, what we did most likely prevented some catastrophic events from happening.* But then he starts laughing. "I can't believe you did that," he says, "but if you're taking fire, technically, it fits the ROE. Good job." And that was that.

It's such a good feeling to operate in an atmosphere where you can trust the leadership to have your back and not second-guess every decision you make. It's not easy to make some of these decisions, and quite honestly, I am sure there have been times when I should have made better decisions. Perhaps this was one of them, or maybe, as I said before, *sometimes a mosque needs to be blown up.*

The gold standard would be to make the best decision every time. But that would require more information, better situational awareness, more time for analysis, or more experience to guide me. But this is combat, and the simple fact is, we often have to make full-impact decisions based on partial information. Action is almost always better than freezing, which is what happens to guys whose commanders second-guess them with lots of armchair quarterbacking.

Of note, at the next ops meeting with Major Alia presiding, the briefer reported OEF accounting on what ordnance units had been firing, referencing their effects on CENTCOM's (Central Command's) inventory. When he got to Hellfire, it showed that line item was in the red. Dangerously low or out of stock. Alia interrupted the briefer and actually read the Afghan breakdown: "Salerno—zero. Bagram—one. Kandahar—thirty-three. It appears A Company is nearly single-handedly putting CENTCOM in the red on Hellfires." For a moment, I thought that Capt. Nervous was going to have the last laugh, but Maj. Alia, an aggressive war fighter who gets it, actually took this as a point of pride for the task force taking it to the enemy. He looked directly at me and said, "Good job, Capt. Slade."

"Just doing our part, sir." I shoot Nervous a sideways smile. It's not always good to rub it in, but from my perspective, supply-and-support types often miss the big picture, and this was definitely one of those times. I am so thankful the leadership here gets it.

Occasionally, our guys would have time to enhance our rockets. I doubt if the Taliban had time to notice. Courtesy of CW4 Kevin Eaton.

By the way, a week or so later, my faith in the purchasing power of the Department of Defense is rewarded, as a new shipment of Hellfires and rockets is delivered to our FARP in larger quantities than we had been getting. "Crunch all you want. We'll make more."

Good thing too, because the scuttlebutt about that upcoming assault on Musa Qala is picking up. Looks as though we're going to need them.

You may have noticed I haven't talked as much about Katie recently. That isn't accidental. My new approach of simply letting things lie has definitely led to fewer conversations and thus less contention, but it has also started to build a wall between us that is more palpable than the 8,000 miles of actual separation. Not bringing things up has also resulted in a very empty savings account. Although it's been helpful that she doesn't occupy my thoughts nearly as much as before, I feel that a growing apathy can't be good for a healthy relationship. This increases my internal conflict of wanting to be a good husband versus my sanity and safety while executing my missions here. Have I effectively decreased the damage of one aspect of our relationship but at the same time opened a new fissure? Am I overthinking it?

CHAPTER 17

OP. MAR KARADAD– D-DAY MINUS 2

UPDATE YOUR WILLS

Use Tension to Build Positive Momentum

Kandahar, December 5, 2007—*Wow! Things are getting real cloak and dagger around here.* I'd just been challenged by armed military police (MPs) guarding the secure, basketball-sized marquee tent where the intel guys from battalion S-2 had constructed a giant sand-table model, built to scale, depicting Regional Command South and the Musa Qala area in northeast Helmand Province. It includes the area we'd be assaulting in two days and is actually big enough so that during the briefing, I physically walk the route we'd be flying on the model, experiencing the hills and valleys, roads, tactical reference points, and civilian residential areas. Nerdery is usually something I just look at and say, "Yep, that's what those guys do," but I'd never seen mission preparation at this level in the eleven months our unit has been in Afghanistan.

I guess the effort makes sense. Operation Mar Karadad ("Snake
Bite" in the native Pashto dialect spoken in the region) is being
billed as the largest air assault in OEF history, with 600 American
paratroopers to be flown in by helicopter for the climactic battle.
We have been getting bits and pieces briefed to us for weeks, and
rumors about plans to take back the city from Taliban forces have
been circulating since October, just after International Security
Assistance Forces (ISAF) and Afghan army units killed sixty insur-
gents in a six-hour battle near Musa Qala. I'd attended a briefing
run by the Brits at Lashkar Gah on November 28, where it was
obvious to me that Lt. Col. Brian Mennes, a West Point graduate,
had already had a significant impact on the Brits' mission plan.
Mennes had successfully stymied the notion of splitting his force
into two separate units, assaulting from opposite sides of the city.
At the same meeting, he'd also made clear his unhappiness with
the notion of a helicopter-borne air assault conducted in daylight.
He'd already led six such assaults during his 82nd Airborne unit's
time in country, all of them under cover of darkness. I shared this
concern.

Ironic that they've got MPs guarding this tent but just dropped thou-
sands of leaflets over Musa Qala telling everyone that we're coming.
Yeah, they didn't say exactly when, but I don't like it. It's concerning,
to say the least, that we're pretty much telling the abadabas to
gather the SAM missiles and anti-aircraft guns they've hidden in
the surrounding mountains and set them up poised and ready for
my Arrows and the twenty-plus other rotary-wing assets that are
coming. We know the Taliban is doing just that because it's been
reported in newscasts on Al Jazeera English as well as in London
media. Those are in addition to the already formidable stash they
have in Musa Qala, according to intel.

Then there are the intel briefs we have been getting that assess
the Taliban's military capabilities in Musa Qala city as being

much better than anything we've fought thus far in all of Afghanistan. The way it sounds to me, they're saying, "We want you to swim through this tank of piranhas, okay?" And when I respond, "Okay, I guess we can do that for you," they add a little something: "Not so fast, Capt. Slade. First, we're going to dump in some blood and chum to put them in a proper frenzy. There we go. Now you can go."

I get that reports on social media and in the world's press about mass civilian casualties—collateral damage—caused by the American military don't help us win hearts and minds and that those leaflets might convince some noncombatants to get while the gettin' is good, which is definitely a hope of the Brits who planned this op. I understand it's part of a strategic effort to convince the Taliban that their very survival depends on them leaving Musa Qala long before the actual assault begins. But the way I see it, it's a political calculation big-footing smart planning. No book I've ever read on military strategy has said it's a good idea to let the enemy know you're coming. *Hmm, I wonder why that is?* I'd already been confronted with political realities a week or two earlier, when we were told that irrespective of who is really doing the fighting, credit for successful execution of the operation would go primarily to the Afghan National Security Forces.

Again, the reasoning is nuanced because this is a war where it seems political considerations trump military ones. When it's all over, the lasting impression on the Afghans who actually live in Musa Qala is supposed to be that they were liberated from the predations of the Taliban by President Hamid Karzai's Afghan national army forces—their fellow countrymen—who were careful not to destroy the city in order to save it. (It's a storied Vietnam War reference you can look up.) The plan is theoretically designed to drive the Taliban out of Musa Qala, not kill them or anyone else inside its borders.

In his comprehensive book on the battle, *Operation Snakebite*, British combat journalist/author Stephen Grey writes:

> In theory, this whole operation was still to be led by the Afghans...
> But talk of Afghan "leadership" of the forthcoming battle was a
> fiction. The primary role of the Afghan troops was not to win
> the battle but to influence the town's population to believe
> that it was the Islamic national government who had returned
> to control the town, and not foreigners. The use of the Afghan
> troops was also to influence the Afghan government. It had to
> feel Musa Qala was its victory—and feel responsible for what
> happened next.

Although the British leadership bought into—or more likely, originated—the notion that no ordnance should directly impact the city's center without their command's express approval, our 82nd division's ground force commander refused to agree that the rules of engagement precluded firing into the city, *even if they were taking fire from Taliban sheltering there.*

I was a fly on the wall and watched Lt. Col. Mennes insist that if his troops were fired on from within the city, they had the right of self-defense, and that included the use of heavy weapons and airstrikes. The dispute between Mennes and British Brigadier Andrew Mackay, commander of the Helmand Task Force, was heated, with Mackay insisting that in order to use heavy weapons, the Americans would have to secure British approval, and Mennes arguing that if his troops are taking fire, no such approval is needed.

As to the Afghan army, Grey recounts in *Snakebite* a story told to him by Maj. Guy Jones, Mennes's operations officer. It's an exchange at the Lashkar Gah headquarters between Lt. Col. Mennes and Brigadier Muhammad Mohaydin, commander of the Afghan brigade of

2,500 men who made up the bulk of the 5,000 troops to be deployed in Mar Karadad.

"Hey, boss," said Mennes as they shook hands. "They say they want me to go in there with you. What are you needing me to do?"

Mohaydin gave him a puzzled look. "I can't do this on my own. You go in and we'll be partners."

"I agree we need to be partners. I said we will get you in there. You come and meet up with us and we will get you in there."

It was clear, recalled Jones, that Mohaydin wanted the US troops to go much further than the plan on paper actually called for. Mohaydin, it was clear, had no desire or intention to do much fighting. No US troops nor even any NATO troops were supposed to enter the town. But Mohaydin had his own idea: "I'm not going into town. At night, you all clear it, and make sure it's good, and I'll go in, in the morning."

Of special concern to me was the matter of our Apaches' role in the operation. The first plan that came down had us playing backup to the British Apache helicopter unit based at Camp Bastion. I was told they'd be going in immediately after an artillery barrage (Brit) and heavy bombing (mostly American, by Gulf-based bombers) softened up the area, while we'd be flying circles five miles away, waiting to get called if we're needed.

That didn't sit well with me or my guys, but fortunately, we had some powerful supporters in our corner. I wasn't privy to the actual conversation, but the word I heard was that Mennes made it clear to whomever was counting on him to win this one that direct support by British-flown Apaches was not acceptable. He wanted our Arrow Apaches, and he got his wish. *Place at the table! Alpha Company is in play.* This carried with it mixed emotions to be sure. We're going to be embarking on a dangerous mission against known, dug-in, fore-warned enemy forces—and doing it when we are only weeks away from going back home to Arizona after a yearlong deployment. I wondered if everybody would be onboard, but to a man, they were. Everyone wanted to be involved with what we'd started calling the Big Mish. I felt blessed to have the soldiers I had. Other compa-nies—noticeably those *not* flying Apaches—did not have the same experience. I learned there were aviators who asked to not be part of this one after receiving intel briefings on enemy strength and the risky nature of the planned daylight/twilight assault.

With regard to the rejection of British Apache support, it's not that the British pilots couldn't do the job; they just do it in a way that doesn't give American infantry commanders the warm fuzzies. The Brits are trained to fly high and shoot from altitude, something the Apache helicopter is definitely designed to do. However, in our way of thinking, its capabilities for stand-off distance engagements are typically reserved for more conventional-type warfare. If your targets are tanks, bunkers, convoys, and the like, the Apache can stand off at a great distance and execute exit-the-planet direc-tives at will. Our tactics, on the other hand, have been adapted to maximize lethality in under-tree-canopy, pop-out-shoot-and-hide engagements for which the Taliban are notorious.

In order to do that, we get down low and make our presence known. It's more dangerous for us, but we believe it gives us a better abil-ity to find, fix, and kill the enemy—and experience tells us that the ground pounders appreciate the effort. They can feel our presence and know we are much more likely to see what they see. The enemy, too, can feel our presence and most often are less likely to engage. These tactics are what earned us the title "the special mosquitoes marked with the tail flash" by enemy fighters. Intel had intercepted this type of communication on several occasions. The special marking the Taliban are referring to is the Arizona flag on our tail.

As you can imagine, the British commanders and aircrews—who see us as overaggressive fliers—weren't happy with the perceived diss. Honestly, not my problem. I would give them the mission if that's what was called for. We could go home, content with the service we have provided up to this point. But if we are going to be in this fight, right in the middle is where my guys need to be. That's who they are now, pilots who not only stare adversity in the face but narrow their eyelids with intensity. I call it "getting the squints."

My only real concern with the mission requirement for Alpha Company is that we keep two Apaches on station over the battle space twenty-four hours a day and be prepared to do it for two to three weeks. That would be tough for us to staff by itself, but we also have to maintain the ability to fly escort on the daily ring routes resupplying all the FOBs in the southern part of the country. Even more, we need to have two Apaches instantly available 24/7 to fly as part of a quick reaction force (QRF). There's no way I can do that with the resources we've got right now. There's some discussion about having the Dutch Apaches based up at Tarin Kowt fly ring route escort, but they already had their own taskings to take care of, and US Black Hawk and Chinook pilots flying those missions apparently vetoed that idea.

After mapping it all out with my team, I tell the planners we need two more Apaches and two more crews, minimum—four additional pilots—to make this happen. They run it up the chain and decide to give us four pilots and two helicopters from Charlie Company up at FOB Salerno, which had already blessed us with CW5 Chris Walker weeks earlier.

Typically, you will not find a CW5 in a line company—they're in HQ playing a management role—but Chris, who is a great pilot and a solid God-fearing man, couldn't keep his mouth shut around Desert Hawk 0-6 when the boss was saying or doing things detrimental to the folks he had stewardship over. A smart man would have listened to Chris and even solicited more feedback. I know that's what I did when he came to us, and his wisdom is something I truly value. Desert Hawk 0-6, however, just dealt with him as he did with everybody who dared offer an alternative plan—he shipped him out.

So with Chris and the four other Salerno-based pilots, we now have a total of ten Apaches and ten crews. That's if everyone stays healthy and the maintainers can work their magic. We can make that work, I think.

With four birds committed 24/7 just to Operation Mar Karadad, that'll leave us four to five to do the routine operational missions, including Dustoff escorts, and the potential QRF. Typically, one or two birds are always down for maintenance, so, yeah, it'll be tight.

My interaction prior to the deployment with the augmenting pilots from Salerno was varied. I knew them all but none of them well. My most immediate problem is that all four of them arrived with the misguided impression we were calling on them to take the lead on the Big Mish. *Why would we do that?* I quickly disabuse them of the notion, saying it's not going to happen, at least not immediately. I tell them, "I don't know your capabilities as aircrew like I do my own guys. I'm not saying you're not capable. In fact, my assumption is you are, but it is still an unknown versus a known. You also don't know the territory as well as my guys do. The fighting and tactics here are different than what you've flown in Salerno. We need some time to figure it out and integrate you into our routines. Only when it makes sense are you going to get in on the mish. And it definitely does not make sense to put you in on the first wave. When you do go in, you're going to be paired up with one of my pilots. If you have a problem with that, you can go back to Salerno, but that's the way it's going to be."

Yes, I'm absolutely favoring my guys. Tactically speaking, that's the smart way to go. I know what they're going to do and what they're not going to do. Not to mention, I wouldn't sideline my guys for something like this. The very fact they've been going toe-to-toe with Johnny TB down here, having my six, equates, in my book, to me owing it to them. They have shown the courage and commitment to fight and have developed a stalwart confidence along with a solid capability to do so. It's that same recipe for success I learned in high school football. Only the stakes here are much higher.

As for the guys from Salerno, they sent me two aircraft commanders and two copilots. One of the ACs is CW4 Ken Jones, nicknamed Iron Ass because he loves to fly and doesn't care how many hours he spends in the seat. He's got lots of hours and this isn't his first deployment. Never heard anything but good things about him, so I think he will indeed be an asset. The other AC is CW3 Bitch'n'Moan. I'm not sure why, but he feels entitled to be in the Big Mish from the start and has already vocally complained. I'm hoping I can get ol' Bitch'n'Moan to lockstep; otherwise, he'll have to go.

One of the two copilots is CW2 Garrett Radigan, who earlier in the year had been the front-seater on an Apache that crashed into a mountainside. He lived to tell the tale of evading enemy contact till he and his pilot, Sean Hoover, could be picked up by rescue choppers. Actually, two Apaches had crashed in separate, but similar, incidents that same night. Breaking out of a blinding fog, they pitched up at the last second and managed to match the angle of the helicopter to the slope of the mountain, hitting flat and then sliding back down on the belly of the aircraft until they were eventually stopped by rocks and trees. Fortunately, they were able to exit immediately from their burning aircraft. The fact that all four pilots managed to get out safely is amazing. Bitch'n'Moan was actually on one of those two birds as well. The difference between how he thought he was entitled because of that incident and Radigan's perspective was stunning.

CW2 Thomas "Otto" Malone is the other copilot from our Charlie Company up at FOB Salerno. He's a jovial, quick-witted twenty-seven-year-old who had essentially no experience prior to this deployment, but as was the case with most young guys/gals, he had been afforded many hours of practice to become proficient in his craft. I didn't talk much with Otto that first day, but the first and only time we crewed together, I sat down and chatted with him, just to give him my expectations of a solid copilot. He shared with me some of his experiences in Salerno, which, quite honestly, weren't eye-popping, but they were combat experiences, nonetheless. They had easily won the engagements he'd flown, and he told me they left him feeling invincible. To this, I drew in a deep breath, saying, "Whoa! Don't say that, man." I am not typically a superstitious type, but things like that give me an uneasy feeling. Truth is, I had felt similarly off and on during the deployment, and my flying showed it at times: I was too bold, too stupid, or too confident. If I'm being honest with myself, I, too, would admit to occasional feelings of invincibility. I just don't believe I could ever bring myself to say it out loud.

Once I explained my crewing plan to the Salerno augmentees, all but one bought into it. Go figure, Bitch'n'Moan still thinks that because of his crash survival, he's God's gift to military aviation. I try to deflate him a bit because I need his ego checked if he is going to be useful to us. "First of all, dude, you crashed. I get that you lived, that you pitched the aircraft up perfectly. That's cool. Hopefully, if I were in your situation, I would have done the same thing.

But crashing and surviving does not mean you walk on water in my book." That's what I say, but what I'm truly thinking is, *Thank God these guys made it out of that situation, and the fact they are all alive deserves a book of its own, but I'm not going to let Bitch'n'Moan know that. Right now, he's becoming a nuisance and needs to come down a peg or ten.*

But he wouldn't stop complaining to everyone but me about being mistreated. My guys are loyal, and we had fostered an atmosphere of "can do; don't complain without a solution." They brought it to me immediately because they didn't want to deal with his attitude either.

Initially, it infuriates me. The last thing I need is a self-obsessed, thirty-something toddler to deal with at a time when it's critical that everyone in the company be focused only on making sure the unit pulls off this mission perfectly. I take some time to calm down, since I know if I don't, it will be a borderline violent conversation because I'm that incensed at his behavior. Once I've talked myself down, I take him aside for a frank talk. "Here's the deal. I don't put up with that here. If I hear it again, you're out. To be clear, I don't mean you'll be out of the mission; you will be out of my AO [area of operation]." I look him in the eyes, with the squints, and ask, "Are we clear?" I can tell he wants to retort but is wise enough not to, spilling out a reluctant, "Yes, sir."

Unfortunately, he wasn't wise enough to heed the warning. Later, my guys tell me he's still complaining about his assignments. I don't have time for this. I call him into my office and close the door. I stare at him for probably thirty seconds, so angry I could spit. When I finally do speak, it is not a yell; rather, a piercing assertiveness exits my mouth. "You have ten minutes to gather your crap and leave my company area. I don't want to see your person around this TOC, near our hooches, or talking to anybody here who actually understands selfless service. You're going to get on a plane, a helicopter, a convoy, a donkey, or whatever you can get on, and I want you off Kandahar within twenty-four hours. You hear me?"

He looked at me as if to say, "What the hell?"

"I warned you, man, and I'm not messing around. I don't have time for this whining and moaning and soap opera junk. We're getting ready to do real stuff, and you're just causing problems. We're done. Leave." With a stunned look on his face, he turned and left, and I'm told he made it back to Salerno. Identify and excise the tumor early, and you need to cut out only one. It didn't take long for word to spread. After that, we had no issues with anyone else. To be fair, I don't think we would have anyway.

I want to be clear. I wasn't being a hard-ass just to be one. We're getting ready to fly the most complicated, most dangerous mission we've flown here, with the greatest chance of injury. How danger-ous? None of us truly know, but consider this: the task force S-2 came down to our command post to provide us an intel brief and ended it in tears when she said, "My assessment is at least one Apache will get shot down the first day of this mission." How's that for the power of positive thinking?

Under the guise of a one-armed hug, I pulled her out of the limelight and corrected her on what the heck she had just done. "Look, LT, I am touched that you care about us enough to shed a tear, but your tears help nobody in there right now. You need to be your strongest self around men who are getting ready to take the very risks you just described." She nodded and apologized. "No apology necessary. Your understanding of what I just told you, though, is essential." I stared at her with eyes that asked, "Do you understand?" Again, she nodded. "Thank you for what you do, LT. It's important, know that."

Not long after that disquieting briefing from the S-2 lieutenant, CW5 Chris Walker comes to me and asks if he and Capt. Adam Smoot can pray with our aircrews. He felt that given the potentially dangerous and kinetic nature of our upcoming mission, "reading from Scripture might lend some meaning to this if it doesn't go well." I was grateful for his suggestion; it was another one of those "why didn't I think of that?" moments.

Chris chose to read Psalm 91, part of which says,

If you say, "The Lord is my refuge,"

and you make the Most High your dwelling,

no harm will overtake you,

no disaster will come near your tent.

For He will command His angels concerning you

to guard you in all your ways...

Adam chose Scripture more offensive in nature, reading from Deuteronomy,

The Lord will cause your enemies who rise against

you to be defeated before you. They shall come out

against you one way and flee before you seven ways.

The group experience in our TOC was quite touching. These are words my guys needed to hear right now. Silently, I prayed for the Lord to put a cloak over us, to know that we were protected.

Later that day, Maj. Alia takes me aside, one-on-one, to say that after the softening artillery barrages and air force bombing runs, my Apaches will be "first on station." I knew this already and wonder why he's emphasizing it. Then he adds—unnecessarily to my way of thinking—"It goes without saying on a mission this big, command leads from the front." I guess he was taking the opportunity to mentor me. I had no intention of it being any other way. I didn't cherry-pick missions as the previous CO had done, but on a mission like this—one where we had been told to update our wills—you're damn right, I am in the first helicopter on station. Never ask your men to do anything you're not willing to do yourself, and remember, lead with intensity.

"Absolutely, sir," I said, my back stiffening. Alia expecting that from me is not a surprise. What was a surprise had come earlier from Fury 0-6, Lt. Col. Mennes, while I was walking the sand table. As I reached the area of our landing zone, he bored in on me:

"Capt. Slade, when the Apaches get to the LZ, the ROE is weapons-free. If anybody is on that LZ, I don't care who they are, they go away."

What he said is, "Kill anyone on the landing zone." We've never been weapons-free. It literally means you're cleared to shoot basically anything and anybody. And just in case I didn't fully get the message, he added, "Anybody on that LZ? They go away. You understand?" He looked me right in the eyes with laser-focused intensity, and man, I could tell this commander had seen and done stuff and would do a lot more in his army career.

"Got it. Yes, sir."

CHAPTER 18

OP. MAR KARADAD—
DAY 1

MUSA QALA TAKEDOWN

Lead from the Front

Kandahar Air Base, December 7, 2007—It's always fun to watch Pooh Bear squeeze into the front seat of an Apache. Lockheed's designers never anticipated that the army would choose to train a six one, 265-pound competitive bodybuilder as a pilot for their beefy-but-cramped gunship, but that's somehow what happened when Adam Smoot joined up. Before the army, the captain—who's on loan to us from the 82nd—had competed multiple times in the Collegiate National Powerlifting Championships and had a dead-lift best of 622.8 pounds. You'd think a guy like that would have a nickname like Jackstand but no. One of his buddies in the 82nd told me that his reportedly petite wife calls him Pooh Bear. Of course, his secret is safe with me—until maybe, uh, the next time I see him.

So here we are, walking around the aircraft on the pads at Kandahar, waiting for our precisely planned time to launch, officially kicking off Op Mar Karadad. We have briefed, preflighted the aircraft meticulously, and talked contingencies until we are blue in the face. We are prepared, but still, there is that anxiousness. We're not nervous but definitely not relaxed. It's kind of like a mix between waiting for a spanking you know is coming as a kid and waking up on Christmas morning. Both are anticipatory in nature but very different. This was both of those feelings at the same time. I know I should eat something, but that's risky. I have adrenaline gut. It takes me back to any number of key sporting events: a wrestling tournament or a crucial football game. You know your opponent, you've studied them, and now you're staring at them (or in this case, know where they are). You practice, you train, and you're ready, but there is that tense eagerness that persists until first contact, until kickoff. Until we lift off. Until we pull a trigger. Once that initial event happens, a type of adrenaline-fused relief and calm replace the anxiousness and it's game on. Everyone's lost in their own thoughts; we can still hear the S-2's ominous prediction. Screw that; we got this. Crap! Let's go already. Let's do what we do!

I'm flying with Jack Denton in my front seat, and in Chalk 2 is Jeff Lynch, with Pooh Bear as his copilot. We are geared up with rotors at 100 percent now, minutes away from the most deliberate op any of us have ever been a part of. I can see all the infantry getting loaded onto the assault birds that will take off about twenty minutes after us. I am sure their anxiety rivals ours. I know there's only one thing we can give them to quell that game-day tumult: they need to hear from us that the LZ is ICE—meaning cold, meaning the chances they'll get shot down are reduced. I like that we will be in front. We know it's the most dangerous place to be, but my guys with this awesome machine are a force to be reckoned with. If a tone needs to be set, my guys are the right ones to do it, and you want that done from the onset. Punch first, punch hard, and you will likely not have to go as many rounds.

The clock clicks down; finally, liftoff in *five, four, three, two.*

It's a clear day, with the sun still well above the horizon when we get airborne and head north-northwest over desert toward our first checkpoint in the execution matrix, where "Milwaukee" is our call. That's the call that I'd already walked through in that tent back at Kandahar, the call that triggers the assault to lift and start heading our way. The plan is to stay west of the green zone and well west of FOBs Robinson and Inkerman, where Royal Marines have begun lobbing artillery rounds to sow confusion and begin softening up the outskirts of Musa Qala in preparation for the ground troops.

Actually, the prep involves both DEAD and SEAD, acronyms for "destruction of enemy air defenses" and "suppression of enemy air defenses." The idea is to not only physically knock out Taliban surface-to-air missile (SAM) sites and anti-aircraft artillery (AAA) but to render their guidance and tracking systems impotent by using a variety of electronic warfare schemes deployed from specialized aircraft flying high over the battlefield.

As we approach the primary landing zone, we can see the artillery rounds finding their targets a quarter to a half mile out my right door. The explosions are powerful, sending clouds of dirt and debris flying. Through the canopy of the Apache, we can only see the explosions, but the visual is striking enough I can almost feel the impact; I imagine what it must sound like. What we don't see is any evidence that B-52 and B-1 bombers flying from Al Udeid Air Base in Doha, Qatar, have arrived on schedule to play their part in Operation Mar Karadad. They have missed their first two ex-check calls; we should have heard when they lifted off and declared their readiness to initiate the bombing runs.

The intricate plan had the air force bombing all the known sites that could overwatch the landing zone ten minutes prior to the arrival of the sixteen Chinooks and ten Black Hawks carrying the infantry. Then we're supposed to show up five minutes prior and see if the LZ is clear. And then five minutes later, the air assault begins. But the air force has screwed the pooch.

"We're running ten minutes late. You guys need to get out of there; we need a ten-minute rolex [delay]," is what they tell us.

Jack responds, just to me on the intercom, "No man, we're not turning this six-hundred-person air assault because you guys are ten minutes late. Sorry, you got out of the pool a little late in Qatar, but we're not turning this thing around."

He wasn't being flippant. With daylight waning, there's no lag time in the schedule for us to wait for the air force. The assault birds are now en route and that's a lot of helicopters to put in a holding pattern.

Hearing this, I preemptively call C-2, the command-and-control bird, and tell them we are comfortable pressing without them. My hope is we give Fury 0-6 a warm fuzzy, and we don't push this back; there are a lot of dominos to stop, and the chances of somebody not getting the word could cause a colossal cluster. It's in those moments, historically speaking, that a primed enemy can turn the tide of a battle.

"Arrow, this is Corsair. Continue as fragged to clear LZ and report when ICE."

"Arrow copies all. Wilco." Yes! Either my plan worked or they're thinking the same thing I am. Either way, we are moments away from officially being the first friendlies in the Taliban stronghold's airspace for quite some time.

The full responsibility to clear the area is now on us. But as we get within visual distance of the LZ, I can't believe my eyes. It's a full-on bazaar right where those inbound helicopters are aiming to set down. We see literally hundreds of unarmed dudes—men, women, children, goats, dogs, pigs, and chickens—all doing their thing on the western side of the LZ. This is no good.

I tell Jack to double-check the grid coordinates. *We couldn't be in the wrong place, could we?* "The grid checks, sir. This is the LZ." Heavy on my mind are the words of Lt. Col. Mennes. "You're weapons free. Anybody on that LZ goes away. You understand, Capt. Slade?" We're right where we need to be, over a flat spot southwest of the city, not far from the Helmand River, now mostly a two-hundred-foot-wide dry riverbed. Now what? We can't just blow them away. We all know that. Orders are orders, but we're not robots. *I know. I'll pop some flares. Maybe that'll encourage them to expeditiously move their place of commerce elsewhere.*

Nope. That didn't work. We might as well have been sponsoring a fireworks show; they all just looked up as if we were the evening's entertainment. What's going on here? They're excited at seeing us, not worried. After a few more seconds of thought, I get on the interplane radio and describe my plan. "We're going to use the gun to herd them off the LZ." Denton's semi-verbal, "Uh...okay?" response on the intercom is best interpreted as, "You're going to do what?"

My wingman's response requires no interpretation. Jeff says, "Say again, sir?" His misgivings are clear. I've just decided to use a machine gun that pretty much fires grenades to clear the landing zone. You won't find the technique taught at Rucker. Let's call it a field expedient. Our mission? Clear the LZ without collateral damage, and do it *posthaste*. Will it work? I'll know in a few seconds.

"We are going to use the 30 mm to encourage these guys to get."

I wazz up the 30 and fire a short burst at the eastern perimeter. The reaction was cartoon-like. One dude in black man-jammies jumped up in the air, and I swear his legs were pumping as though he was riding an imaginary bicycle. I almost expected to see the word Z-OOO-MMM spelled out in a cartoon smoke trail behind him. Dogs, goats, chickens, and people are now in full get-the-hell-out-of-dodge mode, and they knew which way to run due to the exploding ground showing them which way not to.

In a matter of minutes, I relay up the chain to Fury 0-6 that the LZ had a bazaar on it, but we were able to clear it. It is now ICE. We quickly get a message back that—I'm guessing because the LZ was full of folks and the air force was a no-show—a decision's been made to go to the alternate landing zone, which is at least four kilometers to the west. We instantly realize this means the troops will be forced to ruck their hundred-pound packs for several hours in the dark before they're in positions surrounding the city.

I feel this added effort by the ground guys truly isn't needed because I'm certain the LZ is ICE and because I like our visibility on any potential threats at this site. I remember studying the imagery of the alternate LZs and thinking they were not nearly as good as the primary. So I try one more time. "Be advised, I think you're good for the primary LZ. It's clear, nothing on the berms. We see nothing suspicious. The LZ is ICE." I know there are also intel and reconnaissance platforms above us—manned and unmanned aircraft—providing them with real-time imaging that would have backed up my report. Of course, those same platforms may have caught just how many 98.6s were on the LZ before our ballistic herdsmanship took place. The response comes back quickly; they're going to stick with the alternate landing zone.

"Okay, guys, let's do this again."

"Jack, get us a fly-to."

"Uh, yes, sir, just head west and I'll get it punched in." Our two birds immediately head west of Musa Qala, looking for the new LZ. What I didn't realize is that Jack hadn't built the coordinates for the alternate into our flight plan. Since there were so many tactical reference points, targets, and checks on this mission, he had to cut out some points. His thought was, *we never use the alternate*, so when he directed me to fly west, it was navi-guessing until he could find the grid coordinates on his kneeboard and fat finger them into our nav system.

When we quickly arrive at the spot, the first thing we notice is elevated ground all around the LZ, which is great cover and concealment for our infilling infantry; however, that elevated ground also serves as high ground for the enemy. Worse yet, there are also several caves in that high ground. I didn't like the idea of abadabas lying in wait in even one of those caves.

We need to deal with this now. I key the mic. "Hey, Jeff, your helicopter sluggish?"

"Yeah, kind of. What're you thinking?"

"Let's get rid of some weight and fix that. We are going to stick a Hellfire in each of those caves." We were flying Hellfire heavy based on the intel briefs.

"Sounds good, sir!" *Weird how no one ever turns down launching Hellfires.*

Between our two ships, we put one one-hundred-pound, sixty-four-inch-long guided missile into every cave that could harbor bad guys. The AGM-114 missile is thermobaric—it uses oxygen from the surrounding air to generate a high-temperature explosion and pressure wave. It's especially destructive when used against fortifications including tunnels, bunkers, and caves because of the sustained blast wave that has a devastating effect on internal organs.

"Corsair, this is Arrow 0-6. The alternate LZ is ICE."

"Copy, Arrow. Package is two mikes out." I could see the long string of helos on the horizon snaking their way toward us, pretty awesome really, and I begin hearing Wagner's "Flight of the Valkyries" in my head. *Da Dun da da DUN dun, Dun da da Dun dun. Well, that's stuck in my head now.*

"Jeff, let's climb up a bit into overwatch."

This is the most vulnerable these guys would be, on short approach loaded with infantry. They land in pairs, the troopers pouring out rapidly, just as they'd rehearsed, over and over. One aircraft getting hit would not only be catastrophic for those onboard, but it would significantly complicate the rest of the insertion. On full alert, we scan the high ground and any nook or cranny where a bad guy could be lying in wait. But one by one, the helicopters land, infantry spilling out of them like ants, and then they take off, no issues. *Okay, last two, aaand that's it; they're airborne. What a relief, but now they get to go home; we get to stay and play. We don't have it as bad as the guys on the ground, though. Those guys are in for a night.*

Bottom line: the infill of those 600 troopers is uneventful. Step one has proven intel predictions incorrect. I'm hoping it's the first of many erroneous predictions. Now the infantry must start their slog to get through a dry valley to their preplanned overwatch positions surrounding the city. The ground guys have NVGs, but they depend on gathering ambient light and using it to provide a green-tinged image of whatever they're pointed at. But when it's almost pitch-black out there, it's a struggle.

Our new assignment is to recon their path of movement. Given the lack of ambient light, we are relying much more on FLIR images than NVGs.

Not long after we begin flying the route, we spot several military-aged men alongside a truck with a tarp over the cargo, parked just outside a walled compound. "Don't think those guys are barbecuing." We contact Fury 0-6 Actual, who is leading his troops on the ground, and he tells us, "Keep an eye on it, and if they don't get out of the way, you guys are going to have to make it happen." A few minutes later, we get a message from the Predator drone overhead that they've spotted several men alongside a truck with what appears to be a heavy machine gun (HMG) under a tarp. They give us a grid. It's the same truck we've already spotted. I relay that info to Fury 0-6. That's enough suspicious activity for him. He tells us to take it out.

On the radio, I coordinate with Jeff in Chalk 2. "Okay, we'll line up and run from north to south and engage through the compound wall." The wall will act as additional fragmentation when our rockets hit it, and we should easily destroy all the military fighting-age males as well as the truck. I roll in, setting up on a long inbound leg to shoot rockets while Jack is heads down locking them up in the TADS (Target Acquisition System and Designation Sight). Just as I'm about to pull the trigger, my naked eye catches this eight-to-ten-foot flame that crosses right in front of us. It looks like the flame from a blowtorch on steroids and leaves a corkscrew smoke trail I can see in the FLIR. My mental computer goes into overdrive. *RPGs don't leave smoke trails like that or have that big of a flame. What was that? Holy crap, I think it was a SAM.*

"Jack, I think we had a SAM cross in front of us. Probably a seven, possibly a fourteen." I'm thinking, *It must have been a SAM-7 because our systems will make a seven go dumb in the air, if it even makes it out of the tube. Okay, the intel said they had SAMs and the capability to fire. I guess they got that prediction right.*

The SAM-7 is a lightweight, shoulder-fired, surface-to-air missile system. It uses passive infrared homing guidance designed to target low-flying aircraft, destroying them with a high explosive warhead.

Then Jack, who was looking at his tactical display when the missile flew by, says to me, "I didn't see it. It didn't happen." It's a monotone soaked in sarcasm. That's Jack. I doubt he even looked up from the TADS. He knew there was no sense worrying about it now; we are still on our gun run.

From the Apache right behind us, I hear Jeff ask, "What was that?"

"Jeff, Jack said he didn't see it, so I guess it didn't happen." It's always good when you can have a little levity on a rocket run.

This all happens in a few seconds. I am still lined up and fire three rockets. *Pffft...* First one is over the wall. *Dangit! Pffft...Pffft...* Next two are through it. "Good hits, 0-6 out."

"Arrow 2-1 in," Jeff calls as he finishes the job on the truck, leaving pieces scattered everywhere, presumably including the bad guys.

Just a few moments later, our replacements arrive; we execute a handoff giving them a sit-rep and encouraging them to keep their heads on a swivel. "SAMs out here, guys. Make sure your counter-measure systems are up and running." Then we turn south and head back to Kandahar where we'll hand the birds to the next crews and then bed down.

The op plan has us right back here tomorrow at noon, just about the time the Taliban likes to attack. The fact that nothing serious has happened yet just adds to my concern that tomorrow is going to be hellish.

Considering the dark premonitions that had been presented to us at pre-op briefings, the first day of Operation Mar Karadad was little more than routine, except for the SAM. We'd made sure to cover for the air force. We'd actually cleared two landing zones. We had done what we could to make the going easier for our 600 buddies on the ground. I'll hesitantly call that a success so far.

As I try to sleep, my thoughts are with the guys who are still flying, knowing that by now the Taliban we'd routed earlier in the day could be regrouping and planning something. This is going to be a long night.

* * *

Twelve hours later and we're doing it all over again, back in our aircraft, headed up to Musa Qala. Same crews as last night. I was right about the long night, pretty sure I didn't sleep. I actually headed back to the TOC and slept in my office, just in case something bad were to go down. But not much activity had been reported on the radios through the night. The infantry got to their spots and by now were dug in.

"Fury 1-1, Arrow 0-6 checking in. Two AH-64s, full load of rockets, 300 rounds 30 mm, four Hellfires each. Two hours plus thirty playtime. Anything going on? Or anything you want us to check out?"

"Arrow 0-6, so far it's pretty quiet. If you want to check out the wadi just to our east, we will be moving down through it in the next couple hours."

"Wilco." *Pretty quiet? Was the intel on this place really that far off? We were expecting so much more resistance. Maybe the whole pacifistic approach of warning and threatening made the Taliban hightail it rather than prepare to fight.* I wouldn't call it tactical blue balls but more like tactical dissatisfaction. Yet at the same time, part of me is grateful, considering our timeline to RIP (relief in place) out of here and return home.

We do check out the wadi, and it's NSTR (nothing significant to report). We fly some circles over the ground guys, using our sensors to scan the city. Still NSTR. "Hey, Jeff, let's go check out that compound we engaged last night."

"Roger that." Jeff and his copilot, Adam, follow us back to the grids of that engagement. We fly over, and Jack locks it up on our multifunctional display, scanning over the disintegrated wall, the burned hulk of a truck, terrorist body parts, and what's that? As I look closer, I see it's half of a donkey; the other half is about ten feet away. I do vaguely remember seeing a donkey on our first pass over the area last night but not on our gun run. I can't resist. I key the mic. "Looks like Pooh Bear killed Eeyore." Sorry, PETA.

Time flies when you're having fun. We're now bingo on fuel, and our replacements are here. As we leave the area, I can't help but think, *Is this what Musa Qala is going to be? I guess I should be grateful, but wow, there was so much buildup to this mission. We're headed to Bastion just to refuel, not rearm, because we didn't shoot at anything.*

My discomfort with how it was painted to be versus how it's panning out would be short lived. That whole regrouping thing I was thinking about last night? It was actually happening. We just weren't aware of it. Yet.

CHAPTER 19

OP. MAR KARADAD— DAY 2

THE PRETZEL MANEUVER

Good Teams Trust Each Other

Camp Bastion, Helmand Province, December 8, 2007—Waiting to refuel at the FARP in Bastion, my mind begins to wander, and I begin to conceive of a new plan to engage the Taliban leaking south out of the conflict area. *What if, instead of flying straight up north to relieve the guys currently overhead at Musa Qala, we cut over to the green zone and verify the abadabas aren't wanting to fight on our way up?*

I'm doing my best not to think about going home after a long year dealing with everything Afghanistan has thrown at us. That's the proverbial light at the end of the tunnel. But even though I'm doing my best not to focus on it, it's still there, in my peripheral vision. Every once in a while, I can't help myself and I dream about the cool breezes on a mountain I own, relaxing in a cabin surrounded by pine trees, a personal chef, a private plane standing by to take me anywhere, and a blissful reunion with my wife. Okay, so I said it's been a long year. A guy can dream, can't he? I mean, I know the blissful reunion may be a lot to ask for.

Truth be told, this morning was pretty much like most others—no weather. It's not hot, but it is still warm enough to make the glass canopy act as a greenhouse, cooking its contents. It's always a treat to climb into the Apache and feel hotter than two mice doing it in a wool sock under a furnace.

This morning, I actually did wake up laughing. The instructional presentation my wingman, Jeff Lynch, gave the company the other day cracked me up. Jeff is a very intelligent guy with a propensity to talk fast when he gets nervous. So he gets up in front of the company and says, "I'm going to go over this forbatim," instead of *verbatim*. I could tell he didn't just misspeak. He actually thought the word was *forbatim*. Not one to let an opportunity for a laugh or to bust his balls get away, I stop him mid-mile-a-minute speaking. "Say that again."

And he does, pausing though, since he can see I caught something in how he said what he said. Reluctantly, he repeats, slower this time, which only emphasizes his misspeak more. "I—am going to go over this—forbatim." But it sounds like *for Batim*.

Most of the company saw where I was headed, trading glances with each other grinning, which caused Jeff to shuffle a little, anticipating a shoe coming but not knowing yet from where or why. I couldn't resist. "Anybody else know who Batim is? If not, I don't know who we're doing this for." Jeff stood there smiling obliviously, but that landed; everybody gut-laughed. One thing was for certain: the day would come when Lynch would give it back to me. Probably sooner rather than later, but ever the professional, I am sure he will put a "sir" on the end of it. It's all good; I expect nothing less. Don't dish if you can't take.

"Looks like the tanks are full," my front-seater, Jack Denton, says, breaking me out of my headspace.

"Jack, what do you think about us heading east from here, then turning north to travel up the green zone?"

His response is pitch-perfect. "If that's where the bad guys are, that's where we should be." He says this in his matter-of-fact minimal-emotion voice. *That's exactly what I was thinking. I just wanted to sanity check it against Jack.* He is a mild-mannered professional, but that in no way means he is timid; Jack has a level of intestinal fortitude many lack. Make no mistake, this is flexing and taunting at its best. We want to send a message: "Johnny Taliban, we know where you are and if need be, we'll deal with you. Best get to farming. Or keep moving on." I relay the plan to Jeff and his front-seater, Capt. Adam Smoot, and they're instantly onboard with the plan. Got to love true attack guys.

The Helmand River Valley is essentially a big river of green in the middle of a vast desert of brown. We call it the green zone, but don't get that confused with, for example, the green zone in Baghdad, which is a fortified, usually safe area for the allies. This green zone is not the safe area; it's where the bad guys hide. It's both urban and rural. We have forward operating bases interlaced along its edges, and the ground pounders routinely patrol into the green.

We knew that our psy-ops unit had papered Musa Qala with leaflets urging the locals to leave before our attack, and the result of that would likely cause enemy troops to filter down into the green zone. Now, as we're flying a patrol as low as one hundred feet but keeping our speed up, we're pretty much saying, "Go ahead, shoot at us, and it's going to be a bad day for you."

Part of the Green Zone, from an Apache ready with rockets and Hellfire Missiles. Courtesy of Kevin Eaton.

We'd been flying for about fifteen minutes without drawing any fire that we knew of, when the common air-to-ground (CAG) frequency erupts. "Apache in the area, this is FOB Rob."

"This is Arrow 0-6. Go ahead."

"We got a truck that we believe is launching IDF. We'd like you to check it out."

"Yeah, absolutely. Send grid." The IDF in this case is most likely mortars. The Taliban uses different kinds of trucks, usually little Nissans or Toyotas, including one that we call a bongo truck. They look like the love child of a minivan and a flatbed truck. They would Mad Max those things out, welding mortar base plates or heavy machine-gun mounts onto the flatbed.

I'm in the lead, and we both fly to the grid we'd been given by the FOB radio operator. Our plan is to circle back and sweep the area with our sensor, but we don't need it. Score one for the Mark One Eyeball; with our bare eyes, we can see the bongo right away. Jack slaves the tactical acquisition and display system and tells me, "That truck looks weighted down." I've heard that before; might be time to give a bongo truck wings.

"Let's go down close and look," I tell Jack, which is probably overaggressive or flirting with that line. We drop down to maybe twenty or thirty feet but see nothing. No people in the truck. It looks pretty benign, but months of experience here tell me they might have hopped out and taken cover in the tree line. If they're smart, that's what they should do and stay there, because although we may be hanging it out a little, Jeff has our six from above. Anyone decides to get froggy, the club's coming.

I call the FOB, which is about two or three miles away, and tell them we're not seeing anything suspicious, and I'm actually in the middle of describing the scene when I interrupt myself. "Rob, standby. We're engaging. I'll get back to you." Muzzle flashes off my nose. Jack is quick with the 30 mm answering back. Jeff can see we are engaging even before I say anything.

Usually, Jeff would be behind me in a supportive role. But we had been circling the bongo truck, and once we did our low pass, we took a straight-line path out of there. For some reason, Jeff stayed in the circle for a bit, leaving him ninety degrees out from our position and spit out in distance, meaning he was farther away from us than we typically were for mutual support. I think, *This may be why these jackwagons decided to open fire on us.* I look his way and see a flaming basketball headed right for him. It's red, round, pretty big, and getting bigger. The bad guys have targeted him with a recoilless rifle and it looks as though it's going to hit him head-on. I'm sure he can't see it coming at him because the visibility looking down, directly in front of you in the Apache, is pretty crappy.

"Break right, now!" I call, a lot of urgency in my voice. We'd been in a lot of engagements, so this wasn't something unexpected, but I'm thinking, *Oh, guess there's a few dudes here wanting to dance.* But what compels the urgency in my voice is that I can see the trajectory is right on target. *If Jeff doesn't do something instantly, he's going to get hit, and that's a big round. That isn't a let's-fly-it-home-with-battle-damage round; it's a freakin' let's-try-to-make-this-a-survivable-crash round. Not good.* I don't get amped up too much in these moments; my voice stays relatively calm most of the time. But there's an inflection, like, "Break right, now! I'm in hot!" It needs to be immediate, and he knows it, complying just in time to avoid a lead enema.

Our default for patrols like this is that my front-seater has the 30 mm wazzed and slaved to his reticle or the TADS, and I've got rockets selected. Why choose TADS over the eyeball view through the reticle? There could be a number of reasons, but here's one that comes up often: the effective range on the 30 mm is just over 2.5 miles—not that we are engaging at those distances. But with my eye, I can't see detail at distances beyond a few hundred meters, but the TADS can. We can switch off in an instant if we see something pop up or a muzzle flash by just saying, "Pilot gun"—select it on my cyclic castle switch, fire ten rounds with one pull of the trigger—"you have it back." It's all just a move of the thumb and trigger finger. The reason for the default is that the chain gun can fire pretty much in whatever direction the gunner is looking—as much as 120 degrees off the nose.

Knowing that Jeff has reacted to my warning, my job is to move so I can cover him. I saw the point of origin (POO) of the fireball, so I kick it off by firing two or three rockets. POO obliterated; now it's a party. In the meantime, he's yanking around to cover me because I'm shooting at what was just shooting at him. I figure he's going to get in the gunfight by hitting the same spot I did.

But as Jeff comes around, he sees something that's coming at me from yet another POO and directs me to "Break!" He catches me a little target-fixated on what I had just destroyed. His directive call brings me back instantly. No way he'd say that unless there's a reason, so in the middle of my shooting, I break right. Immediately. He's got tactical situational awareness on something I don't. I've got to listen. No time for "I'll get 'round to its." I already know I eradicated that first target. That guy's done, so there's obviously another one out here. I'm yanking the war machine around and looking for it. As I come around, he says, "You were taking fire from three o'clock; we're rolling in hot, zero nine zero."

"Copy, I got your six. Wait. Wait. Break left." I see him taking effective fire from yet another POO. He abbreviates his gun run, breaking out early due to my directive call. We roll in hot on that POO with 30 mm vibrating the airframe and rockets in between bursts. Okay, that one's gone.

On our breaks, we're not only changing direction, but we're climbing and descending as well. It's partially to make ourselves a harder target—a three-dimensional jink. But it's also to get that aircraft around quicker. So this time, I'm diving and coming back around. Almost doing a pirouette. Pitch up and turn around the nose. We call it a return target. We're flying right over the targets, in some cases giving them hell on the inbound, so that complete turn has to be quick to get weapon systems back on them before they have time to shoot up our tail feathers.

It's all rhythmic reaction: *Don't let them shoot him down; don't let them shoot us down; don't let them shoot him down.*

This is probably a good time to recall that an instructor once told me that flying an Apache in combat is like balancing a beach ball on a toothpick while riding a unicycle and reading a book while someone is hurling crap at you. I've never ridden a unicycle, but I have done the toothpick bit. Trust me, it's much easier than flying while you're shooting and getting shot at, not to mention a little bit safer.

They're throwing everything in their arsenal at us now. Muzzle flashes everywhere, with their white sparks looking like popcorn exploding from its kernel state. I yank my aircraft around to cover him only to see effective fire coming at him from his nine o'clock. I direct him, "Break right!" and I swear the rounds miss him by feet as he breaks. Big, flaming basketball rounds, recoilless rifle fire, no doubt. I haven't seen this much recoilless in one spot before and skillfully timed coordinated firing too. Next, I roll in hot on that POO only to hear Jeff tell me to break, as I'm now taking fire from—you guessed it—yet another POO. He rolls in on them; then I cover. *Hell, how many dudes are out here?* This dance goes back and forth like a sadistic tango. The whole earth decides to shoot at us from every direction with recoilless rifles in multiple positions, heavy machine guns, RPGs, AKs, and other small arms interspersed throughout.

I am on rocket runs, and Jack is hitting pop-up targets while we are on the runs, left and right. Both weapons systems can't fire at the exact same time, so rockets and 30 compete for air time, leaving basically no dead time. *GUGUGUGT.* The 30 hammers. *Pffft. Pffft. Pffft.* Three rockets away. *GUGUGUT, Pffft, Pffft, Pffft.* And so on. The problem is, we're fighting and covering, but we're also staying right in the kill box.

At one point, Jeff keys the mic, stuttering on the radio, "RRRR-RRR PG." He's stuttering because as he's saying it, it's happening, and he thinks it's lights out for us. It misses, and then he tells me it looked like it went right through our rotor system. It was that close. Possible, I suppose. God seems to be picking sides today, and so far it looks like he has chosen team Arrow! Another RPG airbursts right in front of Jeff, and he literally flies through the cloud, getting peppered with grenade bits.

We engage until all our rockets are gone, all our 30 mm is gone, but we're still taking fire. I tell Jeff, "I'm Winchester," then immediately interrupt myself. "Scratch that. We have Hellfires." Keeping Captain Nervous in the back of my mind, we would usually save Hellfires for buildings, vehicles, caves, and the like, but this pickup game calls for more lead. Crunch all you want! So we start flinging Hellfire missiles at enemy firing positions.

There's no discussion between our two aircraft about breaking contact and getting away. We can't. We're in the middle of a hornet's nest, and we are killing every damn hornet who reveals himself.

"You're taking fire. I'm killing that."

"I'm taking fire. You're killing that." It's all, *Bring it to the enemy; don't worry about the enemy bringing it to us.* The cousins came to play, and man, their game was solid, but we killed a lot of skilled fighters in only fifteen to twenty minutes of vehemence and fury. It seemed like hours in some ways and only seconds in others. It left me with my heart beating so hard that I think I can hear it, mouth open, and a primitive desire to beat my chest. *What the heck just happened?*

We go back to Bastion to rearm and refuel and to check the aircraft for holes. I'm thinking, *Those guys were on target, but we laid the hate. I am sure our birds are riddled with holes.* I'm still not clear on what we'd just been through. I just hadn't put it together yet.

We finally land at the end of the day, and that's when the tumblers fell into place and the picture of what happened made sense: that was a sophisticated, well-executed air ambush. By every measure, they should have gravity-checked at least one of our aircraft with that setup.

Adam would later tell me that he didn't believe he'd survive this engagement, that what saved us all was our training: the evasive maneuvers, the lightning-fast returns to target, the determination to cover the other person that was embedded in every fiber of our being, and the Almighty's hand watching over us.

During the fight, it was just like, WOW! There was lead flying up from everywhere. We didn't have time to figure out their game plan, and none of us had ever been in something orchestrated to that degree prior to that day.

Our after-action debrief is somewhat difficult. That's where we can clearly see there was a fallacy in our thought processes during the fight. I like the aggressiveness; we need to be aggressive. I love the mutual support and understanding of what the other bird would do, how the fight—albeit chaotic as hell—had a fluidity to it, creating a clarity of action in the midst of a tumultuous exchange of ordnance. Although there is solidarity in that, we also have to know when to break contact, tactically speaking. The argument could be made that we didn't *need* to break contact. We did it, after all. We swatted an overwhelming force, but to be honest, I feel there was a lot of grace of God in that.

Jeff and I both talk about it. I ask him, "Did you ever think of just bee-lining out of it?"

"No."

"Neither did I. It's because I was covering you and you were covering me, and they just kept popping up and I was covering you and you were covering me with extreme prejudice." This was one of the few times we were outgunned, actually the underdog. I paused and took a deep breath, pondering my own vulnerability and the fact that I flew with men who simply would not let the enemy take my life, nor would I let them take theirs. Individually, we both would have been toast; together, we destroyed an overwhelming force. "Hey, Jeff, thank you."

And the true miracle is that neither one of us got hit with anything. A frickin' miracle. I have no idea how that could be. Not a single hole—how is that even possible?

There's no real answer to that question. So much that happens in war is random and unfathomable. Could just be dumb luck. Or perhaps on that particular day, a higher power chose to watch over me rather than my pious enemy. Jeff and I both laugh, just grateful to be alive, knowing the Angel of Death had been nearby but left in defeat—this time.

I've been on flights where I wasn't even in a fight and there'd be holes and I didn't even know how I got hit. Understand, if small arms fire hits an Apache, we don't feel it inside. Even a 50 cal round we may not feel, unless it takes out something that affects the aircraft. Now an RPG, that's another story. I landed one time with a flat tire, and the ground crew told me, "There's two bullet holes through your tire."

We talk about it again the next day with everybody else because everybody needs to learn from it. Not everyone is getting in engagements, so there's someone who says, "Oh, you got in another one? What was this one?" It would've been real easy for us to just focus on the fact that we wrecked house—after all, we did—but there is a bigger lesson from that one, for sure. "Yeah, we wrecked house, but we did it the wrong way, tactically speaking."

I start off the after-action briefing by drawing on the whiteboard our two little ships, FOB Rob, and then, as best we could recall, the position and sequence of all the enemy fire and our reactions to it. By the time I'm done drawing, there are a lot of wide eyes and "holy craps" going around. What I had drawn was a bunch of curved lines representing our flight paths, and as you can imagine, it was a masterpiece: a twist of overlapping lines in an overall ellipse shape. I said, "So, gentlemen, I present to you the pretzel maneuver, a maneuver we did—for Batim," garnishing some chuckles. But I continue and say, "Now let's talk about how this was the wrong way to execute."

We did share that lesson. In fact, the lesson was put into practice a few days later when Jeff got into it again in the same area without me as his wingman—CW2 Chris Wright and 1st Lt. Will Ruiz got the honor—and this time, they broke contact. But like true warriors, they did not run from the fight. Rather, they fought it from the outside in, instead of fighting it from the kill box out. I was amazed there were still fighters left to fight in that area. Intel told us foot patrols went out after our engagement and they couldn't even count how many bad dudes were now *jihad complete. Maybe this is why Musa Qala has been relatively quiet. All those fancy-pants fighters intel had been warning us about just shifted south a bit so they could still maintain the element of surprise. Frickin' pamphlets!*

A day later, after the S-2 reviews our gun tapes, she tells us that we'd been surprised by the first highly orchestrated aerial ambush executed in Afghanistan by the Taliban. Not only was it deliberate in its setup and execution, but it was intended specifically for Apaches. They knew we would take the bait of indirect fire on the FOB, that it would draw us into their kill box. It was a tactic successfully used in Iraq, and the foreign fighters known as "the cousins," coming here to join the jihad, had brought it with them. Because of this being the first time it was employed in Afghanistan, our gun tapes were taken and classified as secret.

When Jack and I had a chance to reflect on the mission, he acknowledged that we—all of us—"after eleven months had gotten pretty complacent and maybe a little overconfident in our ability." In that deliberate tone of his, he said, "Going to try to stir some things up over there—it was not the right thing to do—from a survival standpoint. We didn't have kids, we're young, and we wanted to punish the enemy. We were just like, *Man, let's do this. Let's get these guys.*"

This was something I have noticed over and over again on this deployment. A righteous desire leads us to effort, which leads us to added confidence, which leads us to overconfidence and risky behavior. The risky behavior, if noticed in time, grounds us again, and we start over with righteous desire. It's the pride cycle and it's something that happens in all arenas of life. However, in this arena, the cycle can be self-critiquing—even terminally so.

Those intense moments, those moments where everything is faster but at the same time slows down, have deep impact on one's soul. How they interact with that soul, in my opinion, depends on how that soul has been prepared. One thing I know for certain is that I am deeply grateful for my brothers fighting with me that day. Captain Adam Smoot, 1st Lt. Jack Denton, and CW3 Jeff Lynch are all studs in my book. We were cohesive and emotionally invested in making sure we got each other out of there, and we did. The impact I mentioned is real; as I write this, I shake a little. Not out of fear. I shake and swell inside out of an awakening, an awakening of a past life's reality that carries with it a Thor-like punch.

To see my conversations with Lt. Denton and Capt. Smoot, go to www. clearedhot.info/pretzel.

CHAPTER 20

OP. MAR KARADAD– DAY 3

TALIBAN TURN THE TIDE

A Prepared Mind Can Literally Save Your Life

Musa Qala, Helmand Province, December 9, 2007—It's midday and the Taliban are right on schedule. Ever since the pretzel maneuver, every coverage rotation has had some interaction with the enemy. This is more what we were expecting, but so far, every time they get bold, we hand them humility, served hot. Yeah, that's tough-guy talk, but it sounds good, right?

In my front seat is CW2 Thomas "Otto" Malone, one of the augmentees down from Salerno for the Big Mish. It's our first time flying together. Normally, since we are flight lead, either I or my copilot would be doing this coordination with ground forces, but I had talked to Gladish and Denton before taking off, telling them they'd be taking TAC lead on the radios. That would allow me the latitude not only to assess Otto's strengths and weaknesses but to also instruct him during real-time interaction with ground forces. He is more than competent; he just needs to understand local area nuance and how we work together in a hunter-killer team down here. In fact, from what I have heard, he had gotten into the most engagements of any of the guys from Salerno. Of course, that is all relative; they didn't have the enemy presence up there that we do down here, so their high-time guy had quite a bit less experience dancing with the Taliban than some of our low-time guys. Otto is anxious to get into the fight, and we get a chance right off the bat. Ground forces had been taking DShK heavy machine-gun fire from an undercut cave above their position. Excellent opportunity for Otto to shoot the king of our ordnance arsenal, the Hellfire. Most guys in Salerno hadn't had the opportunity to fling one of those in actual combat, but Otto had actually fired three already. We are about to make it four. The cave is tucked into the side of a cliff, and since Hellfires hit from a top-down trajectory, our goal is to stick one of the thermo-baric versions right in the opening. It'll cause negative pressure in the cave and eliminate any life within its walls. The problem is that our run in was very short due to terrain, so he would have to get the cave locked up quick, squeeze laser and then trigger, so that we didn't violate the five-hundred-meter-minimum engagement criteria. The book says any closer than that and the missile most likely won't find its target.

We roll in on our first attempt. "Get it on there, man."

"Yeah, yeah, I am getting it."

"Six hundred meters, dude, you need to lock it up and squeeze!" It's obvious it isn't going to happen on this pass, so I break it off. "Okay, man, you see how quick that is? We will come in the exact same way. You just need to be Johnny-on-the-Spot."

"Yeah, I'll get it this time for sure."

We roll in, 600, 500, he still doesn't have it, but I can tell he is almost there, so I don't break; 450, and *whoosh*, the Hellfire is off the rails. We'd busted our minimum engagement range. Nevertheless, I keep trucking toward the target so Otto can hold the laser on it. Just when I'm certain we may have lost the missile, *BOOM!* It smacks the opening of the cave. I break away at 200 meters and let Otto know he just proved the book is wrong. He is pretty stoked, and we actually get a chance to shoot another one into a nearby cave, along with some 30.

Otto is riding the wave of excitement—he'd nearly doubled his entire deployment's worth of engagements in a single morning—when ground forces call us again for assistance.

Fury 1-1, in a command center near the base of Roshan Telco's cell tower on high ground at the southeastern edge of the city, tells us some of their ground patrols have been taking periodic small arms fire from a tree line directly across from their overwatch position. We respond and orbit while 1st Lt. Jack Denton, flying as front-seater for 1st Lt. Stephen Gladish in Chalk 2, works with the 82nd Airborne's HQ to refine exactly where they want us to engage.

Monitoring the radio freqs, it sounds as though Fury's troops, using an acoustic direction detection device on the incoming small arms fire, are close to getting us an azimuth, and I've got us on what would be an outbound leg. I slow a little, hoping we can make this next turn inbound a weapons-hot leg. *Slowing from one hundred knots to seventy at 300 feet above the ground. Don't like being this slow in this area, but I'll gain the speed back on my turn inbound.*

Then we get the call we've been waiting for. "Arrow 2-1, this is Fury. You are cleared to fire 30 mm on a 110 azimuth within two kilometers of the tower."

Okay, here we go. I start my turn as Jack confirms one last time. Otto has the gun and knows where we are going to shoot. "Arrow 2-1 understands clear to fire 30 mm on that azimuth within two kilometers of the tower."

I am in the middle of a fairly aggressive bank, initially trying to line up a shot against our enemies shooting from a tree line, when screams fill my helmet. They're coming from my copilot through the intercom system.

"AHHH!! AHHH, MAN. I AM SHOT. I'm shot in the leg!"

Also in my ear at exactly the same time is the audio warning from my helicopter, an intense, monotone female voice repeating, "Rotor RPM low. Rotor RPM low." My heart rate just jumped from sixty to, I don't know, two thousand beats per minute. That enemy has just given us instant feedback requiring me to alter my plan or succumb to theirs. Crazy as this may sound, I have more important matters to deal with right now than my screaming copilot, who is undoubtedly in excruciating pain.

I deduce quickly that the slow rotor is due to losing power in one engine. Additionally, my flight controls are locked up with the aircraft in a descending forty-degree bank. We are falling out of the sky. *Stay calm, act quick, be decisive.* We've already dropped one hundred feet. In the same instant that I realize my controls are jammed and the rotor is decaying, I know I need to do two things right now: break out of the mechanical control we typically have in the Apache and counterintuitively reduce the collective quickly to regain rotor rpm.

The Apache is designed with a backup control system—we call it BUCS. To engage it, the mechanical linkage between my cyclic—the stick between my knees controlled by my right hand—and my copilot's has to be physically snapped.

It is designed to do this for instances such as the one we find ourselves in, but it does take some force applied through the jam to sever the connection. That literally means I have to slam the cyclic with my right hand to the left. I suspect that the controls are jammed because Otto's mangled leg is entangled with his cyclic. What I have to do is going to hurt him.

According to Boeing, the backup control system requires one second to take effect. They call it a one-second easy-on. The reason for that built-in hesitation is that in order to physically break the linkage, the designers knew the pilot may have to slam the controls to an extreme position, which could cause the Apache to roll over out of control if an immediate correction isn't applied.

This is exactly the situation we find ourselves in. I was already banking left and had already started to correct it when the controls jammed. In order to get into BUCS, I have to snap the controls hard left in the direction of our bank. (Reading this explanation is taking so much longer than the time in which I had to do it.) And that's what I do. I slam the cyclic to the left, breaking the mechanical linkage, praying the one-second easy-on works as advertised, allowing me to recenter the cyclic before it takes effect. If this doesn't work, we'll snap-roll this aircraft, and given the power-limited state we are in, it will likely be unrecoverable, resulting in an upside-down landing. Those never turn out well. Otto's screams increase when I do this, which tells me my assumption about why it was jammed is correct.

Simultaneously with my inputs to the cyclic, I slam the collective down with my left hand, reducing the pitch in the blades, resulting in recapturing flyable rotor rpm. Although it also causes us to lose more altitude, we're flying—I think. All that happens in less than three seconds. Deep breath. Just one, no time for two.

Throughout all this, Otto hasn't stopped screaming. "Ohhhhh, dammit! My leg. Oh, God." My mind's trifurcated, if that's a thing: one part needs to communicate with our wingman, another with my copilot. And the third has to remember everything I was taught and have since learned about what keeps a damaged AH-64 in the air. *Keep the spinny thing spinny.* Try patting your head and rubbing your belly while explaining what you're doing to two different people on opposite sides of the room, all while bad guys are firing rounds at you.

I transmit quickly and succinctly to Chalk 2. "My front-seater's shot in the leg; I'm in BUCS. Headed in." They read my between-the-lines message. *I am still super busy; please don't bug me. Tell the world.* I'm still monitoring external coms and hear Gladish and Denton do exactly what I hoped they would do. As they relay the info to Fury HQ and start the communication back to the house (Bastion), they fall in on my six to provide cover to our wounded bird. I love these guys. (We found out later, they had also taken rounds, some in their tail rotor, which is a very bad place to be compromised by enemy fire. Fortunately, their bird had absorbed the rounds with no ill effects.)

I take a second to talk with Otto, trying to calm him down. Since we're in separate compartments, one behind the other, I can't see his leg. "Put pressure on your blood." Not the clearest of instructions, but it's what comes out of my mouth.

"Oh, jeez, my leg is so jacked up, dude."

"Put pressure on it."

"I don't know where it went in. Sonofabitch! My leg is so swollen right now."

Somewhere in my mind, first-aid lessons kicked in. *If his leg is swollen, then the bleeding might be internal. Not spraying all over. Could be a good thing?*

Since my left engine is producing little to no power, our bird is pretty much imitating a migrating goose with one wing shot to shreds, but I'm eking out every knot I can. *We've got to put some distance between us and this place. If we have to stick it down, so be it, but not in firing range of known Taliban fighting positions.* I'm balancing the power pull between max available and power limiting—too much power, we crash; too little, we crash. The helicopter is on a thin power margin, but it is flying.

I know Otto is hit in his leg, but did it sever his femoral artery? That's a death sentence where we sit. "Otto, where are you hit?" He's no longer screaming, but I can almost feel his pain when he answers.

"My leg is so jacked up, dude." *That's not the answer I need to assess, but at least he's talking and lucid. He's substantially calmer than he was three minutes ago, but I still need him to calm down even more so he can describe his wound.*

"Okay, man. Just calm down, and I need you to tell me where you are hit."

Right then, I hear CW5 Chris Walker's voice on the radio. He's in the area escorting a Chinook. I immediately key the mic. "Hey, Chris, my front-seater is shot in the leg. I am in BUCS and headed back to Bastion." I throw that out there simply because I know Chris is a very

experienced pilot and likely would have some valuable advice, something I would gladly take at the moment. He assesses the situation,
sees my wingman on our six, and urges me to "keep flying south.
Our prayers are with you. We got the fight." No gems of wisdom in
what he said, yet comforting all the same in that everyone's eyes are
focused on getting us back.

Back to Otto. "How's your blood, man?" *Dang it, losing altitude, reduce
power, pitch up a little to gain what I've lost.*

Laboring heavily, he says, "I don't know dude; I can't see anything."

"Keep your pressure, keep your pressure on the blood."

"Tryin'. I don't know where it went in."

"Does it have an exit wound?" *Losing altitude again. Squeeze back into
parameter. Stay calm, prioritize. What else do I need to make sure gets done?*

"Ahh, I don't know. All I know is that my leg is swollen. There's blood
everywhere."

We will need medical support ready for us. "Hey, Chris, relay to Bastion
to have ambulance standing by."

"Oh man, oh man, this sucks," Otto says, as I hear Chris transmit
"Wilco" in the background.

"All right, man, just calm down." *Easy for me to say. I don't have a hole
in my leg, but I need good info from him.* "Are you dizzy?"

"Yeah, a little." *Does that mean he is close to passing out, or is it just due
to the excruciating pain he's in?*

"You need to put pressure on the blood. You need to find the entrance and exit wounds."

"I don't know where it went in."

"Okay, feel down your leg and try to find the hole." *Clock's ticking. If he has a bleeder, we need to identify it. I may need to put this helicopter down in the desert and have the Chinook transload him so they can get him stable. Can he survive the twenty-five minutes we have left to fly to Bastion?*

"Ahhhh, I can't move."

"You're okay, you're okay. Just find that hole." My eyes are scanning over all my engine readouts. *I know we were obviously hit in multiple places; we lost power; the controls were jammed. It wouldn't surprise me if we have another situation developing silently that will cause yet another emergency.* To my relief, it looks as though all my indications are in normal operating range, except power from my number one engine, which I already knew. Then it hits me. I say aloud to myself, "I don't think I let anybody know that." *How could that be? Let's rectify that with a full info dump. They're probably wondering what's going on but didn't want to bother me.*

"Be advised, guys, I am in single engine. I am in BUCS. My front-seater was shot in the leg, but he is talking to me and I think it's under control." *Losing altitude again.* Chris hears the call and must be thinking the same thing I was regarding the transload option.

"Brian, let us know if you need any Chinook support."

"Roger, we will continue to assess. If it gets worse, I may need to roll this thing on in the desert and get him to the Chinook."

Back to Otto. "Did you find the hole, buddy?"

"No, dude. My leg is broken above the knee."

"You need to find where you are hit."

"I think my leg is gone, like blown off, dude." *What did he just say? It's gone? No, that doesn't add up with everything communicated so far. He would know, right? That has to be shock talking. Someone just said something about our engine on the radio. What?*

"Say again, Steve."

"Just to let you know, no smoke or fire coming from your engine." *Finally, some good news.*

"Roger that." Back again to Otto. "I need you to keep talking to me, and I still need you to find that wound."

"I can't."

"Yes, you can!" Much firmer than I'd spoken to him till now. "Calm down, and reach down your leg, slide your hand until you find that wound." He just moans. "Listen, listen, listen to me. Take your hand."

"I'm trying, dude. I think I have my hand on the entrance wound. I don't think there's an exit."

Okay, now we are getting somewhere. Ah, what's that? Erratic control inputs. Oh, great. Come on, girl, I plead in my head to the bird, no more surprises. Just get us home. "You have your hand on the entrance wound, okay. You push down on it as hard as you can."

"I am pulling up on it because it's on the bottom of my leg." *Duh! Of course it's on the bottom. They didn't shoot at us from the sky.*

"You keep pressure on that as hard as you can. We are going to make it. They have medics on standby at Bastion and they'll get you fixed up. You just keep talking to me and keep that pressure on your leg." *Okay, now what? What am I missing? Aircraft is flying, check; communicated to whoever needs the info, check; copilot's wound under control, check. Oh, yeah, where am I flying? I headed south in the general direction of Bastion, but I do not have a flight plan in the nav system. Last thing I want to do is add to our flight time by not taking the most direct route. I can't have Gladish input a flight plan and take the lead. If we fall out of the sky, he's got to be behind us, where he can see where we go down. If I'm trailing him, that won't happen.*

The flight controls in BUCS are not nearly as responsive as they are with the primary system. They are very sloppy, have delayed reaction, like drunk driving, I suppose. I carefully take my left hand off the collective and select control measure C65 (Bastion) and build a direct flight plan.

Otto and I keep talking. I need to keep his mind on task but at the same time distracted from what just happened. First try: "Hey, man, you're alive, brother." *Yeah, that's good, Slade. Tell him he could've died but didn't.*

All that nets is a raw "It hurrrrrrts."

Second try: "Yeah, that's good! Pain is good. It means your nerves are working like they are supposed to." *What the heck am I saying? I have no idea if that's true or not. I am just trying to reassure him.*

"I can't move my leg."

Third try: "Well, you got a hole through it, so I think that's normal." *Where did that come from? I just committed medical malpractice with my mouth.* "Just keep that pressure. You're sure there's no exit wound on top?" *If he has an undiscovered exit wound, he could still be bleeding out and not realize it.*

"I don't have anything through the top."

"Keep talking to me."

"I'm good. I'll let you know if I pass out," he says with a pain-riddled laugh.

"I don't know how you do that... The fact that you're talking to me is money. I mean, it could've been your head." *Did I really just say that? This is where I want to get him mentally focused on what needs to be done but not on what is happening pain-wise. We have been flying for only nine minutes since he got hit, but, man, it feels like a lifetime. Good news is, it can't be a femoral artery or we wouldn't be having a conversation at this point.* "Otto, do you have a water bottle?"

He says he does. "Keep the pressure on your leg. Get to your water bottle, grab that, and take some drinks." I recall the times I have been in excruciating pain with significant injuries like my missing finger; a cool drink of water was so much more than just a cool drink of water. It was sustenance, a refocus tool. Otto needs that right now.

I shoot an update out to my wingman on interplane, making note of how I am giving it all I can, but we are power limited. Chris Walker chimes in and says I should feel free to jettison my wings stores. Aaaand...there's the gem of wisdom I knew he would provide. Why the heck hadn't I thought of that? Getting rid of our rocket pods, the Hellfire racks, and missiles would reduce weight and parasitic drag. "Great idea, Chris."

I find a clear spot over the desert, tell my wingman to take spacing so nothing hits him, and press the jettison button. Never having hit the button before, I'm not sure what to expect. *Maybe there'll be a pop or an explosion.* All we feel is a real quiet little bump. Kind of like a guy pointing a gun at you and pulling the trigger, but the only thing that happens is a flag popping out that says "BANG."

Otto shares my sentiment. "That was it? I thought it would be bigger."

In Chalk 2, Denton has set up the video camera to record the explosive moment, but all he sees are all four missile racks and two rocket pods just falling off our aircraft. Jack serves as our company's property officer. He tells Gladish, "This is going to be a lot of paperwork. Those missile racks alone are fifty or sixty thousand dollars."

That's followed by an attempt to destroy all the munitions on the ground. I hear Gladish save the grid coordinates as Jack shoots them up with ten rounds of 30 mm so they can't be used in the haji's "Your-Weapons-to-Our-IED Modification Program." Unfortunately, they don't explode. The grid is passed to Chris, who comes by later and does get them to explode but only after herding off some locals who hadn't wasted any time moving in on the metal gift that just fell from heaven.

"How far out are we?" Otto wants to know.

I do a quick check. "It's showing fourteen minutes, man. I got as much power in there as I can."

"I understand, dude. Sir, the thing I fear the most is getting out of this bird. That is going to hurt like hell."

We've still got fourteen minutes to touchdown at Bastion, but I'm beginning to think about how I can get us on the ground. *A normal hover landing is out, given our power limitations. I'm gonna have to do a roll-on like a Cessna on the HALS (helicopter air landing strip).* I'm confident I can do it on the HALS now because when I practiced roll-on landings up at FOB Wilson in October as well as a few times on the HALS after that, I had artificially limited my power. Score one for worst-case-scenario practicing.

Of course, I had never done a roll-on landing in BUCS—to my knowledge, nobody has. *How will I do this roll-on? How will I compensate for the sloppiness in the controls on a maneuver that requires fine motor skills?* I go through it a couple of times in my head. Then I check back in with Otto, reassuring him, and verbalizing my plans to him, as much to have something to engage his mind as to solidify the required actions in my own head.

"Hey, you shot four Hellfires today. Two into a cave and two onto the ground. How many Hellfires you shot up until now?" He says three. "You more than doubled it." He manages a sloppy chuckle. Then I add, "Twenty miles. Twelve minutes out."

Meantime, I can hear my wingman being all a wingman could be, coordinating things with the tower and Corsair HQ, passing along crucial information so I don't have to worry about those coms.

"Buddy, we're just ten minutes out now, last four minutes gone just like that."

"I have a feeling it's going by a lot faster for you, buddy." Touché. Even though there is obvious pain in his voice, he is cracking jokes and engaging with me. Every minute that passes makes me feel the likelihood of him making it is exponentially better.

Anticipation is growing in me as I continue to get erratic inputs in the sluggish controls. If I get one of those on touchdown, it could be ugly. Seven minutes out—it's been just over eighteen minutes since we got hit—and I can hear Bastion tower talking with Gladish about where the ambulance should be positioned.

Six minutes. "Ahhh, this is the longest flight ever," Otto tells me. I can hear the fatigue that comes from prolonged severe pain. I declare an emergency landing so Bastion will clear all traffic out of my way and have crash rescue equipment ready. "Otto, if you wanted a Purple Heart, I would have just thrown a rock at you."

"I don't even want it."

"I'm just kidding, man."

Four minutes now, winds verified, I should be able to do a straight-in approach, rolling it on landing to the south.

Three minutes, runway is in sight. I start to set up on my approach path, making it as gradual as I dare so that my required inputs will be minimized. Otto's voice is fading, so I begin tasking him with responsibilities. He starts to do the before-landing check, and then I ask him to keep calling out airspeed. I can't get slower than thirty-seven knots until I am in ground effect, or I could lose control of our rate of descent.

He begins calling airspeed. "Sixty-five right now." Then, "Fifty-five, fifty, looking good."

"Keep that airspeed coming."

He calls, "Forty-five knots, forty. This better be the smoothest landing ever."

"Got it, got it." As we pass through forty feet at thirty-five knots, we're in ground effect now. The aircraft is wobbling, but it's rhythmic, and I am able to keep the nose straight relative to the quickly approaching landing strip. If I can continue this, we should be able to touch down under control. *Deep breath, in through the nose, release slowly through the mouth, relax grip, focus.*

Otto calls, "Seventeen feet. Thirty-five knots."

Looks good. As the ground rush increases, I think, *Nobody's ever done this in BUCS. Damn, I hope I can do this without crashing...I will do this. I will fly this aircraft. I will not let it fly me. Twenty feet, ten, and touchdown. Nice! Barely even felt it.* "I'm looking for the medics."

Otto had apparently seen us roll right past them. "They're behind us."

On the wrong end of the frickin' HALS. I continue to brake using the rotor system to slow the aircraft to a stop, then execute an emergency aircraft shutdown. As I unbuckle my harness, the audio warning voice says, "Rotor rpm low, rotor rpm low."

"Screw you," I retort. The announcement is normal during an emergency shutdown, but I'd had enough of the machine telling me such things today. With urgency, I exit the cockpit, turn around, and open the door to Otto's compartment. I can see the red lights of the British emergency vehicle heading our way but don't want to wait for them.

I reach in and slide both my hands under Otto's armpits and on the count of three, two, one, forklift him up, out of his seat, and onto the forward avionics bay (FAB), but both of his legs are still inside the aircraft. "AAAAAH!!" He lets out a loud string of profanities, understandable given the situation. That's when I actually realize there is blood everywhere.

When the firefighters arrive at the side of our aircraft, I hop off the FAB, and with my feet firmly planted on the ground, I help them slide him out. As his wounded leg comes out, it is actually at my eye level, and the wound seems to pause right in front of my eyes. It's a big hole with exposed muscle hanging and twitching, blood still draining. My arms are supporting Otto as I stare at the wound.

Otto's still conscious, sees me looking, and says, smiling—yes, he was actually smiling—"You got me shot." I know he saw me gaping at his wound and could tell that my mind was processing it. His sarcastic quip was absolutely an attempt to put me at ease—I already knew that's the kind of person he is—but those words actually did the opposite. They struck me right to the core; he was right, after all. I did get him shot. In all my chair flying, I had often mimed what I would do if I were hit, or if our wingman was shot down, but for some reason, I never thought of my copilot being hit and me being fine. We either both get hit or just me. Never just my copilot. Never with me fine and him in surgery with a life-altering injury.

Some British Apache maintainers catch up with me in the makeshift surgical waiting room I'm sitting in. I have no idea how much time has passed; it could have been a minute or it could have been a day. They tell me there is a Chinook headed back to Kandahar in fifteen and they can take me to the bird.

I am in a fog, not really thinking about anything in particular, mentally exhausted and maybe in a little shock. It barely registers when I learn that our bird took hits from a barrage of 50 caliber heavy machine guns, AK-47s, and belt-fed light PKM machine guns.

It's dark when I board the Chinook. I sit in the rear alone, staring toward the front of the cabin, which now glows with ominous red lights. As soon as we take off, the lights are extinguished, and it's just black, noise, wind, and the smell of hydraulic fluid. It's a thirty-minute flight to Kandahar. The same time it just took me to get Otto to Bastion, but this thirty-minute flight seems to take ten seconds. It feels like we just took off, but now I feel the ground as we land at KAF. I exit the bird in much less of a fog now. My mind is now focused on the fact we lost this fight. I lost this fight.

I look up to see the task force commander, Lt. Col. Altieri, and the brigade commander, Col. Kelly Thomas, coming toward me. Altieri grabs my arm, looks at me, and asks how I'm doing.

I tell him, "Well, sir, I have had better days." Col. Thomas opens his arms, signifying he's coming in for a hug. I am not much of a hugger, especially with guys I don't know too well. So for anyone watching, it had to be funny looking as he wrapped his arms around me, with my arms remaining at my side and me standing rigid, noticeably uncomfortable.

He asks the same question just worded a different way. "Are you okay?"

"Yes, sir. They got us today, but I am going to fix that tomorrow."

He stops me, saying, "I don't think it would be a good idea for you to fly tomorrow. Take a few days."

"Sir, I have been fighting in this country for eleven months. I have had many close calls, but we always left the fight as victors. Taliban turned the tide today. I am not okay with that. I want to make sure I rectify that as soon as possible. I am good to go. I am ready to fly."

The colonel looks at me for a minute, saying nothing, kind of cocking his head to the side like dogs do when they are pondering something. I am guessing he was assessing whether he could trust what I was saying or not. Then, to my surprise, he says, "All right, then. You better get some sleep. Big day tomorrow."

While that's happening, back up at Camp Bastion, the British docs have performed basic wound care on Otto and given him enough painkillers to make him comfortable. He's lucid enough to ask a nurse if he can borrow her phone to call his wife, Tara, back in Arizona, where she and their two children were staying with her mother.

It was evening in Afghanistan when Otto called, making it about 6:00 a.m. when the phone rang in Tucson. Tara's mother answered, then woke her daughter, handing her the phone.

They actually chatted for twenty minutes before Otto said, "Oh, by the way, I'm going to be coming home earlier than scheduled."

"That's good. Why is that?"

"Because I broke my leg."

"How did you break your leg?"

"Oh, by a bullet."

That triggered it. "What? You got shot?"

Tara says her husband insisted he was okay, that he actually sounded pretty good. He called because he wanted her to get the news directly from him, rather than in the formal, very bureaucratic, routine call from an army headquarters in Virginia.

Otto was moved from Bastion to the hospital at Bagram, where he received his Purple Heart. Then he was put on the first available flight to the military's largest hospital outside the United States, in Landstuhl, Germany. Doctors there removed fragments from his wound but didn't attempt to repair his shattered femur. They did tell Otto that he'd lost much of his hamstring muscle because the bullet had spiraled up through his thigh.

His next stop was Walter Reed Army Medical Center outside Washington. There, too, no orthopedic surgeon attempted the repair. Finally, Tara says, they found a doctor at the army hospital at Fort Hood, Texas, who was willing to take the case. The doctor's name? Major Chance. Otto took note, but the doc didn't have much of a sense of humor. Even so, Tara says, "He did a phenomenal job in an eight-hour operation, cutting out half of his hamstring, leaving a big chunk out of the back of his right thigh, and implanting a titanium rod that went from his hip down to his knee."

Wounded on December 9, Otto was out of the hospital on the 23rd, staying with Tara and the kids at Fisher House for Christmas. After the family flew back to Arizona, he began two weeks of outpatient physical and occupational therapy at Fort Hood before flying home— still using a wheelchair—in mid-January, to rejoin his family.

A footnote: Five days after Arrow 2-3 got shot up in the Helmand, Jack Denton flew back to Camp Bastion to pick up the now-repaired Apache and fly it home to Kandahar. He told me, "I remember seeing a big red handprint on the outside of the canopy or the door. And I don't know if it's yours, or his, from holding his leg. It was just a perfect impression of a handprint, big and red on the door, and then the whole inside was just covered in blood. I got three large water bottles from the Brits and I think a roll of paper towels, and I just started splashing water everywhere, just wiping everything down. And it smelled like dried blood in there. I had to throw all the seat cushions away and just sit on the Kevlar seat on the way back to base."

I've posted the actual gun camera video of this entire incident at www. clearedhot.info/wounded.

CHAPTER 21

OP. MAR KARADAD– DAY 4

THE RETRIBUTION

Life Will Kick You; KICK BACK

Kandahar Air Base, December 10, 2007—I hadn't gone directly to sleep. I needed to get out of my bloody flight suit and scrub Otto's blood from my hands and face. I have no idea how I got it on my face, but as I stared in the mirror, I thought I looked like someone out of the movie *Braveheart*. I thought I'd just rack out on the cot in my office, but my mind was racing again. I needed a distraction. Otto's *you got me shot* was playing on a loop inside my head; maybe talking would drown it out.

Word had spread that I was back, and some of the company had gathered in our TOC. They wanted details, but I didn't feel like doing a play-by-play on the day's events. It felt good to hear their voices, to receive their support. Camaraderie, right? I gave them the CliffNotes that focused on what little we could call a win today. "Otto got shot.

He's okay. He should be on his way to Germany soon. And I need to go to sleep because in the morning, I'm going to go back and finish what Otto and I started." The guys' reactions to this statement varied from full support to the same reluctance initially shown by our brigade commander. Ironically, both reactions were supportive in nature. Either they showed they had confidence in me to make good on my statement, or they were concerned with my well-being. Either way, I was proud to be part of such a solid group of men—men who were in this together and didn't choose the easy path if it wasn't the right path.

Since I hadn't slept the night before, I am totally exhausted. It didn't hit me until I sat down, alone, at the back of that Chinook, the adrenaline in my body finally dissipating, just as it did in the hours after a big game. Now I just collapse onto the thin mattress and fall into a dream-free sleep.

Sunrise just before 7:00 a.m. comes way too soon. I am still tired, but it's almost like the mornings when you are waking up to go hunting or fishing. At first, you forget that's what you're going to do, so you focus on how tired you are. But then it hits you: I get to go hunting today. Even though you're not rested, you're instantly wide awake. Pushing through the grogginess is not nearly as difficult when you know the new day brings with it a purpose.

Today, I've definitely got a purpose. Before getting breakfast, I confirm that I'm still on the flight schedule and learn that my front-seater will be 1st Lt. Josh Daniels and our wingman will be CW4 Ken "Iron Ass" Jones. I don't have a picture of how this will go down formed in my head yet, more of a mindset that it will happen as I want it to. This sortie is the retribution for Otto. Or is it for Otto? Maybe it's for me, and I am using the "let's do this for Otto" platform to justify me feeling flat-out ticked that we lost, ticked Otto got hurt on my watch, ticked that because the Taliban bested me, he is in a hospital with a devastating wound.

Either way, unlike any previous mission I've flown, this one is personal. Let me be clear: I'm not flying with blind rage but with highly motivated intent. It's my *Enola Gay* moment and Otto was my own Pearl Harbor. I'm dancing around the "r-word" here—revenge. I'd always been taught that belongs to the Lord. But the fine print says I'm definitely permitted to help. Technically, I think it says we can be instruments. So let's be instruments today.

Ironically, my briefing on the pad is almost casual. "Hey, we're going to go to Musa Qala, check in, and do what they tell us, of course. But if we get some free time"—you see where this is headed, right?—"we're going to try to see what we can do with that area that Malone—" I don't get to finish the sentence. My guys are well ahead of me.

"Yup, absolutely. Let's go see what we can do." So I think it's safe to say they are definitely motivated to do it for Otto, even if my reasoning is mixed.

About forty-five minutes later, we check in with Fury 1-1, who tells us the Taliban's been popping up like unwanted rodents more or less continuously, all over the place, ever since yesterday's action. "Anything from that tree line where my copilot got shot at yesterday?" I wanted him to know who I was as well as get a sit-rep. I wanted him to know I was back, thinking he would understand why and do his best to facilitate development of the scenario I am chomping at the bit to execute.

"Every Apache that's been out here since has taken fire from them, and they're still in there." I was hoping we could get straight to it, but Fury wants us to fly west, staying on the south side of the Musa Qala River, and play Whac-A-Mole near a different tree line where his troops are getting harassed. We see no bad guys but put some rockets and 30 mm into it anyway, getting a congratulatory, "You hit it! Thanks for the work, Arrow," from the ground pounders. Usually, that radio com is what I live for. I love hearing relief or excitement in the voices of the guys on the ground, knowing when we take away a threat, it just simplified the complexity of their goal to stay alive. That's normally; but today, I have an agenda—one that I know still has to meet the parameters of ROE and fall within the scope of what Fury wants us to do. When he said they'd been taking fire from that area off and on, it tells me the likelihood of all those stars aligning is pretty good.

Okay, free time has arrived. I tell my wingman that we're going to begin working our way downriver, and I assume—yeah, I know— that he's going to stay on my six because in A Company, we have learned the importance of remaining mutually supportive in this AO. But Iron Ass has been up north in Salerno, where they get away with stuff like spacing out a two-ship sortie. Here, Taliban usually want nothing to do with the business end of an Apache, but if they see the spacing is far enough apart to permit a shot at the back of one bird because the other one won't be able to pinpoint their position, they'll take advantage of that. I fly on toward the spot where we're anticipating trouble, then take a ninety-degree turn away from the tree line just prior to the known area so I can maintain stand-off. That's when I see Ken is currently in a wolf pack of one, hunting, snooping, and poking on his own. "Hey, make sure you stay mutually supportive with me."

"Roger that," and he closes the space between us.

A good thing, too, because not two minutes later, he says, "You are taking fire from your left side." I look, bank left, and even though it's daytime, I can see where it's coming from because the abadabas are firing tracers, which are just barely visible in daytime. *Maybe that's what helped them get lucky yesterday. Oh, you messed up now! Fight's on. Same exact spot.*

I'm looking at a tree line with a fairly large building set back behind it. I take control of the gun from Josh and begin firing the 30 at the source of the tracer fire, then roll back around and switch to rockets, lighting up the tree line, turning trees into toothpicks. My jaw is tightening with every squeeze of the trigger, as though I'm trying to bite through a hunk of rawhide. Usually, I would divide these duties, but this is personal, so for a few moments, Josh is just self-loading baggage. As I complete a rocket run, Fury 1-1 comes up on the net. "You're taking fire from a building just past the trees you just engaged. It's a big, square, white building. Already got a hole in the roof. Those guys are shooting from inside."

"Hey, Josh, I want you to stick some Hellfires in that building." The baggage awakens, frustrated, I am sure, because I had been doing all the trigger squeezing. But all is forgiven with the mention of Hell-fires, especially since the word is in its plural form. It's all happening fast. We're still taking fire as we roll around. *Tshuuu.* Hellfire. Back around. *Tshuuu.* Another leaves the rack. On our breaks, I am throwing 30 down as well, and we see the building crumbling, one quadrant at a time. We break and Iron Ass follows us in, flinging Hellfires as well. We come around again, more Hellfires.

On our next breakout, I'm surprised by a British voice interjecting on the radio. "Apaches engaging the tree line. You are taking fire from a DShK underneath the blue tarp," and he gives us the azimuth from the cell tower, which is behind me. I look down at my heading indicator so I can compare our heading to where he says the fire is coming from. *Yikes, if he is right, we are dead nuts on the gun target line.* My head pops up to see if I can see anything visually and holy crap! Yep! He was absolutely right. Instantly, I can see the flashes from a DShK heavy machine gun in the tree line directly on our flight path. There's no angle in this muzzle flash; it's literally a white flashing circle. It's so clear the fire is coming right at us that I do something that is actually kind of funny (in hindsight of course).

It's an involuntary response. I lean as far back in my seat as I can, cringing, gritting my teeth, and bracing for impact. It's as though some autonomous part of my brain calculated, *Maybe if we lean back enough it'll go over our head.* As if that's going to help.

I simultaneously squeeze the trigger, thinking, *We just got shot here yesterday. Uungggh!* As I grunt, I let loose two more rockets. *Pfffft! Pfffft!* The first hits just to the right of the muzzle flash; the second travels as if in slow motion. I can see the rocket motor burning as it leaves the rocket pod, and the trajectory looks good. I can't help but wonder if the terrorist on the other end of that DShK is doing what I am doing at the very same time, looking down the barrel of the rocket-firing attack helo, leaning back under his blue tarp, cringing, and thinking, *Maybe it'll go over my head.* It didn't. Direct hit.

Up on the radio comes that British voice, one of their elite SAS types. "Arrow 0-6, you were taking DShK fire from underneath the blue tarp. Then you hit the blue tarp, and you are no longer taking DShK fire." I can't help but laugh at the elegant accent and am about to thank him for the guidance when an angry voice cuts in.

"Arrow shooting at the tree line, stop SHOOTING in my AO!" I can tell by the voice that it's Fury 0-6 Actual. He says it again, louder. "Stop shooting in my AO."

"Sir, we're taking fire from the tree line."

He's now screaming at me. "Do you know where all the friendlies are?"

I try reasoning with him with a little ill-advised sarcasm. "Sir, pretty sure the friendlies aren't going to be shooting at us, and we always have the right to return fire." Big mistake. Lt. Col. Mennes wasn't interested in anything I had to say in my defense.

"I understand that, but you need to—" and he blisters me with an angry rant that frankly, just pisses me off. Just yesterday I was almost shot down right here, and my copilot was maimed. I'm not going to just take it. We're totally justified. At the same time, a little voice inside my head reminds me that Mennes is not a leader to mess with, even if he is wrong. We break contact.

That little Jiminy Cricket moment is just long enough for Iron Ass to cut in on the interplane. "You could totally defend yourself, dude. You're in the right. This guy is losing his mind." *Clearly, he doesn't know who Mennes is.*

I'm fuming as I respond to Mennes, "Roger that, sir." I almost add a "but" when Jiminy kicks some sense into me and I simply repeat the same words, "Roger that." Yeah, he did rain on our parade, but we did have the parade and finished what we came here to do today. You readers know me by now, so I won't fake a smile here. I am not happy he chewed us out for doing our job. Instead of opting to argue over the radio with a war fighter I truly respect, I opt to vent by way of a more-or-less one-way monologue to Josh in the front seat.

"Look, I get it. He feels like I feel about Otto. He has stewardship over his guys on the ground. He obviously lost some situational awareness on what was going on. We knew; so did Fury 1-1—the platoon leader on radio who sent us down here. He would have said something if we started engaging near friendlies. After our initial reaction to enemy fire, we told him we're taking fire from the tree line and got his okay to return fire."

My rant serves to vent the pressure that built up inside me because I didn't retort over the radio. Probably a smarter way to do it. Bottom line is, I can actually sympathize with Fury 0-6's position. He is a guy who already had my admiration, but this day, we locked horns a little, both of us driven by our sense of stewardship.

We wait till our replacements check in, give them a very specific lay of the land on interplane (that can't be monitored by the ground), and head back to Kandahar, satisfied that we'd gotten our retribution. The tree line was leveled. The big building behind it is now nothing but a hulk. Unlikely anybody would get shot at from there again. I take one last look at the city before leaving. An eerie layer of dust, residual from our kinetic impacts on enemy positions, now blankets most of the city of Musa Qala. *Fitting that it should be a blanket, since today we put something to bed.*

It had taken a day, but I'd finished my fight. We'd taken one casualty, but we definitely gave more than we took. The Taliban wouldn't have even known about Otto, since to them it looked as though we simply flew away from the scene yesterday, but what they did to him was the catalyst that made this fight so much more visceral to me and ultimately ensured their demise.

Even though this engagement definitely put the dot at the end underneath my exclamation point, it didn't help me feel better about Otto. It also didn't make me suddenly see a purpose to all of this. Rather, it just allowed me to think, *They didn't get the best of me. They didn't get the best of us, Otto.* I guess that's worth something, all by itself.

Tomorrow, we'll be back in Helmand Province. The infantry would be starting a sweep through the city of Musa Qala itself. Operation Mar Karadad is nowhere near over. I can expect two or three sorties a day, almost three hours each, until we begin to train our replacements. Really looking forward to that.

By the way, a few days later, the same platoon leader who had been calling us in on targets near Musa Qala visited our TOC. He came to thank us and deliver a box of cigars as an offering to offset the fact that his boss had wrongly chewed us out during the mission.

When our crews have a chance to reflect on the operation, one particular memory is universal: the gratitude and relief we hear in the voices of the infantry guys on the radio when we show up and lay waste to enemy forces that are harassing them. It's definitely a personal connection we have with them. Perhaps a comparison with the way the Brits fly their Apaches helps explain. It's one thing to have a helicopter 3,000 feet overhead target a tree line with a missile. It's another when a helicopter comes zooming right over your head and takes it to the enemy, guns and rockets blazing. It says, "We're here with you." Maybe it even says, "We love you."

CHAPTER 22

I STILL HAVEN'T FOUND WHAT I'M LOOKING FOR

It's Never Too Late to Start with a Clean Slate

Kandahar Air Base, December 23, 2007—The ground pounders, as always, will be leading the way. The 82nd's infantry contingent is headed home just before us. Man, those guys put in yeoman's work here in Afghanistan. If life were fair, they would all fly back first class, with a dinner of their choice served on a platter, with a crystal goblet of something cool and refreshing. I am envious of how simplified their packing is compared to ours. It's probably the only thing I am envious of when comparing our two realms. We've been watching the troopers of the 82nd Airborne Division packing for their rotation home to the land of twenty-four-hour gas stations, IED-free sporting events, and hamburgers made from real cow. Their packing consists of shoving uniforms into a duffel bag and jamming their Xboxes and off-duty toys, along with acquired items, into new-fangled plastic footlockers purchased at the PX. They'll carry their M4 rifles, just the way they did coming over here. Man, if I were a grunt, I could be packed in twenty minutes.

While I say, "We've got to pack up eight Apaches," it would probably be more correct to say, "Our maintainers had to pack up eight Apaches." Taking those birds apart is not a job for amateurs.

Not us. Not Alpha Company, 1st of the 285th Attack Reconnaissance Battalion of the Arizona National Guard. We've got to pack up eight AH-64 Apache Longbow helicopters, plus all the spare parts our maintainers have squirreled away. When we deployed, we weren't sure what we would need, so they had us bring everything. We packed ISU 90 after ISU 90, 10,000-pound-capacity steel shipping containers chock-full of outdated crap that had been on our hand receipts since Patton. I took this opportunity to purge all that dead weight through the magic of combat loss and DRMO (Defense Reutilization and Marketing Office) paperwork. You are welcome, future property custodians of A Company.

The Apaches had to be folded and stuffed into C-17s to cross the pond, where they would be off-loaded in Corpus Christi, Texas, for a thorough overhaul before returning to Arizona. As the Alpha Company CO, it's my signature that acknowledges responsibility for each of our eight $52-million aircraft. In theory, if there is any negligence resulting in the damage or loss of these military assets, I can be hit with a statement of charges. Last time I checked, Katie hadn't left me with a spare fifty-two mil in our joint checking account to cover a messed-up Apache. In fact, last time I checked, despite my earnings being tax-free and me getting extra pay for hostile fire and imminent danger, the savings I had built up over eight years had been completely depleted while I was gone. Even though I know the likelihood of a financial juggernaut hit like an aircraft is very unlikely, it does give me pause and a little more focus to ensure our t's are crossed and our i's dotted.

But enough of that. It's Christmastime in Kandahar, and our TOC looks like a dollar store threw up—we've been getting decorations in care packages from home for weeks now. Our halls are thoroughly decked, and since we're out of here in less than two weeks, everyone is overdosing on jolly.

Well, let me amend that. Remember when we arrived in country and the unit we were replacing at Bagram had us live the entire two-week transition in a very pungent, waterlogged tent camp, while they stayed in their comfy hooches until they could hear the final boarding call for their flight home? I vowed I wouldn't do that to our replacements. So as the new guys from the 101st Airborne Division arrive, I've been shifting our guys to Kandahar's transition area and allowing the Screaming Eagles to move in. I didn't go so far as putting mints on their pillows, but the thought crossed my mind. After all, we are grateful they are here and in a sense concerned, since we know what lies in front of them. I've moved out of my own deluxe accommodations and am living in my office until the new company commander needs it; then I'll join my company in the tents.

The RIP (relief in place) process with the incoming 101st Airborne aviation company is more complicated than we expected. We had to continue flying ring routes and be ready for the occasional TIC that might pop up. Our assumption had been that as the new guys unpacked and made an Apache flyable, we'd break down one of ours. *Never assume, right?* It turns out that the 101st Apaches had been upgraded with a modified target acquisition designation sight (MTADS) and modified pilot's night vision system (MPNVS) that we'd never seen or used before. Frankly, it pissed us off. Chris was especially outraged, saying, "This is absolutely criminal. You let us fly for a whole year using this [seventies-era] stuff when this technology was available." The FLIR picture provided by the new gear is equivalent to an HDTV, except for the image being black and white. I'd been navigating through slot canyons at night using images that looked like melted film. Time after time, I more or less used educated guesses to avoid smacking into a canyon wall. It's a miracle Taliban granite didn't claim more casualties.

Because we hadn't trained with the modified systems, the bosses at Bagram said we couldn't fly the 101st's birds, even though it was our responsibility to use the two-week RIP period to familiarize their pilots with the area, as well as go over the tactics we'd been using to support the infantry. So how do we pack up our Apaches for their return to the States when we still need them operational? To be crystal clear, we weren't allowed to use a *better* system that operated exactly the same way as ours, the only difference being it gave significantly better visual acuity. Does that make any kind of sense? A compromise was ultimately reached, and the powers that be said our guys could fly back seat with a 101st pilot up front. Hallelujah, common sense prevailed!

Although most of the incoming pilots are eager to learn what we could teach them, there are a few guys who have the "been there done that, we aren't going to learn anything from a guard unit" mentality. Unfortunately, their company commander is one of those guys. He's a young captain, whose ego is one of those obvious overcompensation things. Since he said it so often, he might as well have put, "We were in Iraq two years ago. We know how this is done" on a recorded loop. I would find this funny if I didn't know the significant downside to his not taking this stuff seriously. I did have a very direct conversation with him and showed him a few sobering gun tapes that I hope awoke a sense of reality in him, although I can't be sure. He will either rise to the challenge or ride the struggle bus through it. Those were the same options we'd had, and we did a little of both, ultimately doing more rising than struggling. I feel that's all you can hope to do.

I think I now understand why those Seabees we ran into at the Frankfurt airport on our way here said what they did, the way they did. At the time, "Be safe" didn't really register. But their concern for us was sincere. That's how I feel right now about the incoming captain and his troops. In all sincerity, I wish him good luck.

The New Year's Eve celebration is lackluster—not too much holiday cheer is generated when you're toasting with Grape Nehi. Everyone's focus is still on packing up. Getting an entire company's people and equipment out of a hostile, landlocked country is a huge logistical feat, and everything we were doing at Kandahar was also being done at Bagram and Salerno. The trick is to get the entire 425-person battalion out of Afghanistan at the same time. I didn't know it then, but there was a dog-and-pony show depending on us all getting in at the same time.

As I take my seat on the C-17 that will carry me out of Afghanistan, my feelings are mixed. This country had been my home for over a year. A whole year, or only a year, depending on your perspective.

To me, it was a lifetime of experiences packed in the time allotted. In that sense, it feels as if I am ending an entire life's journey and starting anew in a familiar realm. I had wanted to come here to do my part in the War on Terror. I don't know if I met that mission; I do know that shortly after arriving, my mission changed, at least in my mind's eye. It happened the moment I realized that as an Apache pilot, I was here to try and make sure as many Americans as possible make it back home. That realization is profound.

I feel we did that. I feel we did it well. In the process, this world became my reality, even more so than the life I'd come from in America. That pendulum is about to swing back. Are these guys ready for that? Am I ready for that? The things I've experienced and the growth that's occurred over the past year have been, at times, overwhelming. Even though I am the same person, I am definitely not the same man.

Opting for headphones rather than earplugs to drown out the roar of four huge jet engines, I have U2's "I Still Haven't Found What I'm Looking For" playing in my ears.

I have spoke with the tongue of angels

I have held the hand of a devil

It was warm in the night

I was cold as a stone

But I still haven't found what I'm looking for

How apropos. I'd found a lot of things I wasn't looking for in the past year: things I didn't know I had in me, things I never wanted to be a part of but had to be, things I will never forget. But with Katie, that chorus rings true: *I still haven't found what I'm looking for.* That thought weighs heavy on my mind, not as a point of order to quit, but rather to reengage, and with any luck, find what we are looking for. I let that thought marinate till it's run its course.

As it does, I sit there looking around me at the faces of the men with whom I served. These warrior pilots saved the lives of countless brothers in arms on the ground; some of them saved my life. Our maintainers toiled endlessly to ensure we had flyable war machines. These are the guys who made it through, who passed war's test of human character. (Not all who deployed with us did; some went home early.) I wonder how each of them will come through this final phase of our combat deployment—reentry into a civilization where the rules of human interaction are completely different.

I'm overcome as a sense of gratitude rushes through me. I am not only grateful for these men and who they are to me now but grateful that they, too, get to go home, get to say they served our country honorably. Because they unfailingly did. With these thoughts in mind, I bid adieu to Kandahar's bog of never-ending stench as well as to the rest of Afghanistan. (I didn't know it then, but I'd be back.)

We don't head west toward home but north to the US Air Force's Manas Transit Center at the international airport near Bishkek, Kyrgyzstan. For the past six years, it's been the principal transit point for allied forces and munitions being deployed to Afghanistan.

When we left Kandahar, it was sixty degrees and sunny. We're wearing army combat uniforms—our cold weather gear is packed away because, hey, we're headed to Arizona. Jack Denton remembers that part of the trip well. "We landed in Kyrgyzstan at two in the morning, and an air force guy said it was −17° Celsius outside. I asked,

'What's that in Fahrenheit?' and before he could answer, someone else says, 'Does it matter?'"

The truth is, it didn't matter. We were headed home, and we were already in a place where nobody would deliberately try to kill us.

I remember reconnecting with all my B Company bros, joking, comparing notes, and just sharing the general feeling of *man, we did that stuff and now it's being put in our rearview mirror.* The air force couldn't seem to figure out when we were going to leave and kept giving us conflicting stories. Of course, all our family members wanted to know is, "When will you be home?" and since the date kept changing, everyone was getting frustrated. Joel Mann, the maintainer I'd flown with to Afghanistan a year ago, laughed about this with me. "First time?"

We stayed at Manas for almost a week until nearly everyone in the battalion arrived from the various duty stations in Afghanistan. The plan was for the unit to return home intact, even though there was no way we could all fly on the same plane. We left Manas on a civilian charter jet, most likely an MD-11, with a two-five-two seat configuration. Jack remembers the plane was only about half full, so he took a pair of window seats and made himself comfortable, plugging into the entertainment system and listening to the country music channel that had only a couple dozen songs on a loop. "I still remember hearing 'Moments' by the band Emerson Drive. The lyrics are about a man on a bridge contemplating suicide when a stranger approaches him and starts talking to him about the good moments in his life. One thing he cites as a good moment was *like that plane ride, coming home from the war.* Of course, I couldn't help but relate to that and fantasize about how wonderful my own homecoming would be." His recollection is that we stopped in Turkey, where we weren't permitted to get off the plane while it was refueled, and Shannon, Ireland, before crossing the Atlantic to Bangor, Maine, and then flying on to the airport near Fort Sill, Oklahoma.

When the aircraft stopped in Shannon for maintenance, the duty-free shops opened up for the returning soldiers. Many of the men took advantage, picking up airline bottles of Jameson Whiskey. Chris Walker said, "I was a cheap date at that point. One sip of that stuff and I'm ready to table dance. That was easily the best night's sleep I got on an airplane." (Remember, there was officially no liquor available to American troops deployed in Afghanistan. This wasn't a big deal for the nondrinkers such as myself, but for others, it was a taste of the liberties about to be restored.)

Despite the booze, Chris didn't sleep through the refueling stop at Bangor, where he refueled, too. He clearly remembers being overcome with emotion in the terminal, realizing he was back in the USA. "Just knowing it was American soil was nice. That was nice," he says quietly.

You may have noticed that I'm relying on my buddies' memories to reconstruct our trek home. My memory machine is a little rusty regarding this flight, possibly because I took an Ambien for the first time ever when I boarded the plane at Manas. We had been prescribed them to help us change schedules, and many guys used them on and off during the deployment. Mine ended up in the bottom of my duffel and I never did use them. But when I was packing for the return flight, I found them, and remembering how long the flight downrange felt, I decided I'd pop a couple to help get through the twenty- or twenty-two-hour flight from Manas to Sill. I just wanted to close my eyes and then wake up in America. I think I was sitting in an aisle seat in the center section of a wide-body jet. What I do remember is I had a very vivid dream, which I'll recount if you promise not to think less of me. Actually, think what you will; it's a funny story and if you don't know me by now from this book, I doubt anything I say in the final chapter will get you there.

In that dream, I'm in a boxing match with Broccoli. Yeah, broccoli the vegetable. It had the long broccoli stalk with arms; the top part of broccoli was my nocturnal nemesis's hair. He had boxing gloves, eyeballs, and everything. I'm in uniform, basically fighting *Veggi-eTales*. It's a very vivid dream. Broccoli had some moves and was a lot bigger than me, so he was dishing it out. That wouldn't be problematic except for the fact that when I awoke hours later and came out of my Ambien-induced coma, I noticed that I had crusted food all over my hands. Then I realized it wasn't just my hands; it was all over the front of my ACUs, my face, everywhere. I turned to the PFC sitting one seat over and asked, "Hey, man, why do I have food all over me?"

And he says, reluctantly, "I don't know, sir. You asked for the food. They gave you the food, and then you just started shoving it and smashing it and putting it everywhere, all over." I can just imagine what this kid must have thought: *This guy has complete PTSD*. Nope, just your typical kid-versus-vegetable Ambien-triggered nightmare.

I think I asked, "Why didn't you say something?" Silly question. I'm a captain; he's a private first class who doesn't know me. What's he supposed to say? "Sir, stop being crazy"? That's a for-sure memory of my flight home, probably that kid's too. Man, I am so glad we didn't have smartphones then. That video would have gone viral.

Jack still laughs when he remembers what happened when we got off the plane at Fort Sill. We were bused to a gymnasium on post where local folks had gathered to conduct a welcome-home ceremony. "I think we were all still a little in shock to be back in the US, and although it was very nice of the people to be there, we just felt disillusioned at all the welcome-home banners when we didn't feel like we were home. They put us all in a formation in the middle of the gym and had a band play the national anthem. It was just an instrumental version, but the drummer decided to hit the big drum with everything he had just at the moment we pause for a breath after singing 'and the rockets' red glare...' *BOOOOM!* Instantly, everyone in the formation ducked for cover. I laugh about it now, but we were pretty mad about it at the time. I think a lot of us didn't realize how the hypersensitivity to our surroundings would follow us home. For the next three to six months, I jerked every time a door slammed or I heard some kind of explosion."

We all agree that the out-processing at Sill was a drag. We wanted to get home to our families in Arizona, and we're stuck going through a required demobilization routine that, although necessary, was nevertheless annoying. The army has its protocols, however, and we got medically screened for any injuries we might have sustained, met with a chaplain, got briefings on VA benefits, and were cautioned about the intricacies of family reintegration following combat deployments and told help was available if we needed it.

What especially bothered Chris was the annoyance of "having to go downstairs to this machine and put money into it to get water." In Afghanistan, we consumed free bottled water by the pallet. Whenever we needed more, it magically appeared. So much for returning heroes. "Anyone got change for the water machine?"

We have bittersweet memories of coming back to our home base at Silverbell Army Heliport near Tucson. Our families had been informed of the unit's estimated arrival time, and they'd all been herded into one of the large hangars, and the doors had been closed. Rather than allowing us to run to them, the brass ordered us to stand at attention in formation in front of the closed hangar doors. When they were ceremoniously opened, most everyone anxiously looked for their family members.

This is kind of sad. Although there was some pretty positive emotion, there were a lot of guys whose significant others were not there to meet them because they had run off with somebody else. And in some cases, they didn't even know it. That's heartbreaking. After all of that, you don't just stand a guy up at the airport looking around for you.

We had to endure a formal welcome home by local dignitaries before we could go to our families. I hear none of it. I am locked up at attention in front of my company and all I can think is that *I don't want to stand at attention anymore. I feel like we are a circus attraction.* As I stand there, sweat dripping down my back, I search the crowd for Katie.

When we're finally dismissed, I'm overwhelmed with decidedly mixed feelings. I'm excited to see Katie, but even though we'd talked about it, there's no denying that our relationship has become distanced. We'd had several phone calls in my final weeks at Kandahar, at Manas, and while I was at Fort Sill, during which we'd both expressed excitement about being back together. I tried to focus on the hope of a restart once I got home. For the most part, she seemed onboard and excited to start anew. I knew that what I did upon first meeting up would set the tone. I also knew it would be incumbent upon me to push through the uneasiness in order to make it comfortable again.

And then I see her. Unlike my mid-tour, when she was rocked out with six-pack abs when she picked me up, I notice she's put on about thirty-five pounds. She's wearing a baggy sweatshirt, hair is back in a ponytail, and to top it off, she has her mom and dad in tow. I don't care so much about her appearance. I already was very aware of the bouts of depression keeping her bedridden for weeks at a time, but her parents? I am thinking, *Oh great, she's uncomfortable enough, she brought backup.*

Well, here goes. I walk up to her smiling and can immediately tell she's as apprehensive about this reunion as I am. Neither one of us knows how we're supposed to react. I make the first move, though, and give her a big, tight hug and whisper in her ear, "I love you." It seems to help some. What we're dealing with here is the normal tension of a married couple meeting after a prolonged separation—one made infinitely worse by the uncertainty of war. But layered on top of that is the internal turmoil caused by our roller-coaster ride of relationship drama. We're both suffocating in a cloud of ambiguous discomfort.

Slade, you've got to man up. I tell her I am glad to be home, to which she says, "I am happy you're home too." But then she adds, "Oh, by the way, Brian, we're going to have a barbecue at my parents' house to welcome you home."

I'm thinking, *Really? I don't even get along with your parents. You probably had to beg them to come with you. What are you thinking I want? I'm getting back from a year away from home. I want to go to my home. I want to go have sex and eat a burger—maybe even at the same time. I can multitask!*

So here's that football lesson again. If you're going to complain about how bad something is, then it will be bad, and you may not get through it. Show the commitment and the courage, and increase your capability. So deciding to do just that, I put on a happy face and say, "Oh, great, that will be awesome! What are we grilling?" At the same time, I'm thinking, *How long do we have to stay at Mom and Dad's before we can make the forty-five-minute drive home?* But I opt to be patient. *I have been gone a year. What's one more afternoon?*

Eventually, we do make it home. We agreed to take a few days to enjoy each other before talking about anything serious. When Katie and I finally discuss our life together, we actually find agreement:

the past twenty-three months have been hellish, we'd both let each other down in many ways, and there was nothing for either of us to gain by pointing fingers.

We made a pact to move forward during our next twenty-three months together by setting goals: we would go to church regularly, pray together each morning, and stay focused. But the big one for me—an absolute paradigm shift—was agreeing to show our courage and commitment to each other by seeking marriage counseling. Honestly, I was at my wit's end and knew I didn't have the answers, no matter how much I wanted to have them. What finally dawned on me is that someone had to teach us both how to chair-fly relationship scenarios. We needed to be able to react instinctually in a healthy way when faced with relationship emergencies/difficulties. I desperately wanted this marriage to work.

I have climbed highest mountains

I have run through the fields

Only to be with you

I have run

I have crawled

I have scaled these city walls

Only to be with you

But I still haven't found what I'm looking for

—BONO/U2

EPILOGUE

THE WAY FORWARD (MANY YEARS LATER)

How You Can Experience Post Traumatic Stress Growth

You can imagine a war, you can imagine the fight

No matter what is imagined, you will not be right.

—BRIAN SLADE, "PERMANENT REVISION"

All I can say is that kids grow up way too fast.

In the Utah Rockies, December 2021—My son, Axel, and I are almost at 10,000 feet altitude, looking over a giant snow basin and taking in the natural beauty of cascaded white-covered grandeur that is the Rockies. Can't help but smile at the extreme contrasts in life and soak in the magnificence. Yet all this beauty pales in comparison to the joy I feel when I drop my gaze from the deity-adorned landscape. I look at my eight-year-old boy on his snowboard, grinning ear to ear, his white chiclet smile the only part of his body I can see, as he is wrapped head to toe in brightly colored snow attire, goggles over his eyes, beanie on his head. Doesn't matter that I can't see the rest of him, that smile says it all. So young, so innocent, and ready to conquer the hill with his dad.

Axel and I are a team now; we call each other "buddy" because it just feels right. It's been this way since 2015 when Katie and I divorced.

Our relationship through four subsequent deployments was all tumultuous. Unfortunately, Katie had several miscarriages during this time, which contributed to her emotional and mental health problems. In 2012, we adopted Axel. Not only did it not fix the marriage, but it opened my eyes to my purpose in life: raising that little boy, protecting him, encouraging him, *fathering him*, and doing my best to see that he'd mature into a healthy, happy, responsible, and loving human being. It was apparent that wouldn't happen with parents who were constantly in turmoil. Regretfully, despite considerable professional counseling, I acknowledged defeat, and in 2015 we divorced. I have full custody of Axel, who, as you can clearly tell, is the light of my life.

"You ready?" I ask.

Without pause, he says, "I'll beat you to the bottom, buddy." I do love Axel's commitment, courage, and confidence. One day, he very likely will beat me to the bottom. Not today, though. At the end of the run, I wait as he comes screaming down, snow contrails behind him, and skids to a stop, dusting me with powder. "Why you little..." I say, laughing as I grab him, pick him off the ground, and launch both of us into the ten-foot snow drift behind us. His giggling is infectious, and I find myself laughing like an eight-year-old.

It's been thirteen years since the action described in this book, and I truly love my life. It has been filled with highs like the one I just described, as well as plenty of lows. However, due to lessons learned while in "my Afghanistan," it all amalgamates into one awesome ride—a ride where I even enjoy the lows. My soul is filled with true joy in the anticipation of strength or learning that I know is a consequence of any trial—if your perspective has been honed to catch it. I wrote this book to share those lessons and hopefully aid others in applying them in their own lives. My compulsion to do just that erupted in a single aha moment. Let me take you there.

Salt Lake City, December 2014—My mind is having trouble making sense of the moment. I'd left Kandahar eight years earlier, and now I find myself walking out to center court in the Utah Jazz Arena in Salt Lake City, surrounded by 20,000 cheering hometown NBA fans. I'm way out of my comfort zone, almost wishing myself back into the cocoon-like cockpit of the Apache. I can barely hear the public address announcer reading the citation for my Distinguished Flying Cross, and my eyes are reacting to the spotlights pretty much like a deer caught in headlights. The noise is deafening, disorienting, as Senator Orrin Hatch makes sure I'm securely holding the medal case, guiding my hands to point it toward the cameras surrounding us. I was somewhere in another dimension when one of the stage managers took my arm to lead me off the court.

That moment took me back—not just to Afghanistan but also to my decision to join the army, and to my youth in Utah and Idaho where my values were formed, bringing me to this point. Amid the unrelenting cheers, the memories flooded in: leaving home at age fifteen; nearly losing an arm in a snowboarding accident and then rehabbing as a whitewater rafting guide on the Colorado River; playing football; joining ROTC, graduating, and being commissioned a US Army second lieutenant; ultimately flying the most lethal helicopter in the world, the near-mythic Apache Longbow, in combat. I'd been privileged to be led by, work with, and lead true warriors, men I would learn so much from and always respect. What a tenacious enemy we faced together.

I can't help but effervesce with pride and gratitude for the demonstrated public support we now get, unlike what confronted soldiers returning from some past wars.

This moment is like a finger flicking over the first domino, starting a chain reaction of thought-provoking introspective questions. Why did I get the opportunity to experience and grow from this? It can't have been just for me. There must be a greater lesson or cause here. I looked up at my then-three-year-old boy, my wife, my parents, and every one of my brothers and sisters with their families cheering in the stands. A surge of desire to do something with this hit me. It had been eight years almost to the day since my copilot was hit. I will do something with this, but what?

As I write this now, it's been over fourteen years since I returned from that deployment. I have over twenty-five years of service and retirement is on the horizon. I am getting old; the follicle recession on my forehead tells me this every day when I look in the mirror. But I still love and am grateful for every day. The benefit of time has provided the ability to focus on lessons learned and to add perspective.

I have been deployed four times since the deployment this book covers. During the final one—the only one where I was a father while deployed—my boy was two. This was also the only deployment I had where people were not actively trying to shoot us out of the air, and yet in some ways, it was the most difficult, simply for the fact that I was missing out on my boy's life while I was in a foreign land. How I looked at risk changed as well. I was not nearly as willing to throw caution to the wind, knowing my boy was back home waiting for me. I had to gain that personal insight before I could see the world through the same lens as some soldier parents under my command in previous deployments. And that's only one of many areas that seem so much clearer to me now. I am sure there will be more in the future. In fact, I am hopeful there will be.

With the passage of time, I have had the occasion to observe the lasting impacts on the warriors with whom I served, not only in the deployment chronicled in this book but also the deployments I had as an air force combat search-and-rescue pilot. What I've witnessed is that some are coping well, and those deployments served as building blocks, growth opportunities to who they are and what they have become—a catalyst, if you will, to a greater state of being. Others have moved forward but only with considerable effort to stymie the strain on their inner person. Still others have had difficulty trudging forward at all and are in fact stuck in the damage imprinted on their psyche by intense circumstance.

Finally, there is a small group of vets who, sadly, decided their lives with the residual fog of despair, and perhaps chronic physical pain brought on by experiences downrange, were simply too much to handle, and they took matters into their own hands. This is a tragedy we're seeing play out with too much frequency. It's incumbent on us as a nation—whether it be the Department of Defense, private organizations, or concerned citizens—to expand research and, at minimum, facilitate the application of what mental health professionals have already learned about ways to build mental resiliency into our armed forces. Much of this should be done before putting lives at risk on the battlefield. I acknowledge there is an effort in this realm, and much is being done in these areas already. I don't wish to diminish these efforts, but the number of suicides is proof that we still aren't there and that the doubling of effort is called for.

Frankly, if we're talking about suicide prevention, let's start early and begin teaching mental resiliency in elementary school to head off the rash of suicides we're seeing in our teenage population. And for good measure, my co-author would like to point out that elder suicide is a growing problem in the United States. And it's very preventable—if there's a will to prevent it.

I had a particularly moving conversation with one of my pilots, who shall remain anonymous for reasons that will be obvious momentarily. Unlike some, he's very clear about what he did and why he did it. "When I think of my experience, we went over, we had a job, we did our job, and we accomplished our mission on our rotation. Maybe nationally or globally, we didn't accomplish the mission that was set out, but that was never *my* mission. I could care less about that. I was there for the ground guys and our fellow pilots in the Chinooks and Black Hawks we supported."

Nevertheless, he tells me that "things start to bubble to the surface." And then he got specific. "What I'm finding is, I've got this thing with control. I feel like over there, we were in control of situations, but we couldn't control what was really happening. We could react." Then he makes the correlation between *over there* and *back home*. "I feel like I have this death grip on control in my life right now, where if I get to a point I cannot control the situation, there's something off. That's different about me over the last few years.

"Maybe I'm getting older and that backpack is getting too heavy." What's in his backpack? Memories of exploding bodies, near-death experiences, and people he killed. "Oh well, they were bad guys, right? But that doesn't change anything in my head. It doesn't matter at all to me. It's just the fact they were human." He talks about his mom and her values and acknowledges that his actions didn't meet her standards. He feels an internal conflict, made more difficult when he's honored and rewarded with ribbons and medals for heroism.

"I don't want praise because I have this internal conflict of 'this shouldn't be something that I'm praised for.' That's probably why I never talked to anybody about it. And I have not solved those internal conflicts, and I am at the point where I think I do need to bring in outside support so it doesn't turn into something worse later, you know?"

Here's a man who has served honorably in combat, who notices mental health issues developing, yet he's afraid to seek help. Here's what he told me: "I'm still in the military. I'm still flying aircraft. And I don't want to affect my career in the military. And even though, no matter how many times they tell you that you've got to reach out and get help, even if it's just talking to somebody, talking to other veterans about it or something like that, the army tends to exaggerate things. And as soon as you say anything related to behavioral health, you know, eyebrows perk up. Even if it's simple like, 'I just need to talk about these things with other people that understand what the hell it was about.' And maybe that's all I need. But I have been kind of resistant for a long time."

The military has come a long way from saying "shell shock isn't a thing" to encouraging those psychologically impacted by trauma to seek help. Despite that evolution, though, in some quarters there is still a stigma associated with seeking help. Old habits die hard, and for decades, the armed forces considered acknowledgment of psychological trauma a sign of weakness. Even though this sentiment is waning, its existence keeps many from making the effort to talk to someone.

As I shared my stories in serious settings—as comical anecdotes or with instructional purpose—many told me I should write a book. I had no desire to do so; grammar and spelling are no friends of mine—we know each other but don't exchange Christmas cards, if you get my drift. So why the turnaround? It was incremental; people I cared about began to reveal their pain. I could see it on their faces, hear it in their voices, notice it in their behavior. They needed help. It made me take an inward, contemplative look and ask if I was also damaged in ways yet unperceived. I began to understand that to some degree, the answer to that question was, and is, yes. If I'm being honest, I didn't talk to anybody due to my own belief that I am strong enough and therefore not negatively affected by my experiences in combat. But while writing this book, I had the opportunity to talk to professionals about PTSD; frankly, I wanted them to explain why I hadn't been as negatively affected as many of my brothers in arms. The experience was enlightening. Let's just say that I've come to understand that no one comes back from war unchanged. This process has also taught me to continue to reflect and talk as needed.

But that understanding raised questions. Why do my past experiences largely serve as strength or foundation, rather than a tripwire or hindrance in my life? I know others where this is true in their lives as well. If these experiences, as extreme as they are, served as a strength to me, why were those very same experiences figuratively and literally a killer for others?

That's a roundabout way of saying the Eureka moment that happened silently, inside my head, while standing center court bathed in the roars of approval from the Jazz fans, has come to a fruition of sorts in this book.

I could search my memory, even drill down into my psyche, and extrapolate some commonalities that I can use to help others.

I would be willing to bet that most of you reading this book, whether military or not, have either experienced trauma or know someone who has. In fact, according to the US Department of Veterans Affairs (2022), about 60 percent of men and 50 percent of women experience at least one trauma in their lives. I would also bet that some seem to be stronger for it and others, in varying degrees, are negatively affected by trauma's wake.

What I discovered, with help from professionals as well as through solo self-examination, is that not only are there some things that could be taught but that with proper instruction and repetition, there are some preventative practices that would increase the odds of deriving strength from circumstance, rather than suffering damage to the soul by a thousand festering cuts. What we also found is that while combat has its extreme context, life in general deals trauma out at an alarming rate as well. So these techniques can be used by everyone, not only to prepare themselves for extreme circumstance but to minimize the negative effect of it retrospectively. Everyone has a story; everyone has their own Afghanistan, with more likely to come. Since everyone's story is unique, the efficacy of these techniques will vary, but researchers have found them to aid. Your Afghanistan can serve to make you or break you. So let's dive into how you can prepare yourself so it will make you.

The following are a list of principles I practiced while deployed that unknowingly helped me create a more resilient mind, a Teflon mind, if you will—one where trauma slides off. The pan may still need to be cleaned a bit, but most of the food doesn't stick. This list is not exhaustive. There are many other helpful lessons that I have learned in talking to psychiatrists, psychologists, and clinical professional counselors, but these are the ones I practiced downrange that ended up helping me experience post-traumatic stress growth rather than post-traumatic stress disorder.

- Practice chair flying.

- Build perspective.

- Believe in a higher cause.

- Be part of a team.

- Let the wound breathe by debriefing.

- Don't harbor hate.

- Define and embrace honorable missions.

Let's take them one by one.

Chair flying—I referenced this technique several times in the book but usually referred to it as a preparatory tool for emergencies that allows me to navigate them more effectively when they actually happen. This was the case when my engine was shot out, my copilot hit, and the flight controls jammed. Chair flying helped me navigate that cluster calmly and effectively, but it did something else as well. After sharing this technique with a few psychologists, I learned that this action also serves to prepare and strengthen the mind against lasting effects of trauma. It's called stress inoculation because it works in a very similar way to a medical inoculation. Giving your mind a dose of pseudo-trauma in an environment where you feel comfortable allows it to visualize/experience the event. The more detail you can add during your chair flying, the more effective the inoculation. Traversing the visualization prepares the mind to be more resilient since it's already been dosed with said trauma to some degree. To say this experience did not affect me at all would be a lie, but I am certain had I not chair flown similar circumstances many times prior to its actual occurrence, not only would we likely have ended up impacting the ground, but my psychology would have harbored a significant scar that would need attention for some time. As it stands, we lived, and I have drawn many lessons from that incident that have aided me since.

Military Medicine actually published a study looking at the effects of stress inoculation (SI) among a group of Marines (Hourani et al. 2016). Some of the Marines participated in an SI program prior to deployment, while others did not. Those who did go through the program showed that there was a protective benefit against the effects of PTSD, and the inoculated Marines had reduced physiological reactions in stimulating situations.

We can do this in our everyday life. We can visualize difficult scenarios and consciously work our way through them, being careful to visualize with the purpose of working through the event. Being focused on this purpose will help to avoid causing excessive anxiety. There is a difference between chair flying and obsessing or worrying. Worrying is a misuse of imagination. I currently practice chair flying with relationships, work struggle, possible catastrophes like car accidents, active shooter scenarios, incidents with my son, and such. My belief is that if the catastrophe happens, not only will I likely be better prepared to act effectively, but the residual mental baggage will be minimized.

Take a minute to visualize yourself actually doing this. Don't get overwhelmed; this is simply a tool. Pick a few events. Start with the least daunting and work your way through it mentally. Then change some variables. Once you have walked yourself through it enough times that you feel you could handle it if it were to actually happen, you have reached the goal of chair flying. Now move to something new. Notice I said, *"Handle* it if it were to actually happen." That doesn't mean we always win; often it means we come to terms with the worst-case scenario, understanding we did our best, and life will inevitably move forward.

This can be applied in all aspects of life. I renovate and flip homes. Many people have come up to me and said they want to do this. What keeps most from actually taking that plunge is fear. What if I sink all my money into this and it doesn't sell, or I come up short, or this or that. I tell them, "Well, of course you prepare as much as you can to avoid that finality, but let's say it does happen. Then what? You are not dead; you have family who loves you. You have skills in other areas you get paid for and you can build back, and you have learned an invaluable lesson should you choose to analyze it. Once you become okay with the worst-case scenario, you can operate without fear."

Perspective building—Although chair flying can aid in gaining a better perspective, *perspective* is its own animal. It takes conscious effort to lift yourself above what's happening and look down on it as part of a much larger picture. It takes effort to see that every single occurrence in our life can serve to benefit us in some way. I'm talking about the spectrum of possible negative events we may experience, from the simple things like crashing on a bike to ultimately terrible experiences: the tragic death of a loved one; becoming disabled as a result of injury or disease; even witnessing crimes against humanity.

At the surface, it's easy to say it's impossible that we actually benefit from them. This is where greater perspective is required to see that these events are but a speed bump on our road of life. In the moment, it may seem like these obstacles are the entire road, but like speed bumps, they are really saying, *Slow down, pay attention; there is a lesson to be learned here.* As a seventeen-year-old, I found myself living in a truck during the dead of winter in Idaho. Even in the moment, I actually saw this as an enjoyable adventure, but it also had added benefit. Later in life, I would live in third world conditions, a wood box, and a pungent tent. All no big deal because of lessons learned from previous experience and gained perspective. What that specific lesson is will be as individual as fingerprints, but I promise you, there is one. I'm really not a Pollyanna. I acknowledge that the more extreme the situation, the harder it will be to have good come from it. Sometimes understanding that is the case and revisiting that understanding periodically is enough to lift us while we slog through the darkness, awaiting the growth opportunity to emerge from the mire.

Finding humor in difficult situations is also a priceless skill to hone. Humor frees the mind from excessive strain. During my deployments, we often used humor before and after intense situations. Sometimes even during. It allows us to remain grounded. To that point, research suggests that humor is effective not only at forming relationships and strengthening connections but also at increasing motivation and reducing anxiety (Savage et al. 2017).

Belief in a higher cause—Okay, this isn't where I am going to tell you that you better find religion or you're gonna burn in hell! It is where I am going to say studies have shown that those who believe in a higher cause seem to weather trauma better. I think this dovetails into perspective and its positive effects. If we believe there is a greater cause than ourselves and that we are all part of that cause, it is much easier to understand that even horrible things can be there to serve our overall well-being in the long term.

We can also see guidance in feelings and other occurrences when we believe something greater than us is out there. In the chapter titled "Fireflies On," there was nothing other than a feeling that kept me from squeezing the trigger. To my mind, that was God helping me out, keeping me from accidentally taking the lives of all those infantrymen. Let's suppose I didn't get that feeling and I did commit fratricide. In this instance, my belief in a higher cause would help temper the inevitable inner turmoil that would follow such an event. And yes, I believe that even though in the moment I can't conceive of something positive resulting from this tragedy, in time it will manifest. That's a matter of faith.

What does the research say about spirituality? Well, a recent study looking at approximately 4,000 adolescents and young adults found that spirituality was highly related to positive psychological traits such as forgiveness, gratitude, optimism, meaning, and grit (Barton and Miller 2015). I definitely saw this in my own experience. Having a belief in a higher cause and a God who has a plan definitely allowed me to forgive, not hate, and at the same time take it to the enemy while minimizing residual guilt.

Be part of a team—Being part of a team synergizes everyone's strengths and abilities. It also increases resilience of the mind when we know we are not alone. When we know we are part of a team whom we will fight for and who will fight for us. I mentioned several times in the book the importance of camaraderie in the face of evil or even simply in a game I love. During the incident I've called the "pretzel maneuver," my team's commitment to each other literally kept us alive. We refused to let a very capable enemy kill our teammate, our brother. Alone, we would have both been killed. So if you are fighting your Afghanistan and you don't have a team, do everything in your power to find your people. Fight the fight with them. We all have inner struggles that are ours to figure out, but having a team will aid us in doing that.

According to the Mayo Clinic, feeling we have support and are not alone leads to greater resilience during difficult moments and decreases the physical and mental effects of those situations (Mayo

Clinic Health System 2022). They suggest that nearly every aspect of our lives is organized around belonging to something, and not having that is related to depression, anxiety, low self-esteem, a negative worldview, and mistrust.

There are times we will do things that benefit ourselves only when we see the benefit it has for others. We may lack the self-discipline to do it when it is benefiting only us. For example, I know that working out and eating healthy will have positive effects on me, but I got to a point in my life where finding the discipline to do those things for just me was very difficult. I found renewed willpower when I realized I needed to be healthy to be the best dad I could be for my son. I don't want to watch him throw a ball or hear about his hiking or dirt biking or whatever adventure. I want to be physically able, for as long as he wants me, to join him in doing some of those things. Being part of a team that depends on you as much as you depend on them will aid you in becoming a more resilient person.

Let the wound breathe by debriefing—How often do we hear someone who has experienced some sort of trauma say, "I don't want to talk about it"? This isn't healthy compartmentalization. We have to unpack those compartments, or they will just fester. Accept the fact that intense things happen, and they may sear our soul when they do. But being cut by trauma and simply covering up the wound, never letting it breathe, will only cause it to heal incorrectly. We must clean the wound by talking about it; we have to let it breathe by sharing. Even the pilot who spoke to me about his mental health concerns has recognized that without talking with someone, it's only going to get worse. Try this with your Afghanistan. Be careful with whom you choose to talk about it, though. Make sure it is someone who truly has your best interests at heart or, even better, is trained to listen.

Once you get in the practice of letting it breathe, to whom you talk isn't as important. From here, it can morph into storytelling, where serious events can be injected with humor or lessons learned and actually be an enjoyable and very positive experience for not just you but your listeners as well. *The New York Times* published a piece in 2020 in which they discussed why talking about our problems helps so much. Citing research from institutions including UCLA and Southern Methodist University, they demonstrated how talking to a therapist, venting to a trusted friend, or even just being open about your struggles is associated with being able to more successfully reengage in stressful situations. It also improves your overall health, benefits your immune system, and contributes to improvement in overall well-being.

Don't hate—When we experience trauma, it is human nature to want to blame someone or something. Some guys I served with hated the enemy because of what they "made" us do, or what they did, or what they believed. Most would say that's justified, but honestly, I never truly hated the enemy. I didn't agree with them, but my job was to kill them when they posed a threat to our team. The closest I came to harboring hate was after my copilot was shot. But even when I sought retribution, I made a conscious effort not to hate but rather motivate the destruction of a dangerous enemy location. Sure, immediately after he was hit, I took it personally, but that was an instant, fleeting response, not a permanent condition. It wasn't personal, and even if it was, holding hate in your heart is like drinking poison and hoping the other person dies. In that sense, it is personal; you are personally attacking yourself. Let it go. Hating God, or the drunk driver, or the fence post if a family member is killed are all natural feelings, but they are poison all the same. One hundred eighty degrees from hate is the ability to forgive and let go of negative feelings toward others, which is related to positive mental health, good relationship quality, hope, lower levels of anxiety and depression, and increased self-esteem (Raj, Elizabeth, and Padmakumari 2016).

Define and embrace honorable missions—You desire to be a good person, correct? I am going to assume that answer is yes. Then understand this: being good is a mission, not a destination. You will stumble; you will screw up on this mission. Some parts of the mission you may be able to define as something a good person would never do. Yet if our job was to protect our brothers, we had to kill. Does that make us bad people? No. Our country had given us a moral mission to perform. Yeah, it's complicated. We didn't just blindly follow orders. (Remember the landing zone that needed to be cleared of civilians?) It's a journey, my friend. Define your mission, embrace your mission, trust your mission, and understand that *bad* at times happens along the way; it means you are doing it correctly. Nobody is perfect. *Bad* is inevitable.

I challenge you to prepare for your Afghanistans by focusing on your higher cause, getting back to your perspective, debriefing your pain, chair flying the scenarios, finding humor where you can, eliminating any residual hate, and moving forward. Consider yourself part of the team of all of us trying our best to be our best because you are, and you're not alone. You are not alone in your efforts, and you certainly aren't alone in your stumbles. There are teammates who have had it worse than you who can help you gain perspective, and you can help pull them up. There are those who don't have it as bad as you, and the circle of synergy works there too.

These are a few of the principles I was employing that have scientific support showing they aid in creating a resilient mind—my term is a Teflon mind, a mind where bad stuff simply doesn't stick. I want to acknowledge that every situation is unique. Although I believe these principles will help, there is no cure-all and it isn't magic. We all have our battles. But even though every person's situation is unique, I do believe these techniques increase the odds of having a mind more prepared to grow from trauma rather than be derailed by it. The beauty is that when you truly apply these techniques, it has been my experience that life's peaks and valleys can be enjoyed and seen as a journey worth taking. While in a valley we know there can be growth and should hope to revel in the challenge.

It takes time to create the habit so that you automatically exercise these principles. Stick with it and you won't regret it. If you want to be part of my team and be supported on your journey with insights and techniques, that's awesome. I go into each of these principles and others in much greater detail on my web page. You can definitely do it on your own too; I did. I hope that readers can apply and practice them until they become automatic. In doing so, I believe you are mastering the art of creating a Teflon mind: one where trauma can be thrown at you but your preparation aids in not letting it stick.

For those of you who know me or have gotten a sense of me from reading this book, I want to assure you that I didn't pull this stuff out of my rectal database. I had help. For that, I wish to thank David S. Wood, PhD, a licensed clinical psychologist and assistant professor of social work at Brigham Young University, who is also a major in the Army National Guard, where he serves as a clinical psychologist. I also want to thank Steven Hoffman, PhD, assistant professor of social work at BYU. Various other mental health professionals had valuable input as well.

To those of you who might be wondering what came next for me, well, I became an air force rescue pilot flying combat search-and-rescue and casualty evacuation missions. What a new and awesome set of crazy experiences came from those mission sets. Working with Navy SEALs, Rangers, PJs, and various other customers, deploying multiple times to Afghanistan, Iraq, and the Horn of Africa. Maybe we will capture those stories in a sequel.

I hope this book has in some way inspired or helped you in your life's journey, or with trauma, or in ways I couldn't contemplate. That has been my driving force in writing it. If it has, I ask that you pay it forward to those you know and care about; share anything learned or insight gained.

I named this book *Cleared Hot* with deliberation. In combat, that phrase is a directive given by someone who has the authority to do so, enabling us to engage with lethal force. The implicit understanding is that the required steps to minimize collateral damage, maximize impact, and stay within predetermined rules of engagement have been met. We acknowledge that it's impossible to know every detail in these situations, but sufficient due diligence has been made to bring clarity despite the fog of war. This clarity allows us to proceed and prosecute targets.

Let me draw a connection from that enabling phrase to my intent for this book and suggest how you can be *cleared hot* in your own life. To get that go-ahead means you have taken the necessary steps to proceed forward into a very chaotic world; you have prepared yourself to make decisions, even knowing you do not have all the data. You acknowledge you have absolute authority to dictate the direction of your own life. There will be mistakes, but preparing and collaborating with your team will allow you to move forward while minimizing negative impact.

This is my wish for those who read this book. Take from it the perspective and tools to attack your journey with vigor. Move forward, find comfort in your preparation, and know that you are CLEARED HOT.

If you're inclined to follow up on some of my suggestions, please go to my website: www.clearedhot.info. I would love to hear your story and will read and respond if you write to me at brian@clearedhot.info.

I will leave you with a poem I wrote that I believe helps sum up my journey and can be applied to yours. God bless.

PERMANENT REVISION

You can imagine a war, you can imagine the fight

No matter what is imagined, you will not be right.

I remember well, the feeling that day,

When I saw two planes take the towers away.

A pit in my stomach, began to grow,

I have to do something, but what? Didn't know.

I long to be part of our retaliatory attack

I want my brothers in arms to know, I have their backs.

Already in the service of arms, to defend

This country I love, if need be, to bitter end.

You can imagine a war, you can imagine the fight

No matter what is imagined, you will not be right.

But on the sideline I wait, my turn still not near

To hunt down those, who attack my nation dear.

Go back to school, your time will come, son,

I don't want to turn 'round, rather toward the fight run.

Finish my school, lethal craft learned.

Ever more anxious, feeling my turn I have earned.

You can imagine a war, you can imagine the fight

No matter what is imagined, you will not be right

Finally the day came, for boots on the ground

Of a country lost, now to villains it's bound.

The fight is real, so we practice and plan,

Destruction and death fill Afghanistan.

We do our job, pushing fear aside,

Looking war in the face is a point of pride.

You can imagine a war, you can imagine the fight

No matter what is imagined, you will not be right.

Not what I thought, or imagined indeed,

Fighting for people who have so much need.

Evil fills caverns, so the rest they must suffer,

Can't imagine a place making men any tougher.

You fight not for country, for flag or Great Seal,

You fight for your brothers, and always will.

You can imagine a war, you can imagine the fight

No matter what is imagined, you will not be right.

At last we're back home, in the land of the free,

I may look the same, but I'm a new me.

Things seen and deeds done, now bound to my soul,

In the sum of the parts, that make up my whole.

Using the ugly, to strengthen and teach,

Helping my brothers, the ones I can reach.

Reality's so far from what the mind will envision,

Once experienced, the brain's tattooed
with permanent revision.

You can imagine a war, you can imagine the fight

No matter what is imagined, you will not be right.

REFERENCES
FOR THE EPILOGUE

Barton, Yakov A., and Lisa Miller. 2015. "Spirituality and Positive Psychology Go Hand in Hand: An Investigation of Multiple Empirically Derived Profiles and Related Protective Benefits." *Journal of Religion and Health* 54 (3): 829–43. https://doi.org/10.1007/s10943-015-0045-2.

Hourani, Laurel, et al. 2016. "Toward Preventing Post-Traumatic Stress Disorder: Development and Testing of a Pilot Predeployment Stress Inoculation Training Program." *Military Medicine* 181 (9): 1151–60. https://doi.org/10.7205/MILMED-D-15-00192.

"How Common Is PTSD in Adults?" US Department of Veterans Affairs. 2022. https://www.ptsd.va.gov/understand/common/common_adults.asp.

Raj, Paul, C. S. Elizabeth, and P. Padmakumari. 2016. "Mental Health through Forgiveness: Exploring the Roots and Benefits." *Cogent Psychology* 3 (1). http://dx.doi.org/10.1080/23311908.2016.1153817.

Ravenscraft, Eric. 2020. "Why Talking about Our Problems Helps
    So Much (and How to Do It)." *The New York Times*, April 3,
    2020. https://www.nytimes.com/2020/04/03/smarter-living/
    talking-out-problems.html.

Savage, Brandon M., Heidi L. Lujan, Raghavendar R. Thipparthi, and
    Stephen E. DiCarlo. 2017. "Humor, Laughter, Learning, and
    Health! A Brief Review." *Advances in Physiology Education* 41
    (3): 341–47. https://doi.org/10.1152/advan.00030.2017.

Theisen, Angela. "Is Having a Sense of Belonging Important?" Mayo
    Clinic Health System. December 8, 2021. https://www.mayoc-
    linichealthsystem.org/hometown-health/speaking-of-health/
    is-having-a-sense-of-belonging-important.

ACKNOWLEDGMENTS

So, this part will never capture everyone, but it is an attempt. In no particular order—except for the first one—I would like to thank:

- God for...well, everything

- Dad for discipline

- Mom for unconditional love

- My two best friends, my brothers Nate and James, for encouragement to tell my story, and for product refinement

- The rest of my family for being examples of great human beings to follow.

- Struggles for strength

- Poverty for gratitude

- Coach Srholec for grit and the squints

- Football for team building

- Church mission for altruism

- Farm work for appreciation

- Western River Expeditions for physical therapy

- Rand Curtis for guidance and empowerment

- Need for work ethic

- My ex-wife for empathy

- Boeing for making one hell of a war machine

- Craig J. Alia for the demeanor of a warrior

- Jayson Altieri for doing right by me

- Dan Duffy for righting someone else's wrong

My fellow warriors for camaraderie and for keeping me alive. In particular, the following who helped by sharing their memories with me: Mark Spangler, Ryan Pixler, Jeremy Pfeifer, Chris Walker, Jim Skillman, Garret Radigan, Jim Steele, Jeff Lynch, Kevin Eaton, Brett Brown, Marco Elsner, Ryan McNeff, Tim Wheeler, Adam Smoot, Sean Maiolo, Jack Denton, Steve Gladish, Joel Mann, Gary Benzi, Jennifer Winsley, Eddie Martinez, and Chris Wright. Also, Tara Malone, widow of my copilot, Otto Malone.

Friends who read the manuscript, chapter by chapter, and offered constructive criticism. Among them, Todd Katz, Keith Greenhalgh, Tiffany Long, Nicole Keil, Daniel Moss and Casey Doane.

Kathy Kirkland, for transcribing our Zoom sessions and Zoom interviews.

Saturday Night Live for the term "Abadaba" in the context of war in the Middle East.

A book of the quality we wanted to achieve can't happen without the help of dedicated publishing professionals. To that end we need to thank editor Doug Grad who helped us refine the manuscript, and the staff at Scribe, especially our author success manager Sophie May, cover designer Anna Dorfman, project manager Claire Brudner, design specialist Sarafina Riskind, graphics proofreader Laura Cail, manuscript specialist Vi La Bianca, production specialist Gabe Dyson, publishing specialist Robert Roth, publishing coordinator Lex Statzer, copyeditor Carla Counsil, proofreader Joyce Li, and QA editor Caroline Hough. We also thank the Impact Team at Scribe Media for their marketing efforts.

Michael Hirsh for partnering up with me on this project, dealing with my vagaries, filtering my writing, slaying my grammar and spelling demons, and making this book an infinitely better product. And a special thanks to Mike's wife, Karen, for being supportive of a husband consumed by the process. Thanks also to their kids, Bill Hirsh and Jennifer Weisberger, for fresh eyes and constructive criticism.

And finally, my son, Axel, for life's purpose, daily inspiration, motivation, and joy that continues to grow without limit. I am proud of you, son.

IN MEMORIAM

Staff Sgt. Jonathan "Zingo" Monzingo.

Staff Sgt. Jonathan Monzingo joined the army in April 2002 and served as an AH-64 Attack Helicopter repairer. "Zingo" entered active duty in August 2005 and deployed with the 1/285th Aviation Regiment, Arizona National Guard, to Afghanistan in early 2007. He died on July 12, 2011, at the age of twenty-eight, after a lengthy battle with pancreatic cancer. Zingo was in love with his work. He cared for his helicopters because he cared for us. The National Guard flew a four-bird "missing man" formation over his funeral service. Zingo is survived by his wife, Tamarah, and daughter, Hailey; his parents, Judy and Gary Monzingo; and his sisters, Cheralee Worral and Amanda Ogas.

CW2 Thomas Otto Malone.

CW2 Thomas Otto Malone served just over ten years in the United States Army and the Arizona Army National Guard. He was an attack helicopter pilot with the 1/285th Aviation Regiment and was my copilot on day three of Operation Mar Karadad, when we were hit by enemy fire and he was grievously wounded. After multiple surgeries and rehabilitation, Otto recovered from the wound itself but lived the remainder of his life in constant pain. Despite this, in 2009, he picked up on some unfinished business from before our 2007 deployment, and at the age of twenty-eight, on crutches, made it into the top thirty-six contestants on season eight of *American Idol.*

A year later, Otto was honorably discharged from the army.

Those of us who served with Otto remember him as a jovial guy, though serious about his craft. Undaunted by the rigors of combat, he was a confident aviator, as capable as any who flew his position.

Otto died in 2021 as a consequence of the wound he received in the service of his country. He is survived by his wife, Tara, a nurse practitioner, and three children, Shoshana, Thomas Otto, and Maddox.

GLOSSARY

AC: aircraft commander

AGL: above ground level

AIRBURST: Rockets, bombs, and artillery shells can often be set to explode either on impact with a solid object, at a certain altitude above the target (airburst), or even after penetrating into a target.

AK-47: The Kalashnikov 7.62 mm rifle was developed in the Soviet Union in 1947. It is the most widely used rifle in the world.

AMC: air mission commander

AO: area of operation

BUCS: Backup control system is an emergency fly-by-wire flight control system built into the Apache helicopter to be used if the mechanical flight control system becomes inoperative.

CENTCOM: Central Command

CHINOOK: The Boeing Ch-47 is a tandem rotor heavy lift, ninety-nine-foot-long troop- and cargo-carrying helicopter.

CO: commanding officer

CPG: copilot gunner

DEAD: destruction of enemy air defenses

DShK: a Soviet heavy machine gun

DUSTOFF: term used for medical/casualty evacuation helicopters.

ETL: Effective translational lift is when the lift generated from the rotor disc is more efficient due to increased aircraft speed or wind.

FARP: NATO term meaning forward arming and refueling point or forward area refueling point

FLIR: forward-looking infrared radar creates a video image from heat rather than visible light

FOB: forward operating base

HDU: helmet display unit is a scope mounted directly in front of one of a pilot's eyes that displays a variety of information used for targeting and to fly the aircraft

HELLFIRE MISSILE: Helicopter Launched Fire-and-Forget Missile System

HESCO BARRIER: A collapsible wire mesh container with a fabric liner that can be filled with sand, rock, or other materials. They come in various sizes and can be stacked to provide blast protection for military bases.

HEPD ROCKETS: air-to-surface unguided rocket that can be fitted with a variety of warheads

ICE: the LZ is cold—no enemy fire

IDF: Indirect fire is aiming and firing a projectile on an azimuth, not direct line of sight between the weapon and the target. Mortars and artillery fire are examples of IDF.

IED: improvised explosive device, often made from unexploded artillery rounds

IG COMPLAINT: inspector general complaint, which can be filed by anyone seeking to report wrongdoing

ILUM ROCKET: a rocket designed to illuminate an area

INTERPLANE: radio frequency used only by the formation

ISU-90: Internal Airlift/Helicopter Slingable Container

JBAD: Jalalabad, Afghanistan

KBR: Fortune 500 company providing logistical support for US forces deployed overseas

KOP: Korengal outpost

LDS: The Church of Jesus Christ of Latter-day Saints, often called the Mormons

LZ: landing zone

M-4 Carbine: shortened version of the standard M16 assault rifle

M-9: Beretta semiautomatic 9-mm pistol adopted by the US military in 1985

M-278: A rocket fired to illuminate a wide area. The illuminating component descends slowly on a small parachute.

MAM: military-age male

MFD: multifunctional display

MRAP: mine-resistant ambush-protected light tactical vehicle designed to protect occupants from IEDs and ambushes

MRE: Meals Ready to Eat are the modern version of military combat rations. They require no refrigeration and can be heated in their individual packaging.

NVG: Night vision goggles magnify available light (moonlight or even starlight) to create a green image for the user.

OBC: officer basic course

OD: olive drab color

OEF: Operation Enduring Freedom, the official name for the US mission in Afghanistan

PID: positive identification

PKM: a belt-fed 7.62-mm Soviet machine gun

PL: precautionary landing

POO: point of origin

PSY-OPS: Psychological operations can include audio messages broadcast from airborne speakers and leaflets distributed over enemy territory.

PTSD: post-traumatic stress disorder

PTSG: Post-traumatic stress growth is a theory that explains a kind of transformation following trauma.

QRF: Quick reaction force is on stand-by to respond immediately to emergency situations in combat.

R&R: Rest and recuperation/relaxation is a period of leave granted to military personnel, often getting them out of a combat area for a limited period of time.

RIP: relief in place

ROE: Rules of engagement are specific to military units in specific combat zones. They may change depending on circumstances and location.

RPG: Rocket-propelled grenade is an explosive round fired from a shoulder-mounted tube.

SAM: surface-to-air missile

SEAD: suppression of enemy air defenses

TIC: troops in contact

TOC: tactical operations center

TTP: tactics, techniques, and procedures

WAATS: Western Army Aviation Training Site

WAZZ: means a specific weapon has been selected for next use, e.g., "Wazzed the 30"

WINCHESTER: term used to indicate that the aircraft has no more ammunition to fire

XO: executive officer, usually the second in command of a military unit